Community Energy Options
Getting Started in Ann Arbor

Ronald D. Brunner and Robin Sandenburgh, Editors

Ann Arbor   The University of Michigan Press

85 84 83 82   5 4 3 2 1

"Decentralized Energy Policies" first appeared in *Public Policy*
28, no. 1 (Winter, 1980). Copyright © 1980 by the President
and Fellows of Harvard College. Published by John Wiley
and Sons, Inc. Reprinted by permission.

Library of Congress Cataloging in Publication Data
Main entry under title:

Community energy options.

   Bibliography: p.
   1.   Energy policy—Michigan—Ann Arbor.
2.   Energy conservation—Michigan—Ann Arbor.
3.   Energy development—Michigan—Ann Arbor.
I.   Brunner, Ronald D.   II.   Sandenburgh, Robin.
HD9502.U53A523   333.79'09774'35   82-2048
ISBN 0-472-08025-3   AACR2

Acknowledgments

The editors are indebted to a number of people who have contributed assistance and encouragement toward completion of this book.

In the federal government, Congressman Phil Sharp of Indiana provided the initiative for the Energy and Power Subcommittee's Hearings on Local Energy Policies, the findings from which are summarized in chapter 1 and indirectly reflected in the chapters that follow. Shelley Fidler and Tom Wanley of Mr. Sharp's staff and Phil Warburg of Senator Percy's staff helped interpret findings and prepare legislation. In the Department of Energy, Dick Holt provided a broad perspective on the local role as well as specific advice and comments on portions of the manuscript. Ben Bronfman, Gene Frankel, and Robert Odland shared insights from projects they had directed for the Department of Energy or its contractors.

Mark Croak and Sue Guenther of the National Association of Counties and Tom Graves of the U.S. Conference of Mayors provided a number of valuable leads and contacts in the early stages. In addition to the local officials who testified at the hearings, a number of energy coordinators contributed information on local energy initiatives from personal experience. We are particularly grateful to Leslie Brooks, Michael Bull, Ann Cline, Clara Miller, and Susan Stolz.

In Ann Arbor, the members of the Energy Steering Committee and its task forces reviewed the analyses in Part 2 and provided constructive criticism and support, as well as insights into the organization and management of the community energy initiative. We are especially indebted to John Clark, the committee's chair, and Roberta Booth, Susan Greenberg, Steve McCargar, and Lou Senunas. The Energy Steering Committee was established through the initiative of Barry Tilmann of the Community Development Office and competently staffed by Susie Bell, Randy Derifield, Larry Friedman, and Tom Rieke. In addition, Dan Hanlon of the Ann Arbor Engineering Department worked with us on several program options. The continuing support of Mayor Louis D. Belcher and the city council will be essential in the realization of significant improvements in community energy efficiency.

Only a portion of the members of the Local Energy Policy Seminar are listed as authors of this book, although all members provided comments and criticisms on a regular basis, and some provided initial research or assumed responsibility for implementation. Those who participated in the seminar, in addition to the authors, are Kim Cawley, Gerry Cole, Jim Delcamp, Jim Douglas, Pete Fairweather, Ken Hunter, Ken Jacobs, Jackie Krieger, Sue MacKenzie, Jim Nason, Karen Rutledge, Sydney Solberg, and Dan Weiss. Although not a member of the seminar, Harry Broadman (now of Resources for the Future) contributed in many ways while completing his doctorate in economics. Among the faculty members of the Institute of Public Policy Studies who provided assistance and advice on various projects are Tom Anton, Ned Gramlich, George Johnson, Larry Mohr, and Wes Vivian. Jeanne White typed most of the manuscript with skill and dispatch under the pressure of deadlines.

While acknowledging with gratitude the contributions of all these people—in Washington, in communities around the country, in Ann Arbor, and at the Institute of Public Policy Studies—we also absolve them of any responsibility for the final result. This is especially important where controversial matters of policy are concerned.

The work of the Local Energy Policy Seminar was supported almost entirely through the curriculum budget of the Institute of Public Policy Studies. Editing of this volume was completed with the support of the U.S. Department of Energy (DOE), Grant No. DE-FG02-80ER10125. However, any opinions, findings, conclusions, or recommendations expressed herein are those of the authors and do not necessarily reflect the views of DOE.

Introduction

Since the 1973–74 oil embargo, energy has been widely construed as a national and international problem. However far removed the origins of our energy problems, their impacts nevertheless have been felt by people in the local communities where they live and work. In the early 1970s, several communities began to develop solutions to their own energy problems with impressive results. They quietly reduced unnecessary and inefficient uses of energy, developed local and renewable energy sources, and realized substantial dollar savings. Spurred by word of these success stories, persistent energy price increases, and threatened disruption of energy supplies, leaders in an increasing number of other communities have become interested in the potential payoffs of a local energy policy. Initially, their need is to understand what can be done, and whether and how to proceed. Typically, their response is to begin the search for energy policy and program options by contacting other communities that started earlier and already have some experience.

Through a variety of information networks, an option developed in one community is discovered by (or circulated to) leaders in other communities. Some reject it, but others pick it up and modify it through a priori planning or actual experience to accommodate their own particular circumstances. Among the relevant circumstances are climate, funding, and politics. Thus fresh experience with different versions of an option tends to be developed and accumulated across many communities. Over several years, this process of innovation, diffusion, and adaptation evolves more satisfactory solutions to local energy problems, to the extent that plans and practical experience are well documented and quickly and conveniently accessible through the various networks. The number of communities involved in the process increases so long as energy problems and opportunities persist at the local level.

This book, the work of a Local Energy Policy Seminar, both exemplifies and contributes to the process of innovation, diffusion, and adaptation. The seminar was part of the graduate curriculum of the Institute of Public Policy Studies at the University of Michigan in 1979 and 1980.[1] Like others who live and work in Ann Arbor, seminar members began to identify initially promising energy options early in 1979. For each option, they attempted to assemble information from other communities as well as from other sources. Concurrently, they examined how the option could be adapted to local circumstances, and whether it would be feasible and worthwhile to proceed with the option in Ann Arbor. In March, 1980, the city government established the Ann Arbor Energy Steering Committee, which served as an open forum for consideration of the work of seminar members and many others.

Analyses of six program options by seminar members are presented as Part 2 of this book. Three of the chapters point toward development of local and renewable energy resources: the reactivation of a small hydroelectric site, now owned by the city, at the Barton dam on the Huron River; recovery of energy and materials by various means from the Ann Arbor and Washtenaw County solid waste stream; and an active solar demonstration project at Veterans Park on the city's west side. Three other chapters examine ways of using information to help people identify and reduce unnecessary energy consumption. These include revision of residential gas and electric utility bills to improve consumer feedback; development of a community energy report to clarify local energy consumption norms; and design of an energy monitoring system to improve the energy efficiency of buildings owned and leased by the city government. These options were neither developed from nor justified by a comprehensive energy plan; rather, each was considered on its own merits.

Part 1 reviews the national and local policy processes that affect such energy program options.[2] The first chapter proposes a federal program to encourage and support local energy initiatives, based on an analysis of local needs. The second derives lessons for the organization and management of local energy policy initiatives from the Ann Arbor experience, with emphasis on the work of the Energy Steering Committee. Part 3, which consists of the concluding chapter, brings the various program options up to date, as of mid-1981, showing how they have evolved in response to unfolding events including the comments and criticisms of private citizens and public officials. The evolution of energy program options through a local policy process is both inevitable and desirable.

Although the book is focused primarily on Ann Arbor, it is intended to help people in other communities work out solutions to some of their own energy problems. Obviously, conclusions and recommendations specific to Ann Arbor are not necessarily applicable elsewhere. Each community differs in some important respects, and the differences matter. Nevertheless, analyses of policy processes and program options in one community can help leaders in other communities in at least three ways.

First, each analysis can be used as a guide to information. For example, chapter 3, "The Hydro Option: Reactivation of the Barton Site" considers whether a full-scale feasibility study by professional engineers is warranted in one specific case. It directs attention to a number of sources that are generally useful, including feasibility studies at other sites in Michigan and around the country; technical guides for both initial and comprehensive small hydro feasibility assessments; and federal programs to fund such assessments. Even local information sources can be used to guide the search for similar sources elsewhere. For example, the U.S. Geological Survey has data on the streamflow characteristics of most rivers in the United States, in addition to the Huron River which flows through Ann Arbor; and other utilities, in addition to Detroit Edison, may have produced informative histories of the hydroelectric sites they have abandoned.

Furthermore, each of the analyses employs a framework to help organize and integrate the information collected in order to draw conclusions and make recommendations. Thus, "The Hydro Option" shows how hydroelectric potential depends upon streamflow characteristics and turbine designs; how the value of the power produced depends upon the local market for electricity; and how economic feasibility can be assessed through financial and benefit/cost analysis. Environmental, cultural, and institutional factors also are integrated in the analysis of the Barton site. Other communities can use this framework or model to clarify what information to search for and why it is important, even though one site differs from every other.

Finally, the chapters illustrate the approximate scope of a satisfactory analysis at a sensitive phase in the decision process—after the option has been identified as promising, but before there is a substantial commitment of resources to proceed with it. For example, several copies of the first draft of "The Hydro Option" were circulated in Ann Arbor in the summer of 1979, a time when interest in reactivating the Barton site was growing in several parts of the community. The analysis was one factor in the city's decision to hire an engineering firm to do additional work, which eventually cost about forty-five thousand dollars.[3]

Thus, detailed analyses of policy options in one community can be useful to people in other communities in ways that complement the information now circulating in the local energy networks. Short accounts of local energy initiatives in newspapers and periodicals help identify policy options and, by drawing attention to successes, help sustain interest and enthusiasm. Similar functions are served by community energy plans that summarize conclusions and recommendations for the city council or county commission. Technical guides on program options tend to be most useful to paid consultants *after* substantial resource commitments have already been made. Detailed analyses of policy options in specific cases, however, can help community leaders decide whether and how to proceed. The chapters in this volume are intended to help fill the gap between the promotional literature on the one hand, and the technical literature on the other.

For energy policy analysts, this book is intended to provide additional insights into the role of local energy policies in the realization of national energy goals. The oil and gas price increases effected through decontrol and deregulation at the federal level have begun to curtail unnecessary energy use and to speed the development of renewable energy resources. Local energy policies can address the diverse attitudinal, institutional, and other factors that stand in the way of a smooth transition to a sustainable energy future, and thereby enhance the effectiveness of the price mechanism.

More generally, the emphasis here on the evolution of local energy programs through innovation, diffusion, and adaptation illustrates a partial alternative to neoclassical economics, the foundation of most energy policy analysis. Given the complexity of energy issues even at the local level, the ideal of rational solutions through analysis alone can be sustained only to the extent that problems and opportunities are oversimplified. To accommodate complexity and diversity, a reasonable alternative is to improve the search for satisfactory solutions[4] through open and informed policy processes at the local level.[5] In this way private citizens and public officials, as well as analysts, can play important and respectable roles. The detailed analysis of specific cases—a particular hydroelectric site, a particular consumer's energy bills, or the Ann Arbor energy initiative—is a means to this end.

NOTES

1. The institute was founded more than a decade ago to improve public policy decisions through applied, interdisciplinary research and training. It offers a Master of Public Policy degree and a Ph.D. in Public Policy. The Local Energy Policy Seminar met over four consecutive academic terms. The new students each term initiated new projects or developed projects begun by their predecessors.

2. The distinction between options and the processes through which options are considered is fundamental and often made. See, for example, Harold D. Lasswell, *A Pre-View of Policy Sciences* (New York: Elsevier, 1971), chap. 1. In the search for satisfactory solutions to policy problems, both options and processes merit detailed examination.

3. Letter to Keith Kline, author of "The Hydro Option," from Wayne H. Abbott, Jr., Director, Ann Arbor Utilities Department, February 14, 1980. The additional work by Ayres, Lewis, Norris, and May, Inc., is reviewed in chapter 9.

4. See the work of Herbert Simon, especially "Rationality as Process and as Product of Thought," *American Economic Review* 68 (May, 1978):1–16, and "Rational Decision Making in Business Organizations," *American Economic Review* 69 (September, 1979):493–513.

5. A local or decentralized approach is not necessarily feasible or worthwhile for all aspects of energy policy or all policy areas. However, for energy conservation and renewable resource development where differences among communities and the people in them are important, a decentralized approach can be recommended. For policy planning and evaluation purposes, the U.S. Department of Energy cannot distinguish among the many thousands of local jurisdictions in the United States, nor does it attempt to. One indication is the level of aggregation in the Energy Information Administration's periodic data collection and reporting systems. See the Energy Information Administration, *Annual Report to Congress, 1978*, vol. 1, DOE/EIA-0173/1 (Washington, D.C.: Government Printing Office, 1979), app. 2 and 3.

Contents

PART 1: POLICY PROCESSES

1 Decentralized Energy Policies

Ronald D. Brunner

The United States has been preoccupied with energy policies developed and administered at the national level. The centerpieces of major legislation in the post-embargo period—including mandatory automobile fuel efficiency standards, phased decontrol of crude oil prices and deregulation of natural gas prices, and the proposed crude oil equalization tax—exemplify this centralized approach.[1] The principal exception has been federal support for the fifty states to develop and implement energy conservation policies at the state level.[2] Until quite recently, the possibility of a local role has been overlooked in Washington, despite persistent reports that a number of local communities had been developing solutions to their own energy problems.

In January, 1978, the House Energy and Power Subcommittee under Chairman John D. Dingell scheduled three days of hearings on local energy policies. The purpose was to consider energy policies made and implemented at the local level as means of (1) realizing the national goals of energy conservation and conversion to renewable resources, and (2) accommodating the diversity of energy needs and options that exist across the country. The hearings were held in May and June, and included testimony from fifteen witnesses who had participated in local energy policy processes as private citizens or public officials.[3] Ten of the local witnesses presented contrasting viewpoints on three cases: Davis, California; Seattle, Washington; and Springfield, Vermont.

Briefly summarized, the hearing record together with published material and some field research indicate that some local communities have been very successful with respect to the two goals listed above. They have responded to their own energy problems by discovering or rediscovering and effectively implementing energy programs and technologies appropriate to local circumstances. These typically turn out to be conservation programs and technologies that rely on local, renewable resources. (Large-scale, centralized energy supply projects are not normally among the realistic options at the local level.) The implication is that, in the aggregate, local communities could make a substantial contribution toward realizing national goals for energy conservation and conversion to renewable resources. Only an unknown fraction of local communities, however, have conceived of energy as a local policy problem and begun to search for local solutions. Many other communities have yet to take an initiative.

These findings suggest a federal program to encourage more local communities to become involved (and involved productively) in working out solutions to their own energy problems, without predetermining at the federal level what those solutions should be. This decentralized approach emphasizes federal support for an informal information network that has begun to emerge in response to energy policy planning and evaluation needs at the local level.

The remainder of this chapter reviews *evidence and inferences* about local energy policies as an instrument of federal policy; summarizes *local energy policy needs* that could be addressed productively by the federal government; and outlines a tentative set of *federal policy options* that address those needs. A concluding section reconsiders the local role in national energy policy and policy planning.

Three Cases

A review and analysis of three cases indicates what can be accomplished through local energy policies, and how it can be done.

In October, 1975, the Davis City Council adopted an energy conservation building code that indirectly mandates the use of passive solar heating and cooling processes in new residential buildings.[4] The code stemmed from the initiative of researchers at the University of California at Davis. Several years earlier they had begun research on the energy performance of local buildings that varied in window placement, site orientation, ventilation, and other factors. They proposed development of a new code adapted to the local climate to the city council in May, 1973, and eventually lobbied a number of local commissions and service clubs. The proposal attracted interest primarily for environmental and consumer reasons, but drew additional attention for energy reasons after the oil embargo. Opposition was led by builders and developers who considered the proposed new code ineffective, costly, and restrictive, and who were understandably upset by the threatened disruption of long-standing design and construction practices. The proposed new code was modified a number of times in response to comments and criticisms from many segments of the community.

The new code went into effect in January, 1976. Frustrations were particularly high among the first builders forced to learn how to comply with it. (Although the code is simple in concept, it is complicated in application.) Skepticism and opposition carried over from the earlier phases of the policy process into the evaluation of results. One builder, for example, monitored temperatures in unoccupied units built under the new code in an attempt to prove it ineffective. He discovered to his surprise that the units maintained temperatures more than twenty degrees cooler than outside temperatures on hot summer days, without air conditioning. Another analyzed consumption figures from Pacific Gas and Electric. The figures indicate that since 1973 Davis has realized an 18 percent per customer reduction in residential gas and electricity consumption. The small proportion of the city's physical stock of housing built under the new code is insufficient to account for the magnitude of the reduction. Moreover, the reduction began before the code was implemented. Attitudinal changes arising from the controversy that led to adoption of the code, rather than the code itself, account for most of the 18 percent reduction. By now most Davis builders accept the code as an effective means of cutting energy consumption and utility bills with no increase in construction costs. Some use it for new construction in nearby areas outside the Davis city limits.

In July, 1976, the Seattle City Council turned down an option to participate in two proposed nuclear power plants and adopted instead a vigorous electricity conservation policy.[5] This decision climaxed fourteen months of intensive analysis and debate initiated by a request from Seattle City Light, the municipally owned utility, for council approval of Seattle's participation in the first phase of a regional nuclear development program. The request was highly controversial. Among other things, a full commitment by Seattle would cost more than a quarter of a billion dollars. The council approved a one-year financial commitment up to the beginning of construction, but mandated a study to answer questions raised in public hearings by environmentalists and others about the need for additional generating capacity, the alternatives to nuclear power, and social, economic, and environmental impacts. To carry out the mandate, City Light appointed a citizens committee to select independent consultants and then expanded it into a Citizens' Overview Committee (COC) to monitor the study for comprehensiveness and validity. An important focus of analysis and debate turned out to be the projected annual average increase in electricity demand through 1990. The consultants' estimate was 2.8 percent in contrast to City Light's estimate of 3.7 percent. Small differences in rates compounded over a number of years imply large differences in electricity demand. The lower rate suggested that conservation, the cheaper option, might be relied on to meet Seattle's future needs. The swing members of the COC sided with the environmentalists in recommending the conservation option over the opposition of the business-oriented minority. The majority on the COC and on the council emphasized a lack of demonstrated need for more generating capacity, the high cost of nuclear power, and the need for incentives to make conservation programs work. In addition, they tended to reject charges that the majority had acted against economic growth and nuclear power.

Thirty-two specific programs have been developed to implement Seattle's conservation policy. During 1977, the first full year of operation, City Light estimates these programs saved seventy-two megawatts, an amount well in excess of the seventeen-megawatt annual average savings required to meet the 1990 target. Overall electricity demand decreased 7.7 percent from the previous year. Although City Light attributes most of this decrease to its conservation programs, interpretation is complicated by other factors including a drought and the fourteen-month controversy. Those opposed to the policy have constructively questioned optimistic interpretations of the results, and those in favor of the policy have demonstrated an intense commitment to making it work. Spokespersons for both sides are impressed by the large uncertainties inherent in demand projections, by the lead times required to add new capacity, and consequently by the importance of monitoring results and updating forecasts.

In October, 1977, the citizens of Springfield, Vermont, voted for the second time to establish a municipal utility and to issue $58 million in bonds to develop the hydroelectric potential of nearby low-head dams on the Black River.[6] With 52 percent of those eligible voting, the project was approved by a 72 percent majority. It had been initiated in 1974 when the town's Board of Selectmen looked into low-head hydro as a means of holding down rising electricity costs, and then directed the town supervisor to hire a national consulting firm to study the matter. On the basis of the consultant's report a preliminary application was filed with the Federal Power Commission and the issue was presented to the voters in January, 1975. Opposition was led by Central Vermont Public Service Corporation, an investor-owned utility serving 60 percent of the state. Central Vermont, which stood to lose its customers and facilities in the Springfield area, challenged the consultant's report and distributed others concluding the project was uneconomical. After voters approved the project for the first time in March, 1975, Central Vermont initiated legal action that eventually required the second vote in October, 1977. Whether or not Springfield's project surmounts legal, state, and federal regulatory barriers, it already appears to have induced Central Vermont to take an active interest in low-head hydro. The company has moved from public opposition to the development of several other low-head hydro sites in the state.

Thus the evidence is that some local communities have made substantial progress toward conserving nonrenewable energy resources and converting to renewables. Moreover, policies made and implemented by these communities tend to accommodate the diversity of local circumstances, including both physical factors and citizen viewpoints. What has proved to be effective and politically feasible in Davis is not necessarily so in Seattle, and vice versa.

To be sure, a number of case-specific factors are important in understanding these results. The key inference, however, is that each community in its own way managed to initiate and sustain an open and informed policy process. This appears to be a necessary condition for substantial progress, if not a sufficient one. Without the initiative of a few leaders, energy decisions traditionally made and implemented by one segment of the community—individual builders, certain divisions of a municipal utility, or an investor-owned utility—would have remained so; and a range of considerations that proved to be important to other segments of the community would have had no influence on those decisions. Without independent analyses, each initiative most

probably would have lacked a realistic grounding and a politically effective rationale. The evidence is clear that analysis sponsored by con-
tending groups in each case helped clarify realistic options, but each
analysis also reflected political assumptions and promoted political
conclusions.[7] Moreover, the controversy arising from each initiative
educated and organized constituencies committed to effective implementation and other constituencies committed to monitoring and
evaluating the results from a critical perspective. In Davis and perhaps
the other cases, controversy itself broadened and intensified concerns
about energy problems that were manifested directly in voluntary energy conservation, apart from the effects of the policies and programs
adopted.

An *open* policy process tends to occur where leaders divide
among themselves and where resolution of the issue is expected to
have a relatively large and direct impact on all segments of the attentive public. Under these conditions, leaders on each side have an incentive to compete for popular support in order to approve or block a
policy change. And members of the attentive public have an incentive
to respond as a matter of perceived self-interest, to the extent that
institutional arrangements permit effective participation. Energy
issues in the current period differ from many others in that everyone
has a lot at stake—a point dramatized by the oil embargo and events
since. When these issues are opened up at the local level, the stakes
become relatively immediate and direct from the viewpoint of the individual citizen and the possibility of making a difference in city hall or
the county building appear larger than the possibility of making a
difference in the state capitol or Washington.

An *open and informed* policy process tends to occur where the
major factions have access to independent data and analyses, and
where the attentive public has an independent basis for evaluating
competing claims. Under these conditions, neither faction is handicapped by lack of an important political and analytical resource, and
each may discover that realistic claims based on data and analysis are
more productive in the competition for popular support than emotional
appeals. Moreover, the individual citizen is in a better position to
weigh competing claims and appeals in the pursuit of his or her self-
interest when the issue pertains to local circumstances. The direct
observations and personal experiences of the individual citizen are

concentrated in the local community; for the most part regional, national, and international circumstances are known only indirectly through the media and tend to be discounted in this period of widespread distrust.[8]

The Potential Elsewhere

Davis, Seattle, Springfield, and some other communities are exceptional in results achieved. Many more communities have begun to deal with energy as a local policy problem, but have less experience or experience on less controversial aspects of energy policy. One indirect indication is the degree of interest shown in *A Guide to Reducing Energy Use Budget Costs,* prepared for local governments by the National Association of Counties, the National League of Cities, and the U.S. Conference of Mayors under contract with the Federal Energy Administration. It provides very brief descriptions of energy conservation programs within local governments around the country, together with information for contacting the local official responsible in each case. First published in November, 1976, it is now in its fourth printing and over fifteen thousand copies have been circulated. In addition, in 1977 the National League of Cities and the U.S. Conference of Mayors identified 281 cities involved with energy concerns and surveyed 64 cities that are leaders in energy conservation.

Local officials in such communities put forth the effort for a variety of reasons. The major motivating factor appears to be the problem of balancing city and county budgets in the face of chronic increases in energy prices. No doubt the political popularity of fiscal conservatism has also played a role. Testimony in the hearings suggests, however, that where conservation programs have succeeded in holding down energy costs for local governments, local officials have begun to search for ways of broadening the scope of their efforts to include the community at large. For one thing, leadership on innovative energy policies at the local level is a political asset rather than liability, even before the effectiveness of the policies can be demonstrated. Officials identified with the policies adopted in Davis, Seattle, and Springfield were for the most part reelected in subsequent contests despite controversy about those policies. For another, chronic energy price increases, economic losses and general disruptions arising from intermittent energy shortages, and environmental and social problems aggravated by the energy situation have an impact on public officials and private citizens alike. However remote the origins of these problems, their consequences are experienced by individuals whose primary frames of reference are personal and local in scope.

In these communities the principal constraint appears to be a lack of policy guidance on a convenient and timely basis. Community leaders want a quick and reliable indication of what can be achieved through local energy initiatives, and how it can be done. Technical information alone is not sufficient or even of primary importance initially. The demand is for cases that might be adapted to local circumstances, and that clarify the full range of factors a leader must take into account, including political factors. The search procedure is typically to contact counterparts in other communities, or to contact such organizations as the National Association of Counties, the National League of Cities, and the U.S. Conference of Mayors, which attempt to put communities with energy problems in touch with communities that already have experience with similar problems. Many of the thousands of requests for information about local energy policies received by cities like Davis and Seattle have come from leaders in other communities.[9] The emergence of this informal information network is an important indication that convenient and relevant policy guidance is a significant factor in sustaining local energy initiatives.[10]

There are other indications that policy guidance is a more significant factor than external funding, at least initially.[11] Many energy conservation programs within city or county governments and even some large capital projects are cost-effective from the local viewpoint even without state or federal financial assistance. For example, Dade County, Florida, is constructing a $138 million solid waste facility that (among other things) will use combustible waste to generate seventy megawatts of electricity, enough for about forty-one thousand families—without state or federal assistance, according to testimony.[12] To be sure, other communities have sought and used external funding from a variety of sources. In addition to a small appropriation from the city, the Davis building code was developed with the help of grants from a private source and from the Department of Housing and Urban Development. The total from all sources was about $120,000. On incomplete evidence presented in the hearings, it appears that start-up costs for local energy policies are modest, and that a number of funding programs already exist. They are widely scattered, however, and therefore not always easy to identify, and they are often not well adapted to energy policy priorities identified at the local level.

Still other communities have continued to assume through inaction that energy policy is solely a matter of federal responsibility, with individual consumers adapting in any way they can. The reasons for this inaction have not been systematically studied but one case suggests the importance of perceptual factors. In early spring, 1978, a conservative midwestern community faced mandatory electricity curtailments because of the coal strike. This was the latest in a series of energy-induced disruptions since the 1973–74 oil embargo. Individuals adjusted in a variety of ways, including the use of kerosene lamps for home lighting, cancellation or postponement of school and civic activities scheduled at night, curtailment of business hours, temporary plant shutdowns, and the purchase of small, oil-fired generators to maintain operations through the crisis. The response of local government was limited to such stopgap measures as reductions in street lighting. Community leaders were shocked to learn from outsiders that they had been relying (through inaction) on the federal government to address the community's immediate and long-term energy problems as a matter of public policy. They also began to realize that adjustments by individual consumers were not necessarily optimal. Within a few months the city hired a part-time energy coordinator who has since begun to mobilize a wide range of community interests, secure funding from outside sources, collect energy planning data, and develop local energy programs. Where energy problems have disrupted a community, a little insight can go a long way toward effective local action.

Communities clearly differ in their willingness and in their ability to tackle energy problems at the local level. Whatever the distribution of untapped potential among the communities currently less active or inactive in energy policy, the potential for local energy initiatives will continue to accumulate. Among other things, future energy shortages, local, regional, or national in scope, are possible, if not probable; and domestic oil and natural gas prices are scheduled to increase toward decontrolled and deregulated levels under existing federal legislation. Moreover, the resources and incentives for productive policy responses will increase as successful models like those in Davis and Seattle are developed, documented, and publicized, and local energy policy experience cumulates and spreads.

The principal question for federal policy is not *how much* potential exists, in terms of willingness and ability, but *how to* maximize it. An attempt to develop a quantitative estimate of these human factors on a national scale is much less cost-effective than alternative strategies such as field experimentation or prototyping.

Design Criteria

This analysis suggests that the federal government can encourage more local communities to take an active, effective role in developing and implementing energy policies, without prescribing what those policies should be. Of course there are no guarantees in the use of local policy processes as an instrument of national policy, any more than there are guarantees in the use of market processes or federal regulatory processes. To encourage local energy policies as a means of realizing national goals for energy conservation and for conversion to renewables, the federal government could act to

1. shift some attention to energy policy achievements and potentials at the local level;
2. provide local leaders with quick and convenient access to documented cases that meet their needs;
3. increase citizen and consumer opportunities for informed participation in local energy policy processes;
4. stimulate more energy policy innovations at the local level; and
5. collect and distribute dependable information reflecting the diversity of local energy needs and options for use at the federal level.

The first and last needs arise primarily from the national "fix" on the energy crisis advanced by the Nixon, Ford, and Carter administrations. A preoccupation with national considerations to the exclusion of local ones is apparent in televised presidential addresses on energy policy, energy legislation, and national press coverage. It is virtually institutionalized in a federal energy data base that obliterates local diversity through aggregation of most data series.[13] The effect is to divert attention from local energy policy achievements and possibilities, and to nurture a de facto dependence on federal energy policy and on individual adaptations by consumers. As we have seen in the case of the conservative midwestern community, this inhibits local energy policy initiatives.

The second and fourth needs arise from limitations of the information available to local leaders and the means of finding and distributing it. Both the content and distribution of federal energy information resources are adapted primarily to the requirements of policy at the federal level;[14] no programs are designed specifically to stimulate innovations in local energy policy.[15] The informal information networks that have emerged in response to unmet information needs have not been studied in detail. They appear to be handicapped, however, by insufficient funds even at the present level of local energy policy activity. Moreover, there are no well-documented cases that span the multiple aspects of a given community's energy policy experience, including the historical, political, institutional, and ethical aspects, as well as the economic and technical, all of which are of potential interest to local leaders. The literature is dominated by a few pages (at the most) on each case, and by program descriptions. The effect is to frustrate rather than to sustain local energy policy initiatives, and to render much valuable experience unavailable for possible applications elsewhere. Under ideal conditions, a community leader would have ready access to a wide range of models developed in other communities.

Open and informed participation at the local level needs to be encouraged to minimize the probability that local energy policies are dominated by any one interest to the exclusion of others, and to maximize the probability that realistic, potentially valuable observations and ideas will be introduced, circulated, and developed. Consumer- and citizen-oriented information is currently rather limited. Ranging from conservation tips to how-to-do-it manuals to exhortations, advertisements, and promotional material, it tells the consumer and citizen what he or she should think and do about energy and energy policy, and it is readily identifiable with particular private or governmental interests. The effect is to nurture at least as much public resignation, apathy, confusion, and alienation as active and responsible participation.[16] For market and open political processes to function effectively, consumers and citizens require information to clarify their own interests.

Policy Options

The tentative options intended to meet these needs generally rely on modest amounts of federal funding to produce and distribute information. Information is an important factor in local energy initiatives and is cheap to produce, reproduce, and distribute relative to hardware.

To focus attention on local energy policy initiatives, it appears worthwhile for the Department of Energy to work with experienced local officials to

1. disaggregate existing national goals for energy conservation and conversion to renewable resources by community size and region; and

2. develop appropriate performance indicators for local energy policies.

The other options listed below would also shift attention to local initiatives. Depending on what is interesting at the local level, performance indicators might include not only fuels consumed and technologies installed, but also changes in employment, pollution, attitudes, and life-styles that are influenced in part by local energy policy. For local use, it is not necessary to standardize any particular indicator, or mix of indicators, across communities. Indeed, standardization would inhibit responsiveness to locally diverse circumstances.

To help provide local leaders with ready access to relevant models, it appears worthwhile for the federal government to

3. fund several organizations that have experience as national clearinghouses for information on local energy policies, or a consortium of such organizations; and to

4. fund a small number of local governments (perhaps five to fifteen) with outstanding energy policy and performance records to document and update their experiences, and to distribute the results directly to leaders in other communities on request.

The expectation is that these options, if implemented, would support improvement and expansion of the emerging informal network through which communities now search for policy guidance. The clearinghouse organizations have demonstrated a degree of responsiveness in putting one community in touch with another. And some local communities have records that merit attention as models, and enough motivation (including pride) to be interested in telling the story. A number of communities are specified in order to disperse control over policy information and to increase the range of models available for possible adaptation. Direct distribution is specified in order to avoid unnecessary delays.

To increase citizen and consumer opportunities for informed participation at the local level, it appears worthwhile for the federal government to

5. require utility companies to include bill history in monthly utility bills sent to each ratepayer; and
6. require that community aggregate utility data be made available by utilities on a monthly basis to community groups requesting it.[17]

Bill history can be as simple as the percentage change in consumption from the corresponding month of the previous year, and might also include the percentage change in rate and amount due from the consumer.[18] Aggregate community data might include consumption, rate, revenues, and number of ratepayers for each major rate class. All but the small utilities already collect and store the necessary data in computerized form.[19] Under these options, they would share it with the individual ratepayers and communities from which the data are collected.

Expectations about the results of implementing these options are based partly on experience and partly on theory. Similar options have been implemented as conservation measures in scattered cases. Although the published record is thin, they appear to have reduced energy consumption and to have stimulated informed participation as well. For example, when Atlantic City Electric included bill history in monthly statements starting in 1974, it experienced a sharp drop in electricity demand and a sharp increase in customer questions and complaints.[20] Moreover, the options would provide easy access through individual bills and perhaps local newspapers to existing data that all consumers and citizens could use to clarify their own interests on a continuing basis. The data would put the individual's current energy experience in a context that invites comparisons with his or her previous experience and with community norms, and thereby reduce the institutional barriers to informed participation.

To stimulate additional energy policy innovations at the local level, it appears worthwhile to

> 7. establish a program of small grants for local governments to support energy policy planning for conservation and conversion to renewables.

The intent is to increase the range of models by funding promising local ideas, rather than by adapting local policy plans to federal funding requirements. The need for restrictive federal controls might be minimized by authorizing only small grants and by selecting only those local governments that have already demonstrated a willingness and capability to achieve results in this area.

Finally, to collect and distribute dependable information reflecting the diversity of energy needs and options for use at the federal level, it appears worthwhile to require the national clearinghouses and local governments funded under the options listed above to submit information to the Department of Energy on a timely basis. The department would then

> 8. validate the data and information received on a continuous but selective basis; and
> 9. publish and distribute an annual energy review that coordinates the data and information received.

Validation is intended to deter extravagant and misleading claims. An annual review would include, for example, the number of requests received and local programs identified by the national clearinghouse, disaggregated by request and program type; case documentation from each outstanding city, including program histories and descriptions, methods and sources of funding, institutional barriers identified, and quantifiable trends; similar information from recipients of small grants focused on single innovative programs; and the results of the department's validation studies. This is intended to provide a solid basis for congressional oversight and executive evaluation, as well as policy planning. The diversity of local circumstances could be emphasized by case-wise as opposed to variable-wise presentation of some of the material. Such information would enable federal authorities to identify gaps between the mix of local energy needs and the mix of programs relevant to these needs, as both change through time; gaps among the multiple methods and sources of funding for local energy initiatives; institutional barriers encountered by appropriate technologies and programs; and the contributions of local energy policies to national energy goals.

The available evidence does more to suggest these options than to evaluate the probable effectiveness of any one of them. For this reason, the options should be considered tentative. The point is that the effectiveness of any option, when implemented, does not depend in any significant way on the intent or expectations of policy planners. Realistically, it depends on the responses of the many people who would be involved in implementing the option, and their responses would be shaped by (1) their interests and expectations, (2) the resources (including skill) at their disposal, and (3) the organizational and institutional contexts in which they function. These factors need to be better understood in order to evaluate the options and to modify them accordingly. This requires direct contact with a small number of people who would be involved at key points in order to discover how they would respond, rather than to confirm or refute what policy planners already expected. The matter cannot be resolved a priori by the design of a survey instrument or appeals to theory.

The question, in short, is *how to* maximize whatever potential for local energy policy already exists, or is likely to exist in the future. After the intensive field research described above, the most cost-effective next step would be to implement a modified set of options on a pilot basis. An attempt to estimate through extensive surveys *how much* potential exists on paper would cost a significant fraction of implementation on a pilot basis, would produce results of dubious reliability, and would delay field testing of workable policy options.

The set of options implemented on a pilot basis could be considered an experiment to surface policy-relevant information on local energy policies as an instrument of national policy. In present form, the set is designed to generate dependable and timely information for policy evaluation and planning at the federal level. Costs are flexible, and can be scaled down to the level of a major study by reducing the number of communities funded directly. Finally, because the options do not create a new infrastructure, the experiment could be terminated if results do not warrant continuation or expansion.

Conclusion: The Local Role

In conclusion, let us reconsider the local role in national energy policy and policy planning.

Underlying many federal energy policies is the analytical assumption that price mechanisms can stimulate action toward energy conservation and conversions to renewable resources. For example, decontrol and deregulation of crude oil and natural gas prices will raise those prices to levels that are expected to discourage unnecessary and inefficient energy consumption and to make more attractive appropriate technologies utilizing renewable resources. These effects depend not only on the size of the price increases but also on elasticities that summarize the magnitude of the impact of price changes. Subsumed in these elasticities are attitudinal, institutional, and other factors not immediately affected by price changes.[21] The cases reviewed here suggest that local energy policies can ameliorate attitudinal and institutional barriers and therefore, in effect, increase the relevant elasticities. Over a period of several years, a federal program to encourage more local energy policy initiatives might enhance the effectiveness of price increases already implemented or scheduled. In the longer run, adjustments in attitudes and institutions as well as prices are necessary to accomplish a smooth transition toward a society less dependent on nonrenewable energy resources.[22]

There are many approaches to energy conservation and conversions to renewable resources. The cases reviewed here suggest, however, that energy policy decisions of major significance to specific communities if not to the nation as a whole are the prerogative of local communities. The policies made and implemented by Davis, Seattle, and Springfield would be politically infeasible as well as ineffective if state governments or the federal government attempted to impose them on a wider basis. The relevant configurations of citizen viewpoints as well as physical circumstances are too diverse from one community to the next; effective implementation and evaluation depend upon organized and informed local constituencies that are not likely to exist if policy-making responsibility is removed to the state or federal levels. Moreover, these community-level decisions fall outside the range of options normally available to the individual consumer and citizen acting alone in an attempt to reconcile his or her interests with the energy situation.[23] Yet the consequences of local energy policies may be sufficiently large, immediate, and direct from the viewpoint of individuals in all classes to stimulate widespread interest and options for collective action.

As noted in the National Energy Plan,

> The Federal Government can pass laws and encourage action. State and local governments can play active roles. But this society can function at its best only when citizens voluntarily work together toward a commonly accepted goal. Washington can and must lead, but the nation's real energy policy will be made in every town, city and village in the country.[24]

NOTES

1. Automobile fuel efficiency standards and phased crude oil price decontrol were included in the Energy Policy and Conservation Act of 1975 (Pub. L. No. 94–163, 89 Stat. 871 (1975)). The proposed crude oil equalization tax was deleted from the bill that became the Energy Tax Act of 1978 (Pub. L. No. 95–618, 92 Stat. 3174 (1978)). Phased deregulation of natural gas prices was included in the Natural Gas Policy Act of 1978 (Pub. L. No. 95–621, 92 Stat. 3351 (1978)).

2. See the Energy Policy and Conservation Act of 1975 and the Energy Conservation and Production Act of 1976 (Pub. L. No. 94–385, 90 Stat. 1125 (1976)).

3. U.S., Congress, House, Committee on Interstate and Foreign Commerce, Subcommittee on Energy and Power, *Hearings on Local Energy Policies,* 95th Cong. 2d sess., May 22, June 5 and 9, 1978, Serial No. 95–135 (hereafter cited as *Hearings on Local Energy Policies*). In May, 1978, the Assistant Secretary for Policy and Evaluation, Department of Energy, initiated a Local Roles Study.

4. On Davis see the *Hearings on Local Energy Policies* record and The Elements, *The Davis Experiment: One City's Plan to Save Energy* (Washington, D.C.: Public Resource Center, 1977); Marshall Hunt and David Bainbridge, "The Davis Experience," *Solar Age,* May, 1978, pp. 20–23; James Ridgeway, "A City's Energy Saving," *New York Times,* January 12, 1978; "A California Town is Able to Kill a Watt in Its War on Waste," *Wall Street*

Journal, May 17, 1978; and Gloria Shepard McGregor, "Davis California Implements Energy Building Code," *Practicing Planner* 6 (February, 1976): 24–31, reprinted in U.S., Congress, House, Committee on Interstate and Foreign Commerce, *Hearings on Middle and Long-Term Energy Policies and Alternatives*, 94th Cong., 2d sess., March 25–26, 1976, Serial No. 97-76, pp. 139–43.

5. On Seattle see the *Hearings on Local Energy Policies* record and the multivolume Seattle City Light, *Energy 1990: Interim Report* (Seattle: Seattle City Light, 1976) and Seattle City Light, *Energy 1990: Final Report* (Seattle: Seattle City Light, 1976), both published and circulated widely in Seattle prior to the city council's decision; Seattle City Light, *Energy 1990 Resolutions: An Update Report* (Seattle: Seattle City Light, 1978); U.S., Congress, House, Committee on Banking, Finance, and Urban Affairs, Subcommittee on the City, *Hearings on Energy and the City*, 95th Cong., 1st sess., September 14–16, 1977, pp. 149–75; Greg Hill, "The Politics of Energy 1990," unpublished paper (Seattle: University of Washington, April 17, 1978); and Michael Hildt, Edward Sheets, and Lee Somerstein, "Energy 1990: An American City Tackles Its Energy Future," unpublished paper (Seattle, 1977).

6. On Springfield see the *Hearings on Local Energy Policies* record. For background material on low-head hydro in New England, see Lee Lescaze, "Little Dams Being Revived as Power Source: Big Utilities Balk," *Washington Post*, March 11, 1978; Steven Rattner, "New England Again Turns to Its Streams for Energy," *New York Times*, April 8, 1978, reprinted in U.S., Congress, Senate, *Congressional Record* 95th Cong., 2d sess., April 11, 1978, pp. 9619–20; John B. Oakes, "Taking the Waters," *New York Times*, May 17, 1977; Dick Kirschten, "Hydropower—Turning to Water to Turn the Wheels," *National Journal*, April 29, 1978, pp. 672–76.

7. On the importance of independent analyses, see the written statement and testimony of Brian Lederer, Office of the People's Counsel, Washington, D.C., in *Hearings on Local Energy Policies*.

8. In unstructured group discussions, people tend to support their expressed opinions about energy issues with first-hand observations or with second-hand observations of family members or acquaintances. A participant in one discussion perceived turning on "all those big flood lights on the Wrigley Building" in Chicago as a signal that the energy crisis had ended. Others backed up opinions with these references: "When I see the Army training maneuvers, or the Navy going out . . ."; "the first gas station we came to off the Indiana Tollway—wide open!"; "the rest of the people on the road"; "the electricity bill we just got"; "my electric bill . . ."; "my family in Illinois . . ."; "One of my friends who runs a gas station said to me . . ."; "the people behind us . . ."; "People we know . . ."; "The people I have talked to . . ."; "I've had people in my cab tell me . . ."; and so forth. Opinions expressed by the president and business leaders are not cited for the same purpose. The pattern can be examined in Bee Angell and Associates, Inc., *A Qualitative Study of Consumer Attitudes Toward Energy Conservation* (Washington, D.C.: Federal

Energy Administration, Office of Energy Conservation and Environment, 1975), from which the phrases above have been quoted.

9. On the need for policy guidance and search procedures see especially the testimony of Anthony L. Shoemaker, City Manager, Clearwater, Florida, and Harvey Ruvin, County Commissioner, Dade County, Florida, in *Hearings on Local Energy Policies*. See also note 14.

10. A parallel information network emphasizing energy conservation and appropriate energy technologies by and for neighborhood groups has also emerged in recent years. See for example *Self-Reliance,* published bimonthly by the Institute for Local Self-Reliance, Washington, D.C.; and *People and Energy,* published intermittently by the Citizens' Energy Project, Washington, D.C.

11. See Richard Mounts, "What Cities are Doing About the Energy Crunch, What Remains for Them to Do," *Nation's Cities* 16 (March 1978): 4–11, especially 11, for a discussion of these factors.

12. Testimony of Harvey Ruvin in *Hearings on Local Energy Policies.*

13. See, for example, the data series in the *Monthly Energy Review* published by the Energy Information Administration of the Department of Energy; "Data Gathering Systems," Appendix 2 of the EIA's *Annual Report to Congress, Volume 1, 1977,* which identifies the fifty-nine primary data-gathering systems; and the testimony of Lawrence S. Mayer, Princeton University, in *Hearings on Local Energy Policies.*

14. In the *Hearings on Local Energy Policies,* community leaders reported delays and other difficulties in searching through the maze of federal energy information, and often found the results to be too aggregate, narrowly technical or economic, or otherwise not on the mark. Information provided through regional and state energy offices may be generally more accessible, but only partially meets the requirements of community leaders. The Department of Energy does not have a systematic program for documenting cases in local energy policy. Robert N. Black, city councilman, testified that the Department of Energy had not yet made inquiries about Davis's experience. Moreover, the Department of Energy is understandably reluctant to become involved in controversial local decisions. Jerry E. Thonn, Chairman of the Citizens' Overview Committee, testified in connection with the Seattle controversy that "The [DOE] regional office, of course, would not touch the policy questions that we were discussing with a ten-foot pole."

15. The small grants program for appropriate technologies and the Energy Extension Service are addressed to individual inventors and consumers, respectively, and not community level decisions. The Comprehensive Community Energy Management and Planning Program, a new pilot program, is designed in part to test a planning methodology that was developed under federal contract and that leaves renewable resources out of the community energy audit. Nevertheless, it is a promising first step.

16. See Angell, *A Qualitative Study of Consumer Attitudes.* Although

the results are qualitative rather than quantitative, they vividly illustrate this response pattern.

17. Partial precedents for options 5 and 6 can be found in Sec. 522(c) and Sec. 511(c), respectively, of H.R. 8444, the National Energy Act as passed by the U.S. House of Representatives in August 1977. These provisions were eliminated as the House receded to the Senate position in the conference committee.

18. For theoretical and design considerations, see Fred D. Baldwin, "Meters, Bills, and the Bathroom Scale," *Public Utilities Fortnightly,* February 3, 1977, pp. 11–17.

19. See the *1975 Directory of Customer Accounting Methods and Equipment* prepared by the Customer Activities Committee of the American Gas Association and the Edison Electric Institute.

20. See Kurt W. Riegel and Suzanne E. Salomon, "Getting Individual Customers Involved in Energy Conservation: A Printed Comparative Energy Use Indicator on Customer Bills?" *Public Utilities Fortnightly,* November 7, 1974, pp. 29–32.

21. Many of these factors are explored in *Solar Energy Incentives Analysis: Psycho-Economic Factors Affecting the Decision Making of Consumers and the Technology Delivery System* (Washington, D.C.: Department of Energy, Assistant Secretary for Conservation and Solar Applications, 1978).

22. On the importance of elasticities in long-run analysis of the energy situation, see Charles J. Hitch, ed., *Modeling Energy-Economy Interactions: Five Approaches* (Baltimore: Johns Hopkins University Press, 1977), especially the concluding chapter by Lester Lave.

23. Jeffrey S. Milstein in "How Consumers Feel About Energy: Attitudes and Behavior During the Winter and Spring of 1976–77" (June, 1977), a paper written for the Office of Conservation, Federal Energy Administration, concludes on the basis of many surveys that "people do not want to pay higher prices for energy because higher energy prices are *the* energy problem to most people. Higher energy prices are of great concern to people because they are personally experienced weekly and monthly through gasoline and utility bills" (p. 17).

24. United States, Executive Office of The President, Energy Policy and Planning, *The National Energy Plan* (Washington, D.C.: Government Printing Office, 1977), p. 26.

2 The Organization and Management of a Community Energy Initiative

Ronald D. Brunner, Maryann Friday,

and Eugene Tierney

Community energy initiatives continue to proliferate around the country. The problem is how to sustain them long enough to realize significant improvements in community energy efficiency through energy conservation and the utilization of renewable energy sources. While scattered results are possible in the short run, it takes several years to realize significant results.

In general, sustained progress toward the goal of community energy efficiency depends upon (1) the amount and mix of resources available to the community, including analytical, political, and financial capabilities as well as motivation, and (2) the skill with which these resources are organized and managed. Organization and management strategies are typically made explicit in a work plan, which sets forth structures, procedures, and objectives. The work plan is important. If objectives are unrealistic, or structures and procedures cumbersome and inefficient, the flow of resources necessary to sustain the initiative will tend to be dissipated rather than maintained or increased.

Ann Arbor's energy initiative can be dated from January 28, 1980, when the city government's Office of Community Development presented an energy work plan to city council. Reviewing its own activities over the previous year, Community Development observed that

> the city's energy effort is entering a new phase. It is time to commit ourselves to a broader program that will increase energy savings in municipal operations and to undertake a community-wide effort to develop and implement a comprehensive Energy Policy.[1]

Among the organizations already active in local energy matters were the Chamber of Commerce, several architectural and engineering firms, the Ecology Center, the Cooperative Extension Service, and units of the University of Michigan as well as the city government.

Community Development's energy work plan was modeled after the energy work plan of Portland, Oregon. It proposed an organizational structure consisting of an Energy Steering Committee (ESC), six subsidiary task forces, and a Community Forum, all of which were to be linked to a broader base of citizens and organizations. The procedures to be observed by the Energy Steering Committee were largely unspecified, but it was expected to hold regular meetings and to encourage citizen participation. The basic management objective was to review a proposed comprehensive energy policy and make recommendations to city council within nine to twelve months. The essentials of this work plan were approved by resolution of the city council on March 17, 1980, and reaffirmed by the mayor at the first meeting of the Energy Steering Committee on May 8.

This paper documents and analyzes the evolution of Ann Arbor's energy work plan through the first year of implementation. The evolution of a work plan is both desirable and inevitable. No plan can accurately anticipate and incorporate in advance all of the factors that affect its implementation, and some flexibility in interpretation and application is desirable in order to incorporate new insights as they arise through experience. The evolution of the work plan merits close examination because it clarifies organization and management choices, and their implications for sustaining the energy initiative and eventually for realizing significant improvements in community energy efficiency. What has been learned in the organization and management of Ann Arbor's initiative can be adapted and applied elsewhere.

The first section of this paper examines the work plan and the resources available in May, 1980, when the steering committee first met. Subsequent sections show how the organizational structure, procedural guidelines, and managerial objectives were adapted to constraints and opportunities largely unforeseen at the outset. These are followed by an interim evaluation. While it is premature to assess improvements in community energy efficiency, it is possible to consider whether the resources necessary to sustain the initiative are increasing or decreasing. The concluding section distills organization and management lessons from the Ann Arbor experience and considers these lessons in the light of experience elsewhere.

   A large number of factors and complex relationships are involved in organization and management, and their significance is subject to multiple interpretations. We have presented our interpretation of the Ann Arbor experience in the pages that follow, but we have also attempted to provide enough substantive detail for the reader to formulate and assess alternative interpretations.

Background: May, 1980

In its *1980 Energy Plan,* Ann Arbor's Office of Community Development proposed the following goal, adopted from Portland:

> The goal of the energy policy is to increase the energy efficiency of existing structures and the transportation system of the city through policies and programs which encourage conservation of nonrenewable resources and the application of renewable resources, while maintaining the attractiveness of the city as a place to live and do business.[2]

The goal was affirmed, essentially, by the city council when it acknowledged "a need for the City to provide community leadership in promoting energy conservation and renewable energy resources."[3]

   This section reviews the various and somewhat ambiguous expectations about how this goal was to be achieved. It focuses on the work plan as it was understood in May, 1980, and the resources available to implement it at that time.

The Work Plan

Management objectives specify intermediate outcomes to be realized in the pursuit of some more basic goal. As such, they are intended to affect the directions in which resources are allocated in the near term. The basic objective from the standpoint of the community development office, as noted above, was to have the Energy Steering Committee review a proposed comprehensive energy policy and make recommendations to the city council within nine to twelve months. What was meant by "a comprehensive energy policy" was partially explained in these terms:

> An Energy Policy will establish the objectives and goals of the community's effort to conserve energy and promote use of renew-

able resources. Programs which rely on education, incentives, and mandatory requirements will be assessed in the light of the policy objectives. Program recommendations will be made for final adoption and implementation.[4]

The distinction between *policy* as goals and objectives on the one hand and specific *programs* on the other turned out to be extremely important, as we shall see. It was emphasized in the organization of the *1980 Energy Plan*. As shown in table 1, some fifty-eight objectives under six major policies were proposed in section 2. Appendix C listed seventy-one "example programs"—some proposed, some planned, some implemented—in support of these objectives. In addition, section 3, listing work to be performed by city employees and consultants in 1980, consisted largely of a subset of the seventy-one "example" programs.

To illustrate the distinction, consider the following objective under "Policy No. 2, Retrofit of Existing Buildings (Residential)":

> To assist residential property owners to reach a zero net outflow of capital expended for energy conservation actions through a range of financial and tax incentives. The needs of renters will be satisfied by stimulating owner investment through the same incentives.[5]

TABLE 1.   Distribution of Objectives and Programs by Policy in the *1980 Energy Plan*

Policy[a]	No. of Objectives[a]	No. of Programs	
		ESC[b]	City[c]
Policy No. 1, Role of the City	5	3	2
Policy No. 2, Retrofit of Existing Buildings			
Residential	11	8	2
Nonresidential	11	8	1
Policy No. 3, Land Use	5	4	0
Policy No. 4, Renewable Resources	8	11	5
Policy No. 5, Transportation	7	10	2
Policy No. 6, City Government	11	27	19
Total	58	71	31

a. From sec. 2 of the *1980 Energy Plan*
b. From app. C of the *1980 Energy Plan*
c. From sec. 3 of the *1980 Energy Plan*

One program to implement this objective, as outlined in appendix C, was property tax reduction:

> Develop a program which reduced the property tax liability for residential property owners during the period of voluntary retrofit. The amount is that which is necessary to meet the zero capital outflow mark.[6]

The distinction between policy objectives and specific programs is important because it suggests alternative directions for the allocation of resources. Moreover, policy and program development entail different resource requirements. While it is relatively easy to affirm in principle such objectives as zero capital outflow, it is typically rather difficult to design and justify a specific program to accomplish such objectives. For example, a program to reduce property tax liability raises a number of difficult questions: Who should be eligible? Who should administer the program? What would it cost? Are the costs justified by projected savings? And so on. The program agenda summarized in table 1 is ambitious, to say the least.

The city council and the mayor deleted references to programs from their official statements. Council resolved that "an Energy Steering Committee be established in accordance with the *1980 Energy Plan* (app. B) *to review the Energy Policy objectives and to recommend final policies to City Council.*"[7] In his charge to the Energy Steering Committee at its first meeting on May 8, Mayor Louis D. Belcher said that its first objective was "to recommend to City Council a comprehensive energy policy for the City of Ann Arbor."[8] (The second was to assume responsibility for overall direction of the energy awareness campaign already begun under a grant from the state.) The steering committee was asked "to complete its work and make its recommendations for a comprehensive energy policy to City Council by April 30, 1981."[9] Neither the mayor nor city council attempted to specify what *comprehensive* meant in this context. The committee was left with the task of interpreting its basic objective.

The *1980 Energy Plan* specified procedures for the appointment of steering committee members, but had little to say about procedural guidelines for the work of the committee itself. In particular, it was unclear how policy objectives or programs were to be developed, reviewed, and adopted. The mayor provided some clarification in his charge to the Committee:

> In the process of developing that [comprehensive energy] policy, the Committee should solicit a wide range of opinions from all aspects of the community. . . . The Committee will hold regular meetings and its membership must be prepared to be actively involved in the preparation of the policies.[10]

In addition, the mayor prescribed six general principles to guide the work of committee members. Like the statement of the basic energy goal, the six general principles were adopted verbatim from Portland.[11] The steering committee, in effect, was left with considerable flexibility to work out its own detailed operating procedures.

The organizational structure proposed in appendix B of the *1980 Energy Plan* was established by resolution of city council, as we have seen. The organization chart, reproduced as figure 1, defined various roles and their relationships; the text provided additional guidance about how these roles would be filled. The Energy Steering Committee, to be nominated by the mayor and approved by city council, would be supported by the community development office and by various units of the University of Michigan. Five task forces, each chaired by a member of the steering committee, would be organized under the steering committee to perform the "intensive work on the Energy Policy and related programs."[12] Additional task force members would be drawn from the broad-based Community Forum. Note that four of the task forces correspond to policy numbers 2 through 5 in table 1. Policy number 6, "City Government," was the responsibility of an Energy Management Task Force consisting of city employees organized under the city administrator's office, as outlined in section 3 of the *1980 Energy Plan*. The fifth task force organized under the Energy Steering Committee, "Promotion," was to assume responsibility for the energy awareness program mentioned in the mayor's charge and for information and publicity in general. The internal organization of the task forces would be worked out later.

Resources
The members of the Energy Steering Committee were nominated by the mayor from a list of interested and qualified citizens prepared by

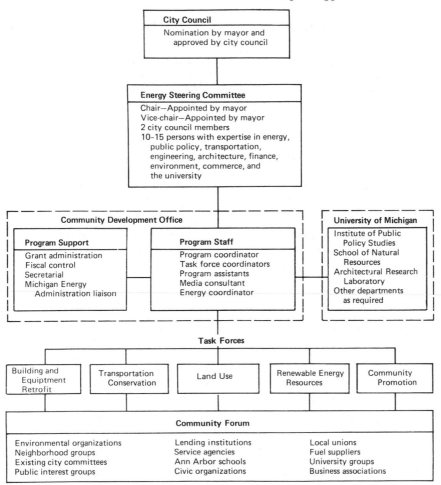

FIG. 1. Organizational structure as given in the *1980 Energy Plan*

community development staff and consultants and appointed by the city council in April, 1980. The backgrounds and affiliations of the initial twenty-three members are noted in table 2.

The common information on local energy matters available to the Energy Steering Committee consisted primarily of the *1980 Energy Plan*, although individual members had been involved in or exposed to other locally focused studies of some relevance. The committee clearly included sufficient analytical capability to extend this information base

TABLE 2.   Affiliations and Backgrounds of Members of the Energy Steering Committee

Architect, Hobbs and Black Associates, and Chair of the Ann Arbor Planning Commission	Solar architect, Sunstructures Inc., and Michigan representative to the Program Review and Planning Board, Mid-America Solar Energy Corp.
Assistant Vice President, National Bank and Trust, and member of the Chamber of Commerce Energy Committee	Engineer, Ford Motor Co., and Member of the Board, Ann Arbor Transportation Authority
Assistant to the Vice President for State Relations and Planning, University of Michigan	Dean, College of Architecture, University of Michigan
Associate Professor of Political Science, University of Michigan, and specialist in energy policy	Principal, Clivus Multrum Great Lakes, Inc., distributors of composting sewage systems and wood burning stoves
Professor of Engineering, University of Michigan, and specialist in comparative energy technologies	Chief Mechanical Engineer, Bechtel Corporation
Professor of Mechanical Engineering, University of Michigan, and former President, Central Solar Energy Research Corporation	Principal, Climate Engineering Inc., distributors and installers of heating and cooling systems
Transportation Policy Analyst, Grefe Associates	Manager, Ann Arbor Division, Detroit Edison Co.
Professor of Civil Engineering, University of Michigan, and specialist in alternative energy systems	Manager, Office of Off-Campus Housing, University of Michigan
Member of the Ann Arbor City Council (Democrat)	Member of the Ann Arbor City Council (Republican)
Professor of Resource Economics, University of Michigan, and specialist in wood and other renewable resources	Member, Mayor's Committee on the Handicapped, and Member, Executive Committee, Community Development Block Grant Program
	Director, Ann Arbor Ecology Center
Administrator, University of Michigan, and former Director, Huron River Watershed Council	Community Liaison Staff Member, Ann Arbor Chapter, Public Interest Research Group in Michigan (PIRGIM)

and develop it into policies and programs. At least three-quarters of the twenty-three members had some prior professional background in energy conservation or energy technologies. There were at least five engineers, three architects, a number of people in energy-related businesses, as well as environmentalists, policy analysts and politicians, a financier, an economist, and a public relations specialist.

The potential for mobilizing support for the committee's work relied primarily on the affiliations of the various members and the formal commitment of the mayor and city council. A number of public and private sector organizations could provide input and potential support through their members appointed to the Energy Steering Committee. For example, in the public sector alone, the committee included members affiliated with the city council, the Ann Arbor Planning Commission, the Ann Arbor Transportation Authority, the executive committee of the Community Development Block Grant Program, and various units of the University of Michigan, including teaching, research, and administrative units. In addition, the formal commitment of the mayor and council constituted an important resource in that it facilitated access to city officials and, potentially at least, would provide a sympathetic audience for the Energy Steering Committee's report a year hence. Aside from support of the March 17 resolution by both the Republican majority and the Democratic minority on city council, the Republican mayor had already made a public commitment to continue his efforts to transform Ann Arbor into a model for energy-conscious, midwestern communities.[13]

The financial resources of the Energy Steering Committee were limited primarily to funds for the typing, reproduction, printing, and mailing of documents, and for staff salaries. The staff consisted of two, and later three, members of the community development staff, two consultants assigned to the committee, and two work-study students. About twenty-five thousand dollars was provided through an energy awareness grant from the Energy Administration of the Michigan Department of Commerce, and a similar amount through discretionary funds from the Community Development Block Grant. The initial energy budget presented to city council on March 17 totaled approximately one hundred ten thousand dollars but most of this was allocated to energy programs within the city government that were largely outside the purview of the Energy Steering Committee.

In short, the capabilities of the committee consisted primarily of information and expertise, the potential for mobilizing political support for its recommendations, funds for producing and distributing documents, and limited staff time. Unlike other communities, Ann Arbor did not have funds to pay for data collection and analysis or funds to implement the policies and programs to be recommended by the committee.[14] The development of such recommendations would depend upon voluntary contributions of time and effort on the part of committee members. Consequently, the intensity of motivation of committee members would be crucial in the effective utilization of the committee's other resources. Although each member had volunteered his or her services, the intensity of motivation was largely untested in May, 1980, when the committee first met.

Organizational Structure

One of the first tasks of the Energy Steering Committee was to get organized. In particular, it was necessary to elaborate the division of work and responsibility set forth in the original organizational structure (fig. 1). It was also necessary to appoint committee members and recruit community members into the five task forces. As we shall see, departures in practice from formal decisions about organizational structure and membership assignments reflected the preferences of the members themselves.

Formal Decisions

The committee quickly organized itself by selecting leaders from its own membership. John A. Clark was elected permanent chair of the Energy Steering Committee shortly after the mayor, at the conclusion of his remarks to the committee at the first meeting, had appointed Mr. Clark temporary chair. Mr. Clark is a professor of mechanical engineering and a nationally recognized expert on solar energy. Robert Blackmer and Steve McCargar were elected vice-chairs at the second meeting on June 5. They are, respectively, a banker affiliated with the Chamber of Commerce Energy Committee, and the head of the Ann Arbor Ecology Center, a nonprofit corporation. In these elections the committee recognized the importance of choosing its leadership from different parts of the community.

Task force organization was carried forward when the community development staff distributed, prior to the third meeting on June 26, organization charts for each of the five task forces proposed in the *1980 Energy Plan*. The organization chart for the Building Retrofit Task Force is reproduced in figure 2 as an example. In each case the charts suggested that membership be drawn from the steering committee and that additional membership, as well as inputs, be drawn from particular interests (such as builders and contractors in the case of Building Retrofit) and from the citizenry at large through the Community Forum. In two cases, Building Retrofit and Renewable Resources, the charts also suggested an internal division of labor. For example, members of Building Retrofit were to specialize in commer-

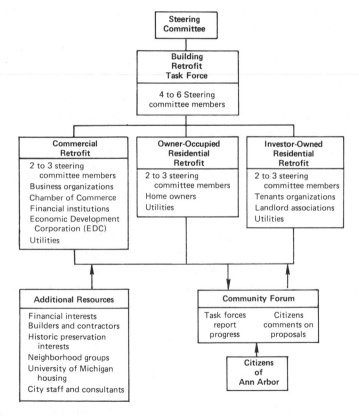

FIG. 2.   Building Retrofit Task Force organizational structure as given in the *1980 Energy Plan*

cial, owner-occupied, and investor-owned residential buildings. The steering committee approved the organization of the five task forces with the understanding that additional task forces might be deemed necessary and approved at some future date.

The process of assigning steering committee members to the task forces began at the first meeting when the chair asked each member to write him a letter regarding task force preferences. With these letters and the advice of the vice-chairs and staff, the chair developed a roster of task force membership for consideration by the committee at its fourth meeting on July 17. Two co-chairs were appointed to each task force to provide for continuity of leadership in the event that one or the other could not attend a task force meeting. In addition, with a few exceptions, each committee member was appointed to two task forces to provide for informal coordination among the task forces. For example, of the committee members appointed to the Building Retrofit Task Force, at least one and as many as three were also appointed to each of the other four task forces.

In the cover memorandum for the proposed roster, the chair noted that "in most cases, I have assigned task force membership in accordance with the requests of the Energy Steering Committee."[15] Inspection of the roster shows that, in fact, the members' particular areas of interest and expertise tended to be reflected in task force appointments. For example, a transportation policy analyst and a motor company executive (who also sits on the board of the Ann Arbor Transportation Authority) were designated co-chairs of the Transportation Task Force. This process of self-selection tended to concentrate particular areas of expertise where they were potentially most useful in the organizational structure. Self-selection also makes sense where it is necessary to sustain the motivation of volunteers to contribute.

Recruitment of additional task force members from the community at large began with a newsprint tabloid, which summarized the *1980 Energy Plan* and included a form that readers might clip and return in order to volunteer for the task forces. The tabloid was designed by the staff media consultant and approved with a few changes by the committee at the first meeting. Twenty thousand copies were distributed free in June through banks, libraries, and other establishments frequented by the public. About twenty-five people responded and were referred to the task forces in which they had expressed an interest. Additional volunteers, graduate and undergraduate students, turned up in September when university classes resumed. (Some students received course credit for task force work.)

Modification and further elaboration of the task force structure continued after most of them began to meet in July. For example, at the committee meeting on August 7, "Transportation" was redefined as "Transportation and Land Use" to address more adequately the close connection between population densities, employment concentrations, and transportation efficiency. Similarly, "Land Use" was reconstituted as "New Construction and Site Design" in order to emphasize energy conservation in the design (as opposed to the location) of new developments. These changes reflected the preferences of cochairs and task force members. In addition, each task force began to define its own internal division of work and responsibility.

The internal organization adopted by Building Retrofit is typical. The work of the task force was projected to proceed in three phases. In the first or investigative phase, eight research tasks described as "action items" were defined.[16] The plan specifies that "the work will be subdivided among the members of the Task Force who will report to [the] overall Task Force at scheduled meetings."[17] Two of the action items were the responsibility of the task force as a whole; the other six were the responsibility of groups of from two to four task force members. In the second and third phases, the information gathered would be distilled and coordinated by the task force as a whole and eventually developed into a statement of policy.

The key feature of the plan was that *groups* would assume work and responsibilities for policy *subareas*. Allowing for variations in detail, this approach was replicated independently by Renewable Resources and, insofar as the records show, by New Construction and Site Design. Transportation and Land Use added a novel feature: its four subcommittees were to meet independently to develop and write sections of the task force report.[18] The obvious advantage of the group approach is that it provides, in principle, for comparison and coordination among alternatives, and a comprehensive overview at the task force level—or, in the case of Transportation and Land Use, at the subcommittee level.

The exception to this internal organization structure was the Promotion Task Force. The key feature of its plan was that *individual* members would select a *program* idea and assume responsibility for developing it into a well-documented, actionable proposal. An open-ended list of more than forty program ideas was generated at the outset. The role of the task force as a whole was to support each "program entrepreneur" with suggestions, criticisms, and encouragement. What was lost in coordination and comprehensiveness through this individual approach was expected to be more than repaid in productivity, in the form of specific programs that could be implemented in the short run. For one thing, the "stick" of personal responsibility and the "carrot" of personal recognition were expected to sustain motivation. For another, coordination costs were avoided by allowing self-selected entrepreneurs a free hand, subject oɪly to the requirement of task force approval of any proposal before it could be reported to the steering committee.

Actual Practice
The formal division of work and responsibility in each task force was modified in practice in several respects. First, as already noted, the areas to be covered by two of the task forces were redefined to reflect the preferences of their co-chairs and members. Second, an advisory group comprised of the committee leadership and the co-chairs of the five task forces was established at the request of the chair on September 4, although it had not been included in the original plan. The advisory group reflected the need to coordinate aspects of the task forces' work in progress in a smaller group than the steering committee as a whole. Third, the Community Forum was never organized as a body that would meet regularly on a quarterly basis.[19] Among the reasons were the press of other matters deemed more important by the committee, and the community response to the tabloid, which was less than overwhelming.

The actual pattern of participation at the task force level also differed from the nominal pattern of appointment and recruitment. First, some participants dropped out. These include an undetermined number of community members and five steering committee members who had resigned by the end of the year. The latter included one co-chair of the original Transportation Task Force and both co-chairs of the original Land Use Task Force. These vacancies were filled in September and October, but the effect was to delay the work of the two reconstituted task forces. Four new members were added to the steering committee at various times up to the first meeting of 1981.[20] Second, after a "shakedown" period of a few months, most steering committee and community members were involved in the work of only one task force. For example, a co-chair of Renewables withdrew from the work of Promotion, and a co-chair of Promotion only sporadically attended the meetings of Renewables. The time and effort required to participate in two task forces was evidently more than most members were willing or able to contribute.

The effective levels of participation in the work of the task forces during the months of September, October, and November, 1980, are summarized in table 3. The figures include attendance at all meetings for which records exist in this period. For each task force, average attendance per meeting by steering committee members is less than half the number of steering committee members appointed in July. Total average attendance per meeting can be compared with the chair's expectation that "I would visualize that an effective task force size should total from 12 to 18 members."[21] Only the Renewable Resources Task Force realized average attendance levels in this range, and two of the others had levels substantially below it. The capability of a task force is constrained not only by *average* attendance per meeting, but also by the number who attend *regularly*. Table 3 shows that if "regulars" are defined as those who attend at least 76 percent of the meetings, there were only two regulars at one extreme (Building Retrofit) and as many as eight regulars at the other (Renewable Resources).

In short, the organizational structure evolved in the direction of the interests and capabilities of those who implemented it, whatever the original intent of the initial design. Given the diversity among the steering committee and community volunteers and the process of self-selection, significant differences began to emerge among the task forces in internal organization and in levels and patterns of participation. If the original organizational structure was intended to provide for coordination from the top down, the effective structure was tending toward diversification from the bottom up.

Procedural Guidelines

While the organizational structure was being worked out in practice, the Energy Steering Committee and its task forces began to clarify procedural guidelines. Operating rules were distributed by the com-

TABLE 3. Attendance at Task Force Meetings, September through November, 1980

Task Force	No. of Meetings	No. of Members	No. attending (by percentage of meetings)				Average Attendance per Meeting
			0–25%	26–50%	51–75%	76% +	
Building Retrofit[a]	6						
Community members		5	0	2	2	1	2.8
ESC members		8	1	3	3	1	3.8
Total		13	1	5	5	2	6.6
New Construction and Site Design[b]	5						
Community members		8	2	1	2	3	4.4
ESC members		9	7	0	1	1	2.0
Total		17	9	1	3	4	6.4
Renewable Resources[c]	9						
Community members		16	6	2	2	6	8.8
ESC members		10	5	1	2	2	4.1
Total		26	11	3	4	8	12.9
Promotion[d]	12						
Community members		14	5	1	5	3	6.0
ESC members		10	4	0	2	4	4.8
Total		24	9	1	7	7	10.8

Source: Task force meeting records
Note: Figures exclude attendance by staff. The media consultant and another staff member attended Promotion Task Force meetings regularly. A third staff member attended meetings of the other task forces regularly.
    The subcommittees of the Transportation and Land Use Task Force are not included, because they met separately.
a. Sept. 15, 22; Oct. 6, 13, 30; Nov. 3
b. Sept. 30; Oct. 7, 21; Nov. 4, 18
c. Sept. 24; Oct. 1, 8, 15, 22, 29; Nov. 5, 12, 19
d. Sept. 8, 15, 22, 29; Oct. 6, 13, 20, 27; Nov. 3, 10, 17, 24

mittee staff in draft form at the second meeting of the steering committee on June 5 and approved with amendments by the committee on October 16.[22] More importantly, the committee began to grapple with questions more directly related to the fulfillment of its charge from the mayor. How were policies and programs to be developed? How were they to be reviewed by the public? How would the committee consider and approve the work of the task forces? This section recounts how answers to these questions were evolved. As we shall see, some of these procedural choices had important substantive implications.

Policy and Program Development
It was recognized rather quickly that policy and program development would have to be done in the task forces, as suggested in the *1980 Energy Plan.*[23] When the roster of task force membership was proposed in July, the chair stated the general understanding that the task forces would meet frequently, and that future meetings of the steering committee (approximately every third week) would be used primarily for task force reporting. With the exception of New Construction and Site Design, the task forces began to meet in July and August. By September each task force had regularly scheduled meetings every week.

Task force members were soon impressed by the magnitude of the effort required. As early as the September 4 meeting of the steering committee, during task force reports, several members expressed concern whether there was sufficient time to consider adequately the volume of material required to produce draft task force reports by February 1, 1981, the tentative deadline. The concern was taken up at a meeting of the advisory group, which reported back at the next meeting of the steering committee on September 25. As summarized in the minutes of the meeting, the task forces were requested to keep the following procedural guidelines in mind:

1. Review the *1980 Energy Plan* . . . and use this report as a reference or point of departure for further investigation and recommendations.
2. *Concentrate efforts in a few energy conservation areas (two to four)* for detailed study and analysis. Criteria for selection should include:

  a) potential energy savings to city,

  b) practical feasibility of proposal, and

  c) demonstration of energy savings and visibility.

3. *Identify other areas with potentials for energy savings* or which are important components of a comprehensive city energy program. *In-depth studies in these areas are not required;* instead, simply list with a brief discussion citing reasons for importance and questions to be addressed in future studies.

4. Strive to meet the February 1, 1981, deadline for submission of a final task force report. The Energy Steering Committee will monitor the progress of task forces toward this deadline.[24]

The logic, of course, was simply to define priorities and allocate effort accordingly, leaving open the possibility of a deadline extension. The references to "areas" of energy conservation are sufficiently ambiguous to be interpreted in program or policy terms. Notice also that *policy* is clearly intended where *program* is used in point 3. Obviously, terminology had not yet been standardized.

This strategy for reconciling the magnitude of the task with the limited time and resources available was reaffirmed on December 11, when the steering committee accepted a common outline for each of the task force reports. The outline, prepared by staff and reviewed by the advisory group, called for detailed discussions of each of the two to four "specific/high priority target areas of study." The outline construed a specific/high priority target area to include both a statement of policy objective and a proposed program. A proposed program was to include specific, detailed recommendations, a rationale, expected impacts and benefits, and implementation strategies.

By late November, when the task forces presented interim progress reports to city council, it was clear that two distinct courses of action had been adopted. Tendencies toward diversification continued to be expressed at the task force level, despite the apparent acceptance of common procedures and format.

One course of action pointed toward development of broad policy recommendations. The Building Retrofit, Transportation and Land Use, and New Construction and Site Design task forces defined three, six, and seven areas of conservation, respectively. Only Transportation and Land Use defined priorities among these areas. The other two task forces gave equal attention to the areas defined. In none of the thirteen areas covered by these three task forces were specific programs selected for detailed analysis of costs and benefits, practical feasibility, or visibility as a demonstration project. For example, the draft task report eventually produced by Building Retrofit recommended seventeen policy objectives across three areas in twenty-eight pages, exclusive of appendices. In general, time, effort, and other resources were allocated broadly but thinly over a large number of policy objectives. The cost of this form of comprehensiveness was a lack of programmatic detail.

This course of action reflected the dominant viewpoint in the three task forces, as well as the resource constraints under which they operated. The members of these task forces took seriously the idea of comprehensive policy review and recommendations, and they believed that individual policy objectives should remain integrated and coordinated with the others. Hence they resisted the setting of priorities and the development of specific programs. These tasks were deferred to a later date, and responsibility for them devolved to someone else. Moreover, the program development option may have been foreclosed to some extent by resource constraints. There was little if any Ann Arbor–focused program research available to these three task forces.[25] In addition, Building Retrofit and New Construction and Site Design had an average attendance of a little more than six members at task force meetings, and only two and four regular members, respectively (see table 3). A co-chair of Building Retrofit drew attention to the problem of "sporadic" attendance on several occasions.[26]

A second course of action was pursued by the Renewable Resources and Promotion task forces. Their status reports to the city council showed they had moved quickly past broad policy review to specific programs that would eventually be recommended. Renewable Resources reported work on nine programs, in spite of the initial intention to emphasize policy areas in its internal organization. Work on some of the nine was later deferred to focus on an energy information clearinghouse; a multimaterial, city-wide recycling program; a solar demonstration project at city parks; reactivation of four city-owned dams to produce hydropower; and waiver of building permit fees for renewable resource projects. The Promotion Task Force listed four programs already approved by the steering committee, two more to be completed by February 1, and three more still under consideration. In general, resources were concentrated on a small number of specific programs and the broad policy review essentially ignored. This course of action precluded the selection or justification of a few programs from a large number of alternatives on grounds of *relative* feasibility, cost-effectiveness, and the like.

A different viewpoint and fewer resource constraints were expressed in this course of action. The general expectation was that to recommend a broad set of policy objectives to city council would be a symbolic gesture at best. While the council might approve such objectives in principle, it would only adopt and commit resources to the implementation of specific programs for which costs and benefits as well as practical feasibility were reasonably clear. Moreover, given the heavy work load of the city council, programs were expected to get more serious attention if recommended one at a time, rather than simultaneously as part of a comprehensive package. In short, effort invested in individual programs, each to be considered separately on its own merits, was believed more likely to be repaid with positive action from council. And such positive action would eventually be necessary to sustain the motivation of task force members.[27] In addition, these two task forces had the opportunity to utilize and extend existing, Ann Arbor–based program research, and levels of participation necessary to do so. Table 3 shows that more than ten people attended the meetings of Renewable Resources and Promotion, on average, and that these two task forces had eight and seven members, respectively, who could be considered regulars. (The Promotion Task Force also enjoyed the services of the media consultant.) Program research and development requires a relatively high level of effort, but it may also be relatively rewarding in view of the level of sustained effort.

Public Review
In his charge to the steering committee, the mayor had urged it to solicit a wide range of viewpoints from all parts of the community. Late in the fall of 1980, as the work of the task forces came into focus in anticipation of the February 1 deadline, public outreach was placed on the steering committee agenda. The Promotion Task Force identified the principal choices in the form of questions at the December 11 meeting, and proposed a public outreach plan at the meeting of Janu-

ary 15. After some discussion, the plan was approved unanimously by the steering committee at that time.

As summarized by the Promotion Task Force,

> *the plan proposes to focus our public outreach efforts on individual policy* [sic] *options rather than on the task force reports or the comprehensive energy plan as a whole.* The task force reports are conceived as working documents from which individual options are selected for public review on recommendation of the task forces and clearance by the Steering Committee. The separate and sequential review of policy [*sic*] options (and their possible adoption and implementation) would proceed in parallel with further work on the task force reports and the comprehensive plan.[28]

Terminology was still not standardized. What the context clearly indicates to be *program* options were referred to as *policy* options.

After clearance for public review by the steering committee, the Promotion Task Force was to develop for each option a plan to forward documentation to those most likely to be interested and affected. Responses would be directed to the staff for purposes of coordination. The task force that developed the option would have responsibility to respond to substantive comments and possibly revise the option accordingly; the Promotion Task Force would have responsibility to report on the breadth and diversity of public input before final action was taken by the steering committee. If the steering committee acted favorably, the option would be recommended to another body, such as the city council, the city's Energy Management Task Force, or the planning commission, as appropriate.

The decision to focus public outreach on program options rather than on task force reports or the comprehensive energy plan as a whole was key. In part, this decision can be explained by the source of the plan. Recall that the Promotion Task Force had adopted program-focused internal organization and procedures for reasons already explained. Additional reasons were provided in the plan itself.

> This plan emphasizes the separate and sequential review of individual policy [*sic*] options in order to *maximize public participation,* to *provide for thorough substantive review,* and to *produce results in the short run.* Results may take the form of policy [*sic*]

options adopted and implemented as well as energy savings realized.[29]

Results in the short run were considered necessary to justify the level of effort already invested, and to sustain participation by volunteers serving on the task forces and the steering committee.

An alternative emphasis on promotion of task force reports or the comprehensive energy plan was described as "self-defeating" in these terms. First, some options would be ready for review well before the other, larger documents. Delay would frustrate those who had worked to develop and document options, and would serve no useful purpose. Second, time, interest, and expertise were limited. To focus on the larger documents would inhibit participation by those members of the community who were willing and able to comment on only parts of them, and would encourage superficial review, unnecessary delays in achieving results, or both. And third, the separate and sequential review of options would permit and encourage everyone to learn how to design and document efficiently: what was learned in one instance might be applied to the next. Simultaneous review of the task force reports or of the comprehensive plan as a whole would delay the lessons of experience and render them less applicable.

Although the public outreach plan was approved unanimously, as we have seen, there remained some ambiguity about what constituted a policy or a program option. Clarification of the ambiguity came through confrontation between the policy-oriented and program-oriented task forces. Building Retrofit tried unsuccessfully to have a large section of its task force report cleared for public review through the outreach plan at the steering committee meeting on February 19. Similarly, Transportation and Land Use proposed to have its entire task force report cleared for public review through the outreach plan on March 5. Instead, a motion to affirm that responsibility for public review of the task force reports be assigned to the task forces themselves was passed with two dissenting votes from co-chairs of Building Retrofit and Transportation and Land Use. (The other co-chairs of these two task forces, and the co-chairs of New Construction and Site Design, did not attend the meeting.)

The motion was justified on grounds that it reaffirmed previous actions by the steering committee (including approval of the public outreach plan) and that the Promotion Task Force, in any case, had neither the time nor the resources to take on the additional responsibility of task force reports, given the number of individual options already submitted or about to be submitted. The effect of the motion was to allow the Promotion Task Force to focus on specific programs, and to allow the other task forces to include formal public review in the development of their task force reports if they so desired. Transportation and Land Use, with the help of the staff, circulated copies of its draft report and conducted a public hearing on it in April.

Steering Committee Approval

Procedures for steering committee approval of the work of the task forces were clarified through precedents and later incorporated into the public outreach plan. Due to a backlog of research focused on Ann Arbor, precedents began to be established and experience gained as early as the fall of 1980.[30]

The first program option was recommended to the steering committee for consideration at the meeting of September 25 (proposal A). Three members of the Promotion Task Force had prepared a seven-page proposal for a community energy report based on research completed a few months earlier.[31] After review, revision, and approval in the task force, the proposal was circulated by mail to all members of the steering committee prior to the meeting, as specified in the operating rules.[32] After some discussion, the proposal was approved unanimously. Among other things, the proposal illustrated acceptable standards of program development and documentation. Its approval demonstrated that a program ready for steering committee action need not be delayed pending completion of the other parts of the energy awareness campaign or the task force report; rather, it could be approved separately on its own merits when ready. Four other proposals (B through E) were similarly considered and approved by the Energy Steering Committee before the end of the year.

These precedents were important factors in the decision of the Promotion Task Force to design the public outreach plan around individual programs rather than task force reports. Indeed, the public outreach plan merely incorporated formal public review into the procedures already established by precedent. The first program processed through the public outreach plan was a solar demonstration project at city parks.[33] When it was ready for final action at the steering committee meeting on March 19, the only differences were that the Promotion Task Force summarized the breadth and diversity of public responses, and the Renewable Resources Task Force pointed out how the option had been modified according to comments received.

The procedures for committee action on the task force reports were proposed by the chair at the meeting of March 5. The proposal was summarized in the minutes of the meeting:

> The task force reports are the views of a particular task force and the Steering Committee will not vote to approve or disapprove them. The Committee will "accept" them and will not agree or disagree with the recommendations made in the reports. Our review [in the Steering Committee] is intended to make comments on the reports and give them to the task forces.[34]

This proposal was accepted by the steering committee. It reflected the realization that the task force reports differed in their emphasis on broad policy objectives or specific programs, and in their formats.[35] It also reflected the growing expectation that the committee had insufficient time to undertake thorough substantive review and revision of the task force reports, and perhaps insufficient consensus to resolve potential points of controversy. A separate document based on the task force reports would be prepared and submitted to the city council in fulfillment of the charge, but detailed consideration of the form and content of that document was deferred to a later date.

In short, the major procedural decisions recounted in this section reflected continuing differences in the interests and capabilities of the various task forces as well as time constraints. To reconcile the magnitude of the planning task with available time and resources, three task forces undertook broad policy reviews and two concentrated on specific programs—despite the formal acceptance of common planning guidelines and report formats at the steering committee level. Amid some controversy, the program focus was built into steering committee procedures for public review and final action, including the decision to accept (but not approve or disapprove) the task force reports. What remained was to reconcile the various task force reports with each other in fulfillment of the steering committee's objective, as specified in the mayor's charge.

Managerial Objectives

As we have seen, the mayor charged the steering committee "to complete its work and make its recommendations for a comprehensive energy policy to the City Council by April 30, 1981."[36] The council would then consider whether to continue the steering committee or to transfer its functions to a commission to continue its work. In addition, the committee was "responsible for the overall direction of the public awareness campaign"[37] funded by the state.

Comprehensive Energy Plan

As the deadline approached in the spring of 1981, attention shifted to the problem of interpreting the first charge. In particular, what would the Energy Steering Committee report and recommend to the city council? The range of possible answers was constrained by the decision to accept (rather than approve or disapprove) the task force reports, and by differences in the format and substantive emphases of the reports themselves.

The question was taken up at a meeting of the advisory group on March 13. The basic problem was how to accommodate the differences among the task force reports. It was clear that little time and less motivation remained to develop detailed programs to implement the broad policy objectives emphasized in some task force reports. It was equally clear that those task forces which had developed several detailed programs were not particularly interested in stating broad policy goals to justify them.

The solution was a rather straightforward compromise. The community development staff, which had recently hired an editor, would take responsibility for working the recommendations and findings of the various task forces into a common format. One main section would summarize the broad policy goals recommended by the task forces, with gaps in the case of Renewable Resources and Promotion filled in by the staff. Another main section would summarize the specific programs and suggested activities (together with directives for implementation) recommended by the task forces, with gaps in the case of Building Retrofit, Transportation and Land Use, and New Construction and Site Design filled in by the staff. These specific recommendations could not be and were not backed by detailed analysis of their feasibility and worth. A third main section would summarize the findings of the task forces. This section, like the other two, would be organized by task force. The draft energy plan produced by the staff would be reviewed by the steering committee in April. As noted in the minutes of the steering committee meeting on March 19, when the solution was announced,

> this document will be submitted to the Mayor and City Council as the work product of the Steering Committee fulfilling the Mayor's charge. It is hoped that the Committee would be able to finish the plan by June 1, 1981, so its activities could terminate.[38]

Another difference among the task forces surfaced at the advisory group meeting and was eventually accommodated in the document produced by the staff. Some participants voiced the opinion that city council could not responsibly commit resources to programs or activities that had not been shown to be feasible or cost-effective, and that some steering committee members might not vote to recommend such programs or activities as action items for council consideration. Yet all the co-chairs who attended the meeting wanted some concrete results to flow from their work as a result of council action.

The solution was again straightforward. The proposed "Resolution of the Steering Committee to Transmit the Ann Arbor Energy Plan to the Mayor and City Council," included as the first page of the draft energy plan, clarified what was being recommended. After noting the committee's charge, the nature of the local energy problem, and the committee's work on the problem, the resolution concluded:

> NOW, THEREFORE, BE IT RESOLVED, that the Energy Steering Committee approves the policies as set forth in the Energy Plan and encourages the City Council to adopt the Plan as a guide for future action.
>
> BE IT FINALLY RESOLVED, that the Energy Steering Committee recommends that the City Council establish an Energy Commission to continue the work of the Steering Committee and consider implementing the programs outlined in the Plan.[39]

The first conclusion, by encouraging council to adopt the plan only as a guide to future action, satisfied those critics who felt that parts of the plan were not sufficiently well developed to warrant immediate action. The second conclusion, by recommending establishment of an Energy Commission, provided a mechanism through which the work of the steering committee might eventually result in the implementation of specific programs. Some construed the commission as the body that would *begin* to develop their broad policy recommendations into actionable programs; others construed it as the body that would *continue* to develop such programs. Moreover, this recommendation to establish an Energy Commission would be a test of the mayor's and council's continuing commitment to the local energy initiative.

The draft energy plan went beyond the five areas of inquiry assigned to the task forces when the staff added two sections. One, on the role of government, included in its statement of policy objectives the establishment of an Energy Commission, contingency planning for energy supply curtailments, and, at the urging of the steering committee, the development of a data system to monitor energy use and costs in the community by sector and through time. The other section, on municipal operations, subsumed the various energy objectives and programs within the city government, most of which had continued to evolve outside the purview of the steering committee. These additions were justified on grounds of comprehensiveness and in effect restored two of the policy areas that had been included in the original *1980 Energy Plan* (see table 1) but deleted in the formation of task forces a year earlier.

The draft energy plan was approved for publication and distribution on April 16. A public hearing was conducted by the steering committee on May 14. With minor revisions, an *Ann Arbor Energy Plan* was approved unanimously by the committee on May 28 and presented to council on June 8. Chairman Clark observed on that occasion that "this is a beginning, not an end."[40]

Energy Awareness Campaign

The proposal for an energy awareness campaign had been submitted to the Energy Administration of the Michigan Department of Commerce by the Office of Community Development and funded well before the steering committee was formed and the Promotion Task Force was functioning. In conjunction with the grant, the Energy Administration designed and conducted two small telephone surveys of households in Ann Arbor and a few other Michigan communities. The first, in December 1979, was intended to provide information to design an effective campaign for marketing energy conservation. The second, in December 1980, was intended to evaluate the results of the campaign.

Because of these timing problems, the Promotion Task Force was not able to complete an energy awareness campaign before the second survey, although it did review the results of the first. However, the Promotion Task Force in collaboration with the media consultant carried out an energy awareness campaign in the ten months after it began meeting in July, 1980. The campaign included a number of news releases, news stories, and personal appearances by steering committee members on live and taped broadcasts and before civic groups, as well as several programs to collect and disseminate local energy information of interest to energy consumers.

Interim Evaluation

A continuing concern in organization and management is the evaluation of progress toward or away from goals as a means of clarifying next steps. The evaluation of a community energy initiative is complicated by the fact that the basic goal—improvements in community energy efficiency—provides little guidance in time frames as short as a year. Apart from early and scattered results produced by initial programs, large and widespread improvements in community energy efficiency cannot be expected in the short run. Such improvements depend upon significant changes in attitudes, behaviors, and structures that are likely to require several years. Meanwhile, the initial enthusiasm that induced contributions of time, talent, support, and funds at the outset tends to wane unless interim results are perceived to be sufficiently promising to justify further investments.

For these reasons, the need to maintain the flow of resources long enough for a community energy initiative to succeed or fail in terms of energy efficiency can serve as a guide for evaluation in the early phases. Resources, as we have seen, consist of various capabilities and sufficient motivation to use them. Among the most important capabilities are information about what is worth doing and the expertise to do it, consensus and support both within and outside a body such as the Energy Steering Committee, and funding. One of these can be substituted for another in an effort to sustain the initiative, but some level of each is necessary. For example, if funding is limited, information and expertise might be mobilized to focus efforts in productive directions with minimal funding requirements, but some degree of funding is necessary for the preparation and distribution of documents, if nothing else. For purposes of interim evaluation, it is easier to know what to look for—increases and decreases in resource flows—than to weigh the evidence and make a judgment about the principal problems and opportunities. However, unless resource flows are monitored and assessed, the probability that the initiative will wither and die is increased.

This section presents data on the first year of Ann Arbor's energy initiative, interprets the data from the standpoint of capabilities and motivations, and provides some tentative judgments about next steps.

Data on Resource Flows

Two streams of data are available and relevant to the question of trends in resource flows. One consists of substantive proposals—programs and policies—that have been formally considered by the Energy Steering Committee. The other consists of participation patterns, most conveniently tracked through figures on attendance at meetings of the steering committee.

Table 4 summarizes the substantive proposals formally considered by the steering committee. Each is identified by name, purpose, and source, and listed in chronological order according to the time of first consideration. Initial action refers to clearance for public review through the public outreach plan, or to clearance for a public hearing in the case of the *Energy Plan*. Where appropriate, action by other bodies and steps toward implementation are noted in the last column. The public outreach plan is included because, as we have seen, it surfaced important substantive issues. The table excludes other organization and management decisions, votes to amend the draft energy plan, and decisions made within the city government but not considered for action by the steering committee.

Twelve specific programs or activities have been considered by the committee (proposals A through L). Of these, nine have been approved, two have been cleared for public review but await submission of additional documentation, and one has been tabled.[41] In addi-

TABLE 4. Major Substantive Proposals Considered by the Energy Steering Committee, 1980–81

Proposal and Purpose	Task Force	Energy Steering Committee Action		Status/Implementation
		Initial	Final	
A. Community Energy Report *To clarify and reduce normal levels of household energy use*	Promotion		Approved 9/25/80; unanimous	Pilot program completed by three members of task force who collected data and reported results through the *Ann Arbor News*.
B. Energy Monitoring System *To monitor energy use trends in all city-owned buildings*	Promotion		Approved 11/6/80; unanimous	Approved 11/5/81 by the city's Energy Management Task Force, but implementation has not yet begun.
C. Feedback for Energy Consumers *To facilitate conservation through improved residential utility bills*	Promotion		Approved 11/6/80; 13 ayes, 2 nays, 1 abstention	Endorsed by council 11/17/81; ESC testimony filed in electric case before Public Service Commission, which has deferred a decision.
D. Ann Arbor Energy Logo/Slogan *To promote energy awareness and focus attention on local energy*	Promotion		Approved 11/20/80; unanimous	Logo and slogan are used on ESC documents and are being reproduced as a decal for general use by the public.
E. Response to Luedtke and Assoc. Analysis of Planning Options *To incorporate energy considerations more fully into planning process*	Transportation and Land Use		Approved 12/11/80; unanimous	Transmitted quickly to the planning commission where it is under consideration.
F. Public Outreach Plan *To maximize citizen input, thorough substantive review, and to expedite results*	Promotion		Approved 1/15/81; unanimous	Used by the ESC (see programs below) and expected to be used by its successor.
G. Solar Applications at City Parks *To initiate a solar demonstration project at Fuller Park pool*	Renewable Resources	Approved 2/5/81; unanimous	Approved 3/19/81; unanimous	Resolution directing review of proposal by city departments and installation of monitoring devices approved by council on 4/9/81.

Item	Category			Notes
H. Change in Capital Budget *To set aside $50,000 in city's capital budget to expand curbside recycling*	Renewable Resources		Approved 2/5/81	$50,000 added to administrator's proposed 1981–82 budget for this purpose by council on 5/25/81.
I. Energy Information Bank *To collect and improve public access to energy information of many different kinds*	Renewable Resources and Promotion	Approved 2/19/81; unanimous	Approved 5/28/81; unanimous	Public library's role as Energy Information Bank is being expanded and coordinated with ESC.
J. Retrofit of Residential Buildings *To improve energy efficiency by voluntary and mandatory means*	Building Retrofit	Tabled 2/19/81		Additional information on feasibility and cost-effectiveness of recommendations requested in the debate.
K. Renter and Buyer Information *To recommend mandatory energy use disclosure at point of housing lease or sale*	Building Retrofit	Approved 2/19/81; 9 ayes, 7 nays		Public review will begin when program documentation is provided by the task force.
L. Curbside Recycling *To recommend city support for expansion of existing nonprofit, private program*	Renewable Resources	Approved 3/5/81; unanimous		Public review will begin when program documentation is provided by the task force.
M. Task Force Report *To state findings and recommend*	Building Retrofit		Accepted 4/16/81	Provides basis for further work by successor to ESC.
N. Task Force Report *To state findings and recommend*	Transportation and Land Use		Accepted 4/16/81	Provides basis for further work by successor to ESC.
O. Task Force Report *To state findings and recommend*	New Construction and Site Design		Accepted 4/16/81	Provides basis for further work by successor to ESC.
P. Task Force Report *To state findings and recommend*	Renewable Resources		Accepted 4/16/81	Provides basis for further work by successor to ESC.
Q. Task Force *To state findings and recommend*	Promotion		Accepted 4/16/81	Provides basis for further work by successor to ESC.
R. Ann Arbor Energy Plan *To establish an Energy Commission and provide guide to future action*	Staff	Approved 4/16/81; unanimous	Approved 5/28/81; unanimous	Transmitted to mayor and council on 6/8/81.

Source: Minutes of the Energy Steering Committee

tion, five task force reports have been accepted, and the *Ann Arbor Energy Plan* approved for submission to the mayor and council. Allowing for a delay of about one month, the latter formally fulfills the major charge of the Energy Steering Committee. However, this action does not necessarily fulfill the expectations of committee members, which have a bearing on motivation or other resource requirements.

Participation patterns over time are summarized in figure 3. The

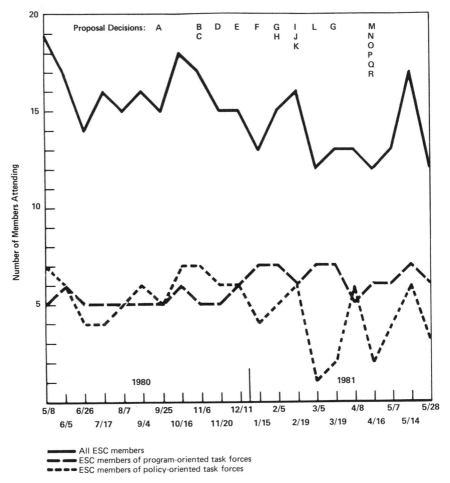

FIG. 3.   Attendance at meetings of the Energy Steering Committee and major proposal decisions by meeting, 1980–81. (*Source:* Minutes of the Energy Steering Committee and task force reports.)

upper curve shows the attendance at each of the twenty-one meetings of the steering committee. The two lower curves show attendance by members of the policy-oriented task forces (Building Retrofit, Transportation and Land Use, and New Construction and Site Design) and by members of the program-oriented task forces (Renewable Resources and Promotion). The two groups are defined by membership lists on the draft task force reports.[42] The three members involved in both a policy-oriented and a program-oriented task force report, and those who were not assigned to a task force or resigned, are included in the upper curve but not in the lower two. The proposal decisions (identified by letter in fig. 3) show the relationship between meetings and attendance data.

Overall, the trend in attendance is erratic but clearly downward over time. Six of the eight meetings with the *highest* attendance occurred in the first eleven meetings, in 1980; seven of the eight meetings with the *lowest* attendance occurred in the last ten meetings, in 1981. The attendance pattern of the policy-oriented group is similar to that of the program-oriented group in 1980, but different in 1981. In the latter period, differences in attendance are relatively large and inversely related: when one group's attendance goes up, the other's tends to go down, and vice versa, except at the end of the period.

The quantitative differences among the attendance patterns of the two groups and the residual category (other) across the two time periods are summarized in table 5. From 1980 to 1981, average attendance by the policy-oriented group declined, but average attendance by the program-oriented group increased. The net difference between the two years is 2.5, or about three persons per meeting. Moreover, five members of each group attended more than three-quarters of the meetings in 1980, but the number of regular attendees (attending 76 percent or more of the meetings) from the policy-oriented group *decreased* to two in 1981 while the number of regular attendees from the program-oriented group *increased* to six.

Interpretations
When the expected benefits of participation are no longer greater than the expected costs, a member tends to reduce the level of participation by doing less work, attending fewer meetings, or at the extreme, resigning. Attendance figures are thus one indicator of net motivational inten-

TABLE 5. Attendance at Energy Steering Committee Meetings by Policy- and Program-Oriented Task Forces, 1980–81

| | No. of ESC Members | No. Attending (by percentage of meetings) | | | | Average Attendance per Meeting |
		0–25%	26–50%	51–75%	76%+	
1980 ESC Meetings						
Policy-oriented	9	0	1	3	5	5.7
Program-oriented	7	0	0	2	5	5.3
Other	10	2	3	2	3	5.1
Total	26	2	4	7	13	16.1
1981 ESC Meetings						
Policy-oriented	8	2	2	2	2	3.9
Program-oriented	8	0	0	2	6	6.4
Other	6	1	1	2	2	3.3
Total	22	3	3	6	10	13.6
Change, 1980 to 1981						
Policy-oriented	−1	+2	+1	−1	−3	−1.8
Program-oriented	+1	0	0	0	+1	+1.1
Other	−4	−1	−2	0	−1	−1.8
Total	−4	+1	−1	−1	−3	−2.5

Source: Minutes of the Energy Steering Committee and task force reports
Note: Other = not exclusively policy- or program-oriented

sity. Of course the incentives and disincentives to participate are multiple and not necessarily the same from one person to the next. Among the relatively personal incentives are the satisfaction of public service, community recognition, the advancement of business or professional interests, making friends, and the like. Among the collective incentives, authorized for all in the committee's charge, are policies and programs that contribute to community energy efficiency. Weighed against these are frustrations and delays occasioned by substantive differences or red tape and the opportunity cost of participation. The latter can be substantial. A member who attended all twenty-one steering committee meetings and perhaps forty task force meetings would have invested about 122 hours (or more than three workweeks) in meetings alone, apart from homework. Every volunteer had alternative and perhaps more rewarding activities in which to invest his or her time.

Why, then, did attendance among policy-oriented members of the committee drop off in 1981, while it increased slightly among the program-oriented members? One interpretation is that the pattern merely reflects only personal incentives and relative opportunity costs that had little to do with the collective task. This interpretation is insufficient because the attendance patterns in 1981 appear to be coordinated across the two groups and through time. The predominance of personal factors would have been manifest in uncoordinated attendance patterns. Another interpretation is that more highly motivated people, on average, were recruited into the program-oriented task forces at the outset. This is unlikely because members were distributed among the task forces through self-selection and because average participation per meeting and regularity of attendance was slightly higher among the policy-oriented members in 1980. A recruitment bias would have been apparent in the first eleven meetings. Still another interpretation is that the motivations of some members were reinforced by early and specific results in the form of programs approved with little difficulty; and that the motivations of others tended to wane in the face of procedural setbacks and deferred results in the form of general policy statements less likely to be implemented.

This interpretation is not easily dismissed. First, the difference in attendance patterns between the two groups began to emerge about the time the public outreach plan (proposal F in table 4 and fig. 3) posed the distinction between individual options on the one hand and task force reports and the comprehensive energy plan on the other, at the first meeting in 1981. Second, the largest drop in attendance among the policy-oriented members did occur immediately after the meeting of February 19, in which the entire residential section of the task force report of Building Retrofit (proposal J) was tabled as an outreach proposal and a subset of it was only narrowly approved pending submission of additional documentation. Moreover, subsequent peaks in attendance by these members occurred in conjunction with meeting agendas that promised recognition of policy statements: the meeting of April 8, in which the draft comprehensive energy plan (proposal R) was initially considered, and the meeting of May 14, in which it was the subject of a public hearing.[43] Finally, the program orientation was reinforced early and often by steering committee approvals beginning with the community energy report (proposal A) on September 25. Formal recognition of the work of the policy-oriented task forces was deferred to April 16, with the acceptance of the task force reports (proposals M, N, O, P, and Q) and authorization of public hearings on the draft energy plan (proposal R).

Whatever the interpretation, the downward trend reflects a continuation of the process of self-selection through resignation and nonattendance. Whether the decline in numbers is compensated by gains in average motivational intensity on the part of those who persisted remains to be seen.

The interpretations of trends in capabilities—such as information, expertise, support, and funding—is also complicated. Over the course of the year, a good deal more was learned about the feasibility and worth of the programs listed in table 4. On the other hand, there is a possibility that the program-oriented, Ann Arbor–focused research base has been depleted rather than replenished. In the case of policy-oriented information, the question is whether the advances reflected in the task force reports and the *Ann Arbor Energy Plan*, over and above the *1980 Energy Plan*, are substantial enough to justify the effort invested and the additional effort required for implementation.

Understanding of how to get things done has no doubt increased among all the remaining members of the steering committee. Underlying the record of proposals and documents accepted, approved, and tabled is a good deal of experience about how to proceed with policy and program information. For example, the amount of detailed analysis and documentation—and what kind—required for committee approval is much clearer now than before.

These gains in "know-what" and "know-how" have been partially documented in order to encourage broader community interest and support. But the effective gains to date are not so much on paper as in the experience of those who have been centrally involved. Most notably, this group includes those ten members of the steering committee who attended more than three-quarters of the meetings in 1981, perhaps those additional six who attended more than half of the meetings, as well as the community development staff and consultants.

The members of the steering committee have been able to mobilize consensus and support among themselves, primarily, and with others to a lesser extent. Most of the decisions reviewed in table 4 were made unanimously. In part this fact reflects the care taken by authors of proposals to work out significant differences before formal action was requested of the steering committee; in part it represents deference toward those members who did their homework, in circumstances where one program or policy was generally not perceived to be in conflict with others. Exceptions to this pattern (proposals C, J, and K) were at least potentially costly in terms of motivation and participation, as we have seen. But the committee avoided a pattern of polarization and retrenchment that could have interfered with the consideration of policies and programs on their own merits. The convergence of attendance patterns of the two groups over the last three meetings, and nineteen votes (twelve attended meeting, seven votes by mailed ballot) in favor of the *Ann Arbor Energy Plan,* are positive signs.

The committee has not yet established an ability to mobilize support from the city government, in spite of positive signs. One program (B) has been approved but not implemented after many months by the city's Energy Management Task Force. Three others (C, G, and H) have been approved by the city council, although only one of these (H) entails a commitment of funds. Similarly, the Energy Information Bank (I) has been approved by the director of the public library but without more than a token commitment of resources. Formal approval alone is less indicative of support than more tangible commitments, such as the time of public employees or funds. Neither particular programs nor the *Ann Arbor Energy Plan* has attracted sufficient outside interest to gauge the trend in community support.

The trend in funding for the overhead expenses of the Energy Steering Committee and its possible successor remains unclear. While the energy awareness grant has expired, the city council on May 25 included thirty-three thousand dollars for energy activities in the administrator's proposed 1981–82 budget. How this money will be allocated between the committee's possible successor and energy projects within city government remains to be seen. Funding decisions for the implementation of energy programs will continue to be made on a program-by-program basis by city council.

Next Steps
With the termination of the Energy Steering Committee on June 8, 1981, the main priority is to ensure continuity. The key steps in this direction are to establish, as soon as possible, an Energy Commission (or an interim body while a commission is under consideration) and to recruit into it a substantial proportion of those ten to sixteen members of the committee who have already played a central role. Otherwise, the policies and programs begun by the committee will tend to lapse before they have had time to produce improvements in energy efficiency, and this group of motivated, informed, and able citizens—the community initiative's main resource—will tend to disperse into other activities. Moreover, the establishment of a successor body with modest funding for overhead and the reappointment of some of the core members of the committee would signal continuing support for the local energy initiative on the part of the city government. To the extent that results in the short run are necessary to justify and sustain such support, the priority should be to carry the most promising policies and programs forward to the point that they produce not only more paper, but more tangible results.

The committee has taken some initial steps to ensure continuity. On May 14, 1981, it approved a recommendation to establish an interim body, and on May 27, 1981, an informal delegation of four members including the chair met with the mayor to suggest that he invite all members of the committee and its task forces to volunteer for it. The mayor was generous in his praise of the committee's work and was receptive to these proposals. Current indications are that letters will be sent soon inviting committee and task force members to serve on an energy advisory board until the powers of an Energy Commission, modeled on others such as the planning commission, can be defined in detail. The board would emphasize analysis of certain energy decisions that the city council is expected to make in the next year, most likely expansion of curbside recycling, a refuse-derived fuel arrangement with the University of Michigan, and hydroelectric development, as well as longer-term issues having to do with retrofit of rental housing and transportation. The steering committee and its task forces have developed some expertise in all of these areas, and it appears there is a continuing need for it.[44]

Conclusion

The Ann Arbor Experience

The organizational structure employed in Ann Arbor over the first year had the effect of decentralizing decisions about the allocation of resources. Recall that the task force rosters were formed and actual levels of participation determined through self-selection—in effect, through decisions made *by* individual steering committee and community members *for* themselves. Moreover, the task forces themselves worked out their own internal divisions of labor. Most assigned groups to policy subareas; one encouraged individuals to take responsibility for a single program idea.

Procedural decisions made at the steering committee level had little effect on the task forces' work. Despite the common approach accepted in late September, the individual task forces devised their own means for reconciling the magnitude of the planning task with the limited personnel and research available. Three undertook broad reviews of policy objectives; two focused on the development of particular programs. Subsequent decisions on procedures for public review and for final action by the steering committee did not deter any task force from following its own course. Some had the effect of legitimizing the program-oriented course as an alternative to the policy-oriented course. (Only the latter was unambiguously authorized in the mayor's charge.) Others—particularly the decision to accept, rather than approve or disapprove—allowed the task forces to retain rather complete and final control over their own task force reports.

Under these circumstances, the managerial objective—a comprehensive energy plan—was more easily realized in form than in substance. Some task forces had provided little or no information on programs necessary to realize the many objectives they had reviewed; others provided little or no information on broad objectives. The staff could only assemble the pieces provided by the task forces (and itself), and paper over the gaps. The form of the result, the *Ann Arbor Energy Plan,* is sufficiently comprehensive in coverage to suggest the possibility of simultaneous comparison of many policy alternatives and selection of the few best. The lack of substantive depth in the *Ann Arbor Energy Plan* precludes this possibility because the value of any policy objective depends in part upon the feasibility and cost-effectiveness of the individual programs necessary to implement it. The steering committee did not attempt to make such simultaneous comparisons and selections, nor can any other body make them on an informed basis unless or until many more programs are researched in detail.

In short, the organizational structure and to a lesser extent the procedures worked at cross-purposes to the objective of comprehensiveness. While the stated objective requires some degree of centralized coordination from the top down, the structure permitted decentralization and diversification from the bottom up. Decentralization and diversification in fact dominated for at least three reasons. First, not all members accepted the viewpoint that comprehensiveness was feasible or desirable in the short run. There was a difference of opinion. Second, no task force enjoyed the resources necessary to develop more than a handful of programs relevant to the fifty-eight objectives suggested in the original *1980 Energy Plan.* The plan was simply too ambitious. Third, the members of the task forces were, after all, volunteers. Any attempt to enforce common procedures or report formats over the opposition of a task force would have resulted in less effort, lower attendance, more resignations, and possibly rejection of the final energy plan by vote of the steering committee. Centralized coordination across many alternatives is simply too costly where the collective effort depends upon voluntary participants.

The Ann Arbor experience demonstrates that citizen volunteers can focus their limited resources on the development of a handful of energy programs and realize substantive review, approval, and implementation of some of them in one year's time. There is evidence that such results might be sufficient to sustain the flow of resources necessary to produce significant improvements in community energy efficiency over several years' time. On the other hand, comprehensiveness in more than a formal sense does not appear to be a realistic short-term objective on the basis of this experience. Those who accepted the goal of comprehensiveness dispersed their limited resources over a large number of policy areas. The results, judging from declines in attendance, did not on the whole appear to justify the effort invested from their standpoint. An energy plan like Ann Arbor's might provide a useful foundation for further work if appropriate resources are forthcoming.

Lessons

Several lessons can be drawn from our interpretation of Ann Arbor's experience in the organization and management of a community energy initiative, but two qualifications should be borne in mind by leaders in other communities. First, ours is only one interpretation, and others are possible. Second, the lessons learned in one context do not often apply without modification in another. For these reasons, we have attempted to provide enough substantive detail and depth to help others formulate and assess alternative interpretations and make the appropriate modifications. There are five major lessons.

1. *Emphasize the goal of maintaining the resource base in the short run.* Improvements in community energy efficiency through conservation and conversion to local and renewable energy resources is the overriding goal in the long run. But without a continuous flow of resources over an extended period, a community energy initiative may wither and die before it can achieve significant improvements in energy efficiency.

2. *Formulate short-run objectives that concentrate initial resources on the development, adoption, and implementation of a small number of programs.* Short-run results more tangible than paper proposals are probably necessary to maintain the flow of resources. Comprehensive planning in more than a formal sense is not feasible within one year unless the resource base is substantially larger than Ann Arbor's. Even then, the tendency to withhold action on programs until completion of a comprehensive plan has the effect of postponing short-run results. A comprehensive plan may eventually be useful to improve the selection and justification of the most promising programs among a large number of alternatives.

3. *Design procedures that encourage the separate and sequential review (and possible adoption and implementation) of program options as soon as they are ready for circulation.* Like the public outreach plan, such procedures avoid unnecessary delays, maximize the potential for public participation, and provide for detailed substantive, as opposed to merely formal, review. Larger packages of proposals constitute bottlenecks in these respects.

4. *Design organizational structures that decentralize control over program planning and allow for self-selection.* Those who are sufficiently motivated and capable to become program entrepreneurs need autonomy in the planning process. Others will assume supporting roles or tend to withdraw. To allow for self-selection, the initial size of planning units such as task forces should be larger than the effective size, except possibly in those communities endowed with large numbers of highly motivated energy activists or paid planners.

5. *Continuously monitor results and resource flows, and adjust organization and management choices accordingly.* For reasons reviewed in the introduction to this book and confirmed in the Ann Arbor experience, evolution of the work plan is both inevitable and desirable. The history and status of major substantive proposals (e.g., table 4) and attendance patterns at meetings (e.g., table 3, fig. 3, and table 5) are among the convenient and informative indicators.

A Comparative Perspective

The literature on local energy policy emphasizes plans over the documentation of results. Thus, what has been attempted in other communities is much clearer than what has worked. Nevertheless, a comparative perspective may shed some light on our major conclusion from the Ann Arbor experience and the major lesson we draw from it: *that the attempt to develop a comprehensive energy plan within one year was unrealistic and costly, and that a better alternative is to formulate short-run objectives emphasizing the implementation of individual programs.*

The program-oriented, relatively incremental alternative to comprehensive energy planning is exemplified by the three cases reviewed in the first paper in this volume. Davis's passive solar heating and cooling ordinance, Seattle's Energy 1990 decision, and Springfield's hydro project were responses to specific problems or opportunities by one or a few local leaders. They were not the results of comprehensive energy plans, although in at least two of the cases they have stimulated the development of additional programs and a more comprehensive approach. It may be easier to evolve a comprehensive energy plan in response to a series of specific problems or opportunities than to produce one full-blown out of a concern for rational program selection and justification.

The program orientation and concern for managing and sustaining limited resources is represented in the general literature as well as cases. The National Association of Counties recommends the following under the heading of "Realistic Goals."

> First, the program should begin with very clear and attainable goals and objectives. It should be manageable within the constraints of budget, staff, powers, and authorities.
>
> Beginning with a limited, specifically targeted program helps to ensure some measure of success. Success will establish the credibility of energy conservation. The program can be publicized and community support generated as the reduction in consumption is documented. Such support is critical for continued funding by an elected body which is responsible to the public for expenditure of tax dollars.[45]

Similarly, a section on "Organizing for Community Needs" in a recent publication of the California Office of Appropriate Technology emphasizes the importance of resource management.[46]

Nevertheless, comprehensiveness in energy planning is the major theme in the literature on local energy initiatives, and particularly those supported by the federal government. In Portland, Oregon, one of three cities supported by the Department of Housing and Urban Development beginning in 1975,

> the project's main emphasis was the development of comprehensive information on the city's current and projected energy use patterns; alternative methods for achieving efficiency in energy consumption by [various] sectors; and possible savings in 1995 energy demand as a result of individual conservation programs. That information provides a base for developing and implementing conservation policies and programs and for monitoring the

achievements of conservation programs against their anticipated effectiveness.[47]

As its name implies, the Comprehensive Community Energy Management Program (CCEMP) took a similar approach. For a two-year period beginning in the fall of 1978, seventeen pilot communities were funded through CCEMP, which was managed by the Argonne National Laboratory for the Office of Buildings and Community Systems of the Department of Energy.[48] In addition, comprehensiveness in energy planning is built into the methodology of the Decentralized Solar Energy Technology Assessment Program, which funded four communities and was managed by the Oak Ridge National Laboratory for the Office of Solar Energy of the Department of Energy.[49]

The meaning of comprehensiveness is apparent from the methodologies adopted. Although there are differences in detail from one program to the next, the major planning tasks specified and their sequence through time are quite similar. The methodology provided to the seventeen CCEMP pilot communities by the Department of Energy has been described as "fairly traditional,"[50] and is reproduced as an example in figure 4. Final selection of alternatives and strategies is based on a comparative impact assessment in part 3 of figure 4.

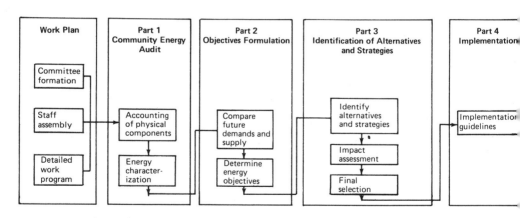

FIG. 4. Comprehensive community energy planning methodology. (*Source:* John L. Moore et al., *Community Energy Auditing: Experience with the Comprehensive Community Energy Management Program* [Argonne, Ill.: Argonne National Laboratory, 1980], p. 3.)

The identification of strategies and alternatives is based on the results of part 2, in which objectives are determined on the basis of energy supply and demand projections. The projections, in turn, are based on a comprehensive community energy audit from part 1. (Ann Arbor's initiative, in effect, started with the identification of alternatives and strategies. From that starting point, the policy-oriented task forces made some progress toward a comprehensive energy audit while the program-oriented task forces made some progress toward implementation.)

Based on informal contacts and incomplete documents, these programs have improved community energy efficiency.[51] The question is not whether there has been success, but what role has been played by the comprehensive planning methodologies. First, the attempt to be comprehensive is costly if not cost-*in*effective. An overview of the Housing and Urban Development program notes that

> all three of the projects experienced difficulties in the development of their information bases. They discovered serious gaps in existing data and encountered numerous problems in data comparability and in gaining access to information from both public and private sources. As a result, the information collection phase of the project consumed extensive amounts of time and money and required the identification of data alternatives and revisions to analytical methodologies.[52]

Similarly, an interim evaluation of CCEMP notes that

> while making a good-faith effort to follow the [community energy audit] workbook, many CCEMP communities eventually departed from it to get the job done within the time, money, and data constraints.[53]

> The time, effort, and cost of producing a comprehensive energy audit does not appear to be worthwhile when measured against its usefulness to setting community energy objectives.[54]

Second, a comprehensive planning process tends to undermine voluntary citizen participation.

> For a number of [CCEMP] communities, there has been a tendency for advisory committees to lose interest in the process dur-

ing conduct of the audit. Reasons given for this difficulty include the long period associated with the audit, the technical nature of the audit exercise, and concerns with the validity and policy relevance of the information produced.[55]

Finally, the attempt to proceed in orderly fashion through the comprehensive methodology tends to be "subverted" by program entrepreneurs from the bottom up.

> A number of communities have proceeded with energy management actions, concurrent with the planning process. Directly or indirectly, CCEMP project staff and advisory committees helped in the implementation of several community energy activities. . . . While CCEMP is an exercise in energy planning, there is a natural and strong tendency for communities to follow lines of opportunity at the time they occur, using the projects later as part of the community energy plan.[56]

To the extent that these interim and incomplete conclusions are confirmed by further evaluation, Ann Arbor's attempt to develop a comprehensive energy plan—and its departures from the ideal of comprehensiveness—appears to be representative of a broader pattern, and not an anomaly.

NOTES

This paper was completed in the week after the Energy Steering Committee was terminated on June 8, 1981. The first and third authors were members of the committee and served on its Renewable Resources and Promotion task forces. We gratefully acknowledge the assistance of Peter Fairweather, who completed the Local Energy Policy Seminar's first paper on organization and management in May, 1979, and of several colleagues who reviewed the draft of this paper and provided valuable comments: Roberta Booth, Cynthia Conklin, Lawrence Mohr, Tom Rieke, and Barry Tilmann. Any errors of fact or interpretation are the responsibility of the authors alone.

1. City of Ann Arbor Office of Community Development, *1980 Energy Plan* (Ann Arbor: Office of Community Development, 1980), p. 3 (hereafter cited as *1980 Energy Plan*).
2. Ibid., p. 7. See also the cover sheet of the *Proposed Energy Policy for Portland* (Portland: Energy Policy Steering Committee, 1979).

3. From the "Resolution to Adopt 1980 Energy Work Plan," Ann Arbor City Council, approved as amended March 17, 1980.

4. *1980 Energy Plan,* p. 3.

5. Ibid., p. 5.

6. Ibid., p. C-5.

7. "Resolution to Adopt 1980 Energy Work Plan."

8. Louis D. Belcher, "Charge to the Energy Steering Committee, May 8, 1980" (Ann Arbor: Office of the Mayor, 1980), p. 1.

9. Ibid., p. 2.

10. Ibid., p. 1.

11. The six principles are the following: "(1) The policy must be aggressive and achieve significant results; (2) the social and economic differences between people and firms must be recognized and accommodated; (3) all sectors of the City's economy must be dealt with equitably; (4) all actions must maintain Ann Arbor's attractiveness as a place to live and do business; (5) conservation measures must be cost-effective; and (6) the City government's role must be to support private activity, not to replace it." See also "An Ordinance adopting an Energy Conservation Policy for Portland and declaring an emergency," Section I.7, which was approved by the City of Portland on August 15, 1979.

12. *1980 Energy Plan,* p. B-2.

13. "City 'Committed to Conservation'," *Ann Arbor News,* September 26, 1979.

14. A number of communities were funded through federal programs identified in notes 47, 48, and 49. Portland, for example, used a $224,000 grant from the Department of Housing and Urban Development in 1975 "to investigate the ways energy is used in Portland and to project the city's energy needs for the next 20 years." Portland Energy Office, *An Energy Policy for Changing Times* (Portland: Portland Energy Office, 1980), p. 3. The result was an eleven-volume progress report on the Portland Energy Conservation Policy.

15. John A. Clark, "Proposed Membership of Task Forces" (Ann Arbor: Energy Steering Committee, July 17, 1980), cover memorandum.

16. For example, the first "action item" was to "develop a program to scope the magnitude of the problem and identify specific areas where the greatest gains can be achieved by means of energy audits, infrared photography, or by any technically feasible cost-effective method." This is quoted from the "Charge to the Building Retrofit Task Force," August 7, 1980, p. 2, which the task force wrote.

17. Building Retrofit Task Force, "Planning and Schedule of Work" (September 4, 1980).

18. The subcommittees were Land Use, Transit, Bicycle and Pedestrian, and Parking Management. Some coordination was effected by the task force chair through meetings with subcommittee heads.

19. One staff consultant, Randall Derifield, attempted to stimulate inter-

est in the Community Forum. See, for example, the steering committee minutes of August 7, 1980, p. 3.

20. The four new members were a member of the planning commission, an architect and developer, the new manager of the Ann Arbor Division of Detroit Edison (who replaced his predecessor on the committee), and a graduate student from the University of Michigan School of Natural Resources.

21. Clark, "Proposed Membership of Task Forces."

22. Steering committee minutes, October 16, 1980, pp. 3–4. The significance of the operating rules was modest primarily because the steering committee per se seldom took up controversial issues.

23. However, the steering committee as a whole did engage in one scheduled discussion on the general question of whether mandatory energy standards were appropriate for the city to impose on its citizens. See the minutes of November 20, 1980, p. 4. It also received several briefings, such as a city engineer's slide presentation on the question of reactivating the city's dams to produce hydropower. See the minutes of September 25, 1980, p. 3.

24. Steering committee minutes, September 25, 1980, p. 4. Emphasis added.

25. One exception was a report on barriers to energy conservation in Ann Arbor and Ypsilanti building codes and zoning ordinances prepared by Susan Mason, a student in the University of Michigan Law School, in the summer of 1980. The report was useful to the New Construction and Site Design Task Force.

26. See, for example, the steering committee minutes of November 6, 1980, p. 4, and Building Retrofit's interim report to city council, November 11, 1980.

27. These expectations were based in part on informal conversations with a member of the Ann Arbor City Council and on fragmentary information on the history of local energy policy initiatives in other communities.

28. Promotional Task Force, "A Public Outreach Plan" (January 5, 1981), p. 1.

29. Ibid., p. 3. Emphasis in the original.

30. The staff encouraged the early consideration of program proposals to liven up the meetings of the steering committee. The regular task force reports were considered to be dull by some members.

31. The three were Jackie Krieger, Sue MacKenzie, and Karen Rutledge. The research on which the report was based has been included as chapter 7 of this volume.

32. According to Article XV of the operating rules, as amended, a substantive matter requiring formal committee action must be approved by the chair and distributed in writing before it can be taken up at the next meeting of the committee.

33. The proposal was based on research included as chapter 5 of this volume.

34. Steering committee minutes, March 5, 1981, p. 4.

35. On recommendation of the staff, *separate* formats for task force reports were approved on February 5. See the steering committee minutes of February 5, 1981, p. 5. Recall that a *common* format for task force reports was approved by the committee on December 11.

36. Belcher, "Charge to the Energy Steering Committee," p. 2.

37. Ibid., p. 1.

38. Steering committee minutes, March 19, 1981, p. 5.

39. Office of Community Development, draft "Ann Arbor Energy Plan" (Ann Arbor: Office of Community Development, 1981), p. 1.

40. Chong W. Pyen, "Council Gives Cool Reception to Energy Conservation Plan," *Ann Arbor News,* June 9, 1981.

41. Two other proposals, one on hydropower development and one on indoor air pollution, were developed and documented too late to be considered separately as public outreach proposals.

42. A membership list was not included in the draft report of the Renewable Resources Task Force. The list included in its final report is the same as the one used for figure 3 and table 5, except that it includes one steering committee member classified here as "Other." The difference does not affect the interpretation of the data.

43. Comments at the public hearing on the draft "Ann Arbor Energy Plan" focused mainly on the retrofit of rental housing, a matter of some concern to the large number of students and others who rent housing in the Ann Arbor area. See Chong W. Pyen, "Renters Support Forced Insulation," *Ann Arbor News,* May 15, 1981.

44. Both the mayor and the city administrator consider the work of the Energy Steering Committee and other local energy activities to be the basis for a bid to have Ann Arbor renamed an All-American City. See William B. Treml, "Is Ann Arbor Still An All-American City?" *Ann Arbor News,* May 25, 1981.

45. Don Spangler, *Establishing an Energy Office: Seven County Programs* (Washington, D.C.: National Association of Counties Research Foundation, 1979), p. 41.

46. California Office of Appropriate Technology, *Working Together: Community Self-Reliance in California* (Sacramento: California Office of Appropriate Technology, 1981), pp. 97–100.

47. U.S., Department of Housing and Urban Development, Office of Policy Development and Research, *Capacity-Building: Local Government Approaches to Energy Conservation* (Washington, D.C.: Government Printing Office, 1979), p. 37 (hereafter cited as HUD, *Capacity-Building*).

48. On CCEMP see John L. Moore et al., *Organizing for Comprehensive Community Energy Management and Planning: Some Preliminary Observa-*

tions, Technical Memo ANL/CNSV-TM-27 (Argonne, Ill.: Argonne National Laboratory, 1979).

49. On this program see Benson H. Bronfman et al., *The Decentralized Solar Energy Technology Assessment Program: Review of Activities (April 1978–December 1979),* ORNL/TM-7189 (Oak Ridge, Tenn.: Oak Ridge National Laboratory, 1980). A related volume funded by this program is Alan Okagaki with Jim Benson, *County Energy Plan Guidebook: Creating a Renewable Energy Future* (Fairfax, Vir.: Institute for Ecological Policies, 1979).

50. John L. Moore et al., *Comprehensive Energy Auditing: Experience with the Comprehensive Community Energy Management Program,* ANL/CNSV-TM-43 (Argonne, Ill.: Argonne National Laboratory, 1981), p. 1.

51. See, for example, Portland Energy Office, *An Energy Policy for Changing Times* (Portland: Portland Energy Office, 1980).

52. HUD, *Capacity-Building,* p. 13.

53. Moore et al., *Comprehensive Energy Auditing,* p. 16.

54. Ibid., p. 24.

55. Ibid., pp. 27–28.

56. Ibid., p. 29.

PART 2: PROGRAM OPTIONS

3 The Hydro Option: Reactivation of the Barton Site

Keith Kline

Small or low-head hydroelectric power (hydropower) projects have become increasingly attractive options to local governments faced with rising electricity costs. This reverses the trend of a quarter of a century, when economic and other considerations led to the retirement of many small hydroelectric (hydro) facilities and channeled most new investments into large fossil fuel and nuclear power plants.[1] By the spring of 1980, a record number of more than 250 applications for new, expanded, or rehabilitated hydropower facilities were pending before the Federal Energy Regulatory Commission (FERC). Of these, more than 40 were submitted by municipalities, and most qualify as small or low-head hydro.[2] A hydro project is considered small if the capacity is 15,000 kilowatts (kw) or less; it is considered low-head if the difference in elevation between the headwater above the dam and the tailwater below is less than 20 meters, or about 66 feet.[3]

Hydropower is an attractive option for a number of reasons. Although the economics vary considerably from one site to the next, hydropower can offset the higher costs of thermal generation under favorable conditions and provide a hedge against future cost increases. According to a recent estimate by an official of FERC, newly installed hydropower costs between one and a half and eight cents per kilowatt, compared to four to five cents for nuclear power and six to eight cents for power from coal.[4] A hydro facility is fairly well insulated from cost increases because it is capital-intensive and utilizes a renewable energy resource. Moreover, hydropower is based on a proven technology refined through years of experience since the first installation in 1882 at Appleton, Wisconsin. With normal maintenance, some installations have operated for fifty years or more.[5]

In addition, small hydro projects entail relatively small environmental impacts, particularly when located at existing dam sites. Because they are less susceptible to challenges on environmental grounds and because FERC has recently streamlined licensing procedures, small hydro projects can be put into operation relatively quickly. Although estimates vary, the time lag between conception and implementation can be as little as three years, compared to the ten to fifteen years often required for major power projects.[6] Finally, substantial hydropower potential remains unutilized although the magnitude of this potential is uncertain. On a national basis,

> the economically attractive sites under present conditions would total significantly less than the 30,000 Mw [megawatts, or thousands of kilowatts] reported potential, but it is generally agreed that several hundred sites are likely to be found economically attractive for immediate development.[7]

In Michigan, a program of the Department of Natural Resources identified 620 existing dams, only 56 of which were generating electricity in 1977.[8]

Four dams on the Huron River—Barton, Argo, Geddes, and Superior—are former hydroelectric sites now owned by the city of Ann Arbor. Plants at these sites once generated as much as 21.9 million kilowatt hours (kwh) of electricity annually.[9] They were retired by Detroit Edison in 1960 at a time when "nobody foresaw what would happen to the cost of oil and gas and coal, to the cost of transporting those fuels or to the cost of constructing huge generating plants and mighty transmission lines."[10] Now these costs are becoming self-evident to electricity users in Ann Arbor, raising the question of reactivation of these former hydroelectric sites.

This chapter presents an initial study of the feasibility of reactivation of the Barton site, located about two miles north of the center of Ann Arbor (see fig. 1). The purpose is to determine whether the site warrants a full-scale engineering analysis. Of the four sites, Barton is the most promising for possible reactivation. The dam has the highest net head, 25.8 feet, and therefore the largest power-generating capacity. The powerhouse still standing at the site would reduce the cost of reactivation. (Only Argo of the other sites still has a powerhouse.) Finally, a convenient market for any hydropower produced at Barton is located just across the river at the municipal water pumping station. If

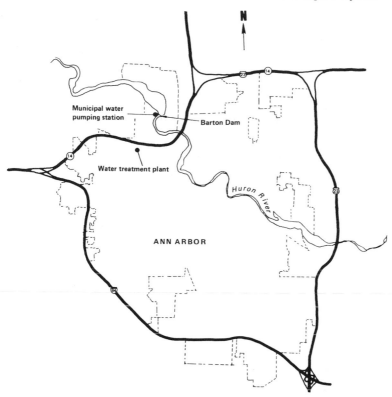

FIG. 1.   Map of Ann Arbor showing location of Barton Dam,
municipal water pumping station, and water treatment plant

reactivation of the Barton site is worthwhile, the other three sites may
warrant detailed analysis.

The next section provides additional background on the Barton
site. The following four sections assess the economic feasibility of reactivation. Three alternative turbine systems with various installed capacities are considered and the total installed costs of each are compared. The effective energy capacity and peak (or demand) capacity of
the three systems are then determined, taking into account the
streamflow at the Barton site. Next, the value of the power that could
be produced at the site is estimated. This amount is the sum of the
pumping station electricity costs that would be offset and the revenue
from surplus power sold to Detroit Edison. Finally, these figures are

drawn together to assess financial feasibility and costs and benefits. (Both simpler and more complex analytical procedures are available.[11]) The remaining sections consider environmental and intergovernmental factors, and summarize conclusions and recommendations.

The results indicate that reactivation of the Barton site would be a profitable investment for the city of Ann Arbor. The net annual profit in the first year of operation could be as high as $49,300 and the present value of reactivation now could be as high as $1,390,000 under conservative assumptions. These results are based on the installation of a 830 kw vertical turbine in the existing powerhouse and the use of the power produced at the site by the municipal water pumping station. There appear to be no significant environmental or regulatory barriers to reactivation. A full-scale engineering study is recommended.

Background

The Barton dam and powerhouse were completed by Detroit Edison in 1913 and 1915, respectively, as the first of a series of five hydropower plants on the Huron River. At one time they supplied the electricity needs of all the communities in the river valley. Detroit Edison retired the Barton plant (along with Argo, Geddes, and Superior) in 1960. One factor was the relatively cheap cost of energy produced at large thermal generating plants at the time. Another was the rising cost of labor and maintenance necessary to operate the hydro plants, which contributed an increasingly insignificant amount of electricity to the growing Detroit Edison system. The dams were also a unique and burdensome public relations liability. Responsibility for these facilities brought up "more and more problems of encroachment, pollution, flood control, erosion of banks, flood damage, low-water damage, high-water damage, public use of the ponds and the shores, policing of our property, and criticism of Edison."[12] The utility seemed eager to pass the responsibility of river flow management over to public authorities.

In 1963 the city of Ann Arbor purchased the four dams, two powerhouses, and more than 945 acres of surrounding water and land. Operation and maintenance responsibility rests with the Water Treatment Division of the Utilities Department. About four work hours each day are spent on a visual inspection of each dam and its impoundment level. Money is also budgeted for dam repairs and maintenance. For fiscal year 1979, the planned expenditure was $155,190.[13] The dams and powerhouses underwent basic structural repairs in 1972–73.

The Barton site includes a powerhouse, a dam approximately 150 feet long with ten arches, and ten electrically controlled sector gates for major flow management. When the author inspected the site in March, 1979, the dam appeared to be in very good condition.[14] Moreover, the city is responsible for dam maintenance and repairs to ensure public safety whether or not the site is reactivated. For these reasons, major costs for extensive dam refurbishment are not necessary and not included in this study.

The sector gates at Barton dam are left open each year from November 1 to May 1, leaving Barton pond about two feet below normal levels, in order to reduce ice damage to the shoreline. This also reduces power costs for side seal heaters on the gates and for the air bubbler system that eliminates ice in front of the gates. In addition, the lower impoundment level provides a small amount of storage capacity for the spring runoff. A telemetering system records the water levels at each dam and transfers this information to the water treatment plant on Sunset Road (see fig. 1). "Alarm conditions" are signaled whenever the water level rises or falls below prescribed levels. The city has had some difficulty coordinating sequences of water control for proper flow at the series of dams due to the timing delays involved and sporadic false alarms. In June, 1968, before installation of the telemetering system, the Geddes dam failed after several days of record rainfall and subsequently had to be rebuilt.

The powerhouse forms about 40 feet of the dam's total length. The building is approximately 68 feet long and 48 feet high from draft tube floor to generator room floor (see fig. 2). The powerhouse structure appeared to be sound although signs of age were apparent. The powerhouse has been stripped of all power generating equipment— turbines, shafts, beaming, governor, electrical equipment, cables, etc.—since Detroit Edison sold the plant to the city. The overhead crane remains, and would "most likely be operable if reconnected" according to Mr. Harvey Mieske, the water treatment plant supervisor. Although rusted, the traveling crane system otherwise seemed in good condition.

In June, 1977, the city signed a lease giving the Washtenaw County Historical Society rights to the powerhouse and adjoining prop-

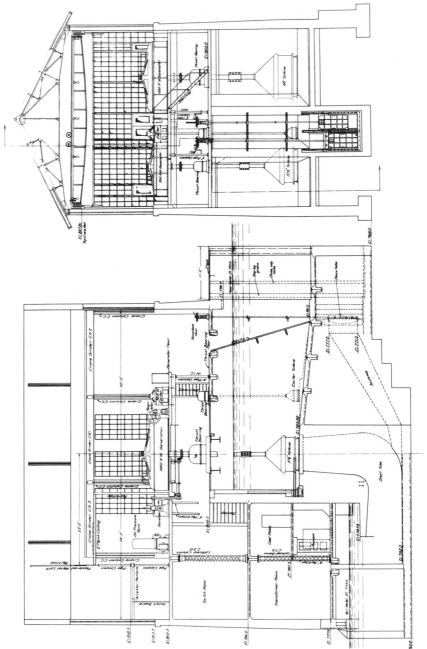

FIG. 2. Barton power house sectional views. (Courtesy of Ayers, Lewis, Norris, and May, Inc.)

erty to the south for the purpose of establishing a museum at the site. The lease lasts for fifty years with the option of a fifty-year extension thereafter. The historical society has spent approximately forty thousand dollars on improvements to the powerhouse since signing the lease, and is presently storing some artifacts there. The society has also decided that the powerhouse cannot meet all the needs for a museum, so plans are under way for the construction of a new museum building at the site. Primary public access to the museum will be by foot, coming from the Huron River Drive side between the railroad and the pumping station, over a footbridge to be constructed, and under the railroad bridge to the museum site. There may also be a separate driveway developed from Whitmore Lake Road alongside the tracks.[15]

Alternative Turbine Systems

Three alternative turbine systems were considered for possible reactivation of the Barton site. Due to time constraints, these alternatives together with cost data have been taken with permission from a feasibility study by Ayres, Lewis, Norris, and May, Inc., of a similar site further downstream on the Huron.[16] The three designs all utilize vertical turbines with the following capacity ratings:

> One 830 kw Leffel turbine;
> Two 500 kw Bofors-Nohab turbines, manufactured in Sweden; and
> Two 830 kw Leffel turbines.

None of these designs is necessarily optimal. The purpose of this analysis is to explore potential costs and benefits of a representative group of alternatives, no one of which is advanced as the "right one."

Table 1 summarizes project cost estimates for these three design alternatives. The costs assume the more expensive synchronous generator machines necessary for speed regulation when power is not supplied directly into a "stiff" utility grid. These would be low-speed, directly driven vertical generators with independent exciters. Turbine costs include an allowance for governors.

The estimate for installation of power equipment is based upon 20 percent of equipment costs. Shipping charges are figured at 5 per-

TABLE 1.   Project Cost Estimates of Three Design Alternatives

	One 830 kw Leffel	Two 500 kw Bofors-Nohab	Two 830 kw Leffel
Materials			
Power producing equipment			
Turbine(s)	$108,000	$358,000	$216,000
Thrust bearing(s)	27,000	incl.	54,000
Gear drive(s)	24,000	incl.	48,000
Generator(s)/exciter(s)	63,000	96,000	126,000
Generator(s)/exciter(s) controls	38,000	76,000	76,000
Automatic synchronizer	10,000	10,000	10,000
Automatic/supervisory controls	20,000	20,000	20,000
Utility interconnection	15,000	15,000	15,000
Subtotal	305,000	575,000	565,000
Non-power materials			
Building/site renovation	30,000	30,000	30,000
Structural modification			
(to retrofit new turbines)	6,000	15,000	15,000
Subtotal	36,000	45,000	45,000
Labor			
Installation of power producing			
equipment	61,000	115,000	113,000
Building/site renovation	20,000	20,000	20,000
Structural modifications			
(to retrofit new turbines)	17,000	34,000	39,000
Subtotal	98,000	169,000	172,000
Shipping			
Power producing equipment	15,000	47,000	28,000
Duty	0	25,000	0
Engineering	80,000	127,000	127,000
Legal, Administration, and Contingencies	48,000	89,000	84,000
Total Project Cost	582,000	1,077,000	1,021,000

Source: Ayers, Lewis, Norris, and May, Inc.

cent of equipment for United States items, and 10 percent for imported items. Import duty is 7 percent of equipment costs in the case of Bofors-Nohab turbines. Estimates of consultant fees are based on similar services on comparable projects, and engineering services are assumed to extend through construction and start-up. A contingency fund of 9 percent of total costs is added for unforeseen problems and expenses. As can be seen in table 1, the 830-kw design is the least expensive and the 1,000-kw design is the most expensive. Project cost estimates range from $582,000 to $1,077,000.

Power Potential

The Huron River watershed has a drainage area of 723 square miles upstream of the Barton dam.[17] Streamflow records have been kept by the U.S. Geological Survey since 1904. Although the flow was measured at the Barton site from 1914–47, the gauge station is now 2.6 miles farther downstream.

The impact of streamflow characteristics on hydropower capacity is conveniently represented in a flow duration curve. The stream discharge rate in cubic feet per second (vertical axis) is plotted against the percentage of time the discharge rate is equalled or exceeded (horizontal axis). The area under the curve represents the theoretical water power available at a given plant capacity. Figure 3 gives the flow duration curve for the Huron River at Barton dam, based on annual streamflow averages.[18] It also relates discharge rates to three levels of installed capacity: 830 kw, 1000 kw, and 1660 kw, as specified in the design alternatives.[19] Installed capacity is the maximum generating potential of a plant with all units operating at their full rated loads.

Figure 3 indicates how much of installed capacity can be effectively used at the Barton site. Consider a plant of 1660 kw installed capacity, for example. At a discharge rate of 770 cubic feet per second (cfs), it would operate at full rated load. The area above the 770 cfs limit (but below the curve) represents water that cannot be put through the turbine. It is either discharged over the spillway or stored for later use during low discharge periods. Notice that the turbine(s) would operate at full capacity only about 14 percent of the time. The rest of the time capacity is constrained by discharge rates lower than 770 cfs.

Turbines can be throttled down to follow the flow duration curve. However, when turbine efficiency reaches about 40 percent of rated capacity (the average minimum acceptable efficiency for most turbines), it becomes better to operate the turbine intermittently. This lets storage build up until it can be passed at an efficient rate. For a plant of 1660 kw installed capacity, the minimal acceptable efficiency would occur at about 300 cfs. The Huron River at Barton dam equals or

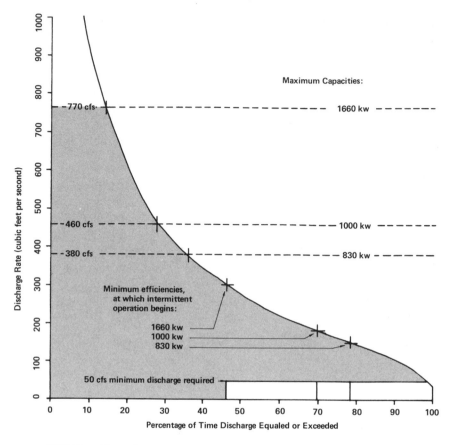

FIG. 3.   Flow duration curve, Huron River at Ann Arbor gauging station (1915–67) with operating characteristics of three design alternatives

exceeds this rate of discharge about 46 percent of the time. While the turbine is shut down during intermittent operation, 50 cfs would still be spilled over the dam as required by the state Department of Natural Resources. This power potential would be lost.

In summary, a given installed capacity has an effective average capacity indicated by the area under the installed capacity limit and the flow duration curve, less the area representing the minimum discharge requirement. For the systems with installed capacities of 830 kw, 1000 kw, and 1660 kw, the effective capacities are 548 kw, 590 kw, and 697 kw, respectively. The average utilization of installed capacity drops from 66 percent in the smallest system to 59 percent and 42 percent in the two larger ones. The average utilization of the *increment* in installed capacity also drops from the smallest system to the larger ones. Starting from zero "installed capacity," the utilization of the first increment is 66 percent; from the first system to the second, the utilization of the increment is 25 percent (based on an effective increment of 42 kw and an installed increment of 170 kw); and from the second system to the third, the utilization of the increment is only 16 percent. This relationship affects the benefit/cost ratio. Although hydro facilities at existing dams have significant costs regardless of installed capacity, some costs are related to installed capacity. The projected annual production of electricity, the main benefit, is based on effective capacity.

The value of an electrical generating facility is a function of demand or peaking capacity, as well as aggregate energy production. Demand is a function of *how fast* energy is produced or consumed at an instant rather than *how much* is produced or consumed over a period of time. The distinction is necessary because utilities must have enough capacity to meet demand at any time, and demand tends to peak at certain times of the day and of the year. The expense of providing demand or peaking capacity used only intermittently is reflected in charges. If a plant at the Barton site could be operated to reliably offset peak demand, its potential would be greatly enhanced.

The demand capacity of a dam site is a function of both impoundment and streamflow characteristics. Barton pond cannot provide significant long-term impoundment, but there is some demand capacity based on the flow of the Huron River. The impoundment *could* be used to offset daily peaks in demand. To do this, flow would be reduced to minimum discharge requirement at night (the off-peak hours) to fill the pond. The turbines could then be run at higher efficiency during the day to offset a greater proportion of on-peak demand. However, variations in the level of the pond would affect use of the river both upstream and downstream, as well as waterfront property. This study does not assume *any* impoundment management for peaking maximization. Furthermore, it recommends a city commitment to avoid such impoundment management practices if the site is reactivated.[20]

To determine the longer-run demand capacity that might be offset by a plant at the Barton site, it is necessary to look at seasonal variations in the river flow. (These variations are not reflected in the flow duration curve, which is based on annual averages.) In table 2, the monthly generating potential of the river is calculated from average monthly streamflow data over the most recent twelve years on record, 1966–77, taking into account the net head of the dam. For this site, potential is approximately 2.18 kw/cfs.[21] The results are compared with the installed capacity of the three systems to determine the average monthly demand that can be offset by each. For the 830 kw system, generating potential of the streamflow falls below installed capacity in July, August, September, and October. Similarly, the generating potentials of the 1000 kw and 1660 kw systems are limited by streamflow in five months and ten months, respectively, as indicated by the boxes in table 2. In all other months, potential demand offset is limited to installed capacity.

Overall costs and operating characteristics of the three alternatives considered for reactivation of the Barton site are summarized in table 3. A conservative projected service life of twenty-five years is

TABLE 2.   Mean Monthly Demand Which Can Be Offset by Hydro Plants

	Average Stream Flow (in cfs)	Equivalent Generating Potential (in kw)	Theoretical Average Demand Offset with Hydropower Using Following Capacities:		
			830 kw	1,000 kw	1660 kw
January	544	1,186	830	1,000	1,186
February	685	1,493	830	1,000	1,493
March	961	2,095	830	1,000	1,660
April	904	1,971	830	1,000	1,660
May	683	1,489	830	1,000	1,589
June	505	1,101	830	1,000	1,101
July	373	813	813	813	813
August	236	514	514	514	514
September	244	532	532	532	532
October	260	567	567	567	567
November	420	916	830	916	916
December	531	1,158	830	1,000	1,158
Mean Average	529	1,153	756	862	1,099

Source: Methodology adapted from Ayers, Lewis, Norris, and May, Inc.

TABLE 3.   Summary of Costs and Operating Characteristics of Three Turbine Systems

	One 830 kw Leffel	Two 500 kw Bofors-Nohab	Two 830 kw Leffel
Projected service life (in years)	25	25	25
Estimated project cost (in thousands)	$582	$1,077	$1,021
Installed capacity	830 kw	1,000 kw	1,660 kw
Effective average capacity	548 kw	590 kw	697 kw
Plant factor	66%	59%	42%
Cost/installed kw	$701	$1,077	$615
Cost/effective kw	$1,062	$1,825	$1,465
Projected annual production (in millions)	4.8 kwh	5.2 kwh	6.1 kwh
Projected annual O&M cost	$32,700	$39,700	$39,500
O&M cost/kwh produced	$0.68	$0.76	$0.65
Theoretical average monthly demand capacity by unit	756 kw	862 kw	1,099 kw
Average monthly demand capacity	659 kw	752 kw	900 kw

Note: Format and O&M costs adapted from Ayers, Lewis, Norris, and May, Inc. Dollar amounts are in 1979 prices.

assumed. Estimated project cost is the total nondiscounted amount in 1979 prices necessary to take the Barton facility from its present condition to operational status, plus a contingency fund for unanticipated expenses (refer to table 1 for details).

Effective average capacity is the projected average production determined from the flow duration curve for the Barton site (fig. 3). Plant factor is the ratio of effective to installed capacity, or the average utilization of equipment. Projected annual production is the effective average capacity of each system times the number of hours per year, or gross annual energy production. The annual energy production of the Barton plant from 1931 to 1950 averaged 5.2 million kwh, about the same as that projected for the Bofors-Nohab 1000 kw system.[22]

Projected annual operation and maintenance cost assumes a labor cost of twenty dollars per hour and

> 730 hours/year operating labor expense, which assumes automatic or remote supervisory control with a daily visit by a mobile plant operator;
> 80 hours/year per generating unit for equipment maintenance;

2 percent of equipment cost/year for maintenance parts and
materials;

Annual insurance and administrative costs of six thousand dollars; and

An annual average dam and building structural maintenance cost
of four thousand dollars.

Theoretical average demand capacity is the electric demand
which could be offset by each system, based on average monthly
streamflow (see table 2). This is biased on the high side for two reasons. It does not include efficiency losses in the system, normally
around 10 percent; and it represents a monthly average that the system cannot support consistently for a whole month. Sometimes demand capacity will be less, sometimes more. Average demand capacity
is an adjustment to accommodate these biases. For months in which
demand capacity is greater than installed capacity, theoretical demand
capacity is discounted by a factor of 0.9. In other months (as indicated
in boxes in table 2), theoretical demand capacity is discounted by a
factor of 0.8 to account for losses attributable to equipment inefficien-
cies and streamflow variations.

Market for Electricity

Electricity produced at the Barton site could be used and valued in
many ways. The "most likely case" analysis assumes that it would be
used to offset electricity costs at the municipal water pumping station
with excess power sold to Detroit Edison. This section estimates the
amount and value of the offset and of the surplus electricity.

The water pumping station purchases electricity from Detroit
Edison at the Primary Pumping Rate E-4. Monthly consumption and
charges for 1978 are summarized in table 4. To illustrate how the
charges are derived from the consumption per month data, consider
the rates effective on and after September 29, 1978.[23] The amount
charged is the sum of:

$150.00 service charge;

An energy charge of 2.0¢ per kwh for all on-peak consumption;

An energy charge of 1.7¢ per kwh for all off-peak consumption

TABLE 4. Electric Use and Charges at the Water Pumping Station, 1978

	Energy Consumption (in kw)	High Demand (in kw)	High Demand June–October of previous year (in kw)	Total Change (in dollars)
January	255,560	577	1,108	$ 9,543
February	318,510	604	1,108	10,637
March	285,900	435	761	11,272
April	318,750	610	751	12,749
May	355,830	694	751	14,666
June	430,350	786	748	12,355
July	444,840	1,050	786	12,080
August	567,930	1,108	1,050	13,700
September	420,930	630	1,050	11,478
October	298,980	496	1,108	10,506
November	291,210	480	1,108	9,697
December	322,680	544	1,108	10,957
Calendar 1978	4,311,470			139,640
Fiscal year 1977–78	3,933,450			124,622
Fiscal year 1978–79	4,528,500			139,583

Source: Water Treatment Division of the Utilities Department, City of Ann Arbor

A demand charge of $6.35 per kw of billing (or high) demand; and

A variable fuel and purchased power adjustment.

On-peak hours are from 11:00 A.M. to 7:00 P.M., Monday through Friday. In simplified form, billing demand is based on the highest thirty-minute integrated reading each week, averaged over four weeks. It cannot be less than half of the highest monthly billing demand during the previous months of June through October. The city also operates pump engines fueled by natural gas. They are used to reduce high demand charges and during electrical power failures. The gas bill for the operation of these engines was about seven thousand dollars for fiscal year 1977–78.[24] This expenditure is ignored in the analysis that follows.

The calculation of the offset is summarized in table 5. The average demand capacity of all three alternatives (adjusted downward for reasons given above)[25] exceeds the average demand of the pumping station for all months except August and September. Average demand (per hour) of the pumping station is the result of monthly energy consumption (table 4) divided by the number of hours per month. In August and September, all three alternative systems are equally limited by low mean river flow and less than 100 percent of monthly charges are offset.[26] In the other months, 100 percent of monthly charges are offset. Therefore, the pumping costs avoided are identical for all three alternatives and amount to $130,200 annually.

The bearing of high demand at the pumping station on costs avoided is highly uncertain, and assumed to be insignificant in the calculation above. Although high demand at the pumping station exceeds the mean demand offset in four or five months, depending on the system, the river may or may not have sufficient streamflow to exceed high demand on occasion. Moreover, the present power purchase agreement would be replaced by a new contract if reactivation occurs. The new contract would be arranged with standby surcharges rather than demand rates. (Standby surcharges are discussed in the next section.) Projected costs avoided could move considerably in either direction, up or down.

Any plant design for the Barton site would produce electricity in excess of that used at the pumping station. (A very small portion

TABLE 5. Determination of Pumping Costs Avoided

	Average Demand Offset (kw)				Pumping Station		
	River	One 830 kw Leffel	Two 500 kw Bofors-Nohab	Two 830 kw Leffel	Average Demand (in kw)	High Demand (in kw)	Costs Avoided (in dollars)
January	949	747	949	949	343	577	$ 9,543
February	1,194	747	900	1,194	474	604	10,637
March	1,676	747	900	1,494	384	435	11,275
April	1,577	747	900	1,494	443	610	12,749
May	1,191	747	900	1,191	478	694	14,666
June	880	747	880	880	598	786	12,355
July	650	650	650	650	598	1,050	12,080
August	411	411	411	411	763	1,108	7,390
September	426	426	426	426	585	630	8,350
October	454	454	454	454	402	496	10,506
November	733	733	733	733	404	480	9,697
December	926	747	926	926	434	544	10,957
Annual	922[a]	659[a]	752[a]	900[a]	492[a]		130,200[b]

a. Average per month
b. Annual total

would be used at the Barton site itself.) It is common for power-producing entities such as a university or industrial plant to sell surplus power on an unscheduled basis to a utility. The utility distributes the power through its system, even though it typically has little incentive to place a high value on such sporadic, generally off-peak sources. Detroit Edison has indicated its willingness to purchase electricity from the French Landing site downstream on the Huron in any amount at any time at an estimated price of 1.2¢ per off-peak kwh and 2.0¢ per on-peak kwh. The actual interchange would be based on the operating and fuel cost of a typical utility plant, on an hour-by-hour basis, which is expected to average to these rates.[27]

Revenue to the city from the sale of surplus energy under each of the three alternatives is summarized by month in table 6. Surplus energy is the kw capacity remaining after the needs of the pumping station are met. It is calculated as the average demand offset of the system less the average demand at the pumping station, both of which are given in table 5. The resulting kw of surplus capacity per average hour is multiplied by the number of hours per month and valued at 1.6¢ per kwh, the average of the price quoted by Detroit Edison. As can be seen in table 6, the larger systems produce more surplus energy and more revenue. Taking these revenues together with $130,200 in pumping costs avoided, the annual totals are $159,300; $172,500; and $193,000 for the three systems, respectively. These enter into the estimates of financial feasibility and benefit/cost ratios that follow.

Financial Feasibility and Benefit/Cost Analysis

An economic summary of the first year of operations for each alternative is presented in table 7 in order to examine financial feasibility. In addition to data already developed in previous sections, table 7 includes a standby surcharge derived from Detroit Edison rates of $1.75 per kw of installed capacity per month.[28] It also includes the annual debt service reflecting the cost to the city of financing the project through the sale of municipal revenue bonds with a twenty-five year term at an interest rate of 7 percent.[29] As shown in table 7, all three alternative systems yield revenues greater than costs during the first year of operation, with the net annual profit ranging from nineteen thousand to about fifty-nine thousand dollars. The smallest system is

TABLE 6. Determination of Surplus Energy Value

	One 830 kw Leffel		Two 500 kw Bofors-Nohab		Two 830 kw Leffel	
	Surplus Energy (kw capacity)	Surplus Energy Value ($0.016/kwh)	Surplus Energy (kw capacity)	Surplus Energy Value ($0.016/kwh)	Surplus Energy (kw capacity)	Surplus Energy Value ($0.016/kwh)
January	404	$4,800	606	$7,200	606	$7,200
February	273	2,900	426	4,600	720	7,700
March	363	4,300	516	6,100	1,110	13,200
April	304	3,500	457	5,300	1,051	12,100
May	269	3,200	422	5,000	712	8,500
June	149	1,700	282	3,200	282	3,200
July	52	600	52	600	52	600
August	0	0	0	0	0	0
September	0	0	0	0	0	0
October	52	600	52	600	52	600
November	329	3,800	329	3,800	329	3,800
December	313	3,700	492	5,900	492	5,900
Surplus energy total		29,100		42,300		62,800
Pumping costs deferred		130,200		130,200		130,200
Total revenue		159,300		172,500		193,000

TABLE 7.   Economic Summary for First Year of Operation

Most Likely Case	One 830 kw Leffel	Two 500 kw Bofors-Nohab	Two 830 kw Leffel
Estimated project cost	$582,000	$1,077,000	$1,027,000
Projected annual revenue			
Pumping cost deferred	130,200	130,200	130,200
Surplus energy value	29,100	42,300	62,800
Total Annual Revenue	159,300	172,500	193,000
Annual Costs			
Standby Surcharge	(17,400)	(21,000)	(34,800)
Projected O&M costs	(32,700)	(39,700)	(39,500)
Total annual costs	50,100	60,700	74,300
Net annual revenue	109,200	111,800	118,700
Annual debt service	(49,900)	(92,400)	(87,600)
Net annual profit	59,300	19,400	31,100
Return on investment	10.2%	1.8%	3.0%

most profitable, even though it generates the least revenue. Reduced outlays for the standby surcharge, operation and maintenance costs, and particularly annual debt service are more than enough to make up the difference.

In addition to estimating first-year profitability, it is worthwhile to compare benefits and costs in terms of present value over the life of the project. The present value concept accounts for the fact that a dollar held today is worth more than the promise of a dollar at some future date. More specifically, a dollar held today is worth one dollar plus the interest it could earn over the intervening period. Thus benefits and costs incurred in the future are discounted by this interest rate back to the present-day value. A discount rate of 2.5 percent is used here because it approximates the current real cost of capital.[30] The analysis also assumes a two-year construction period with full plant operation beginning in year three, and a project life of twenty-five years.

The results of this benefit/cost analysis are presented in table 8. It shows that the total present value of benefits exceeds the total present value of costs for all three alternatives. The smallest system is

TABLE 8.   Benefit/Cost Analysis

	One 830 kw Leffel	Two 500 kw Bofors-Nohab	Two 830 kw Leffel
Total project costs	$582,000	$1,077,000	$1,027,000
Annual benefits (revenue)	159,300	172,500	193,000
Annual costs	50,100	60,700	74,300
Net annual benefits (revenue)	109,200	111,800	118,700

Present Value Determination			
	One 830 kw Leffel	Two 500 kw Bofors-Nohab	Two 830 kw Leffel
Present value benefits	$1,962,900	$2,009,700	$2,133,700
Present value costs	569,200	1,053,400	1,004,500
Net present value	1,393,700	956,300	1,129,200
Benefit/cost ratio	3.4	1.9	2.1
Year present value benefits exceeds present value costs			
From project initiation	7	13	11
From start of operation	5	11	9

again the most attractive one. The benefit/cost ratio is 3.4, and the present value of benefits exceeds the present value of costs of the project in the fifth year of operation or the seventh year from the start of the project.[31]

Reactivation proves to be favorable even when certain key assumptions are varied. To test the sensitivity of the results to the choice of discount rate, for example, the present value estimates presented in table 8 were recalculated using significantly higher discount rates. All three systems yielded positive net benefits using a discount rate of 9 percent, indicating that any conclusions about the project's profitability are not dependent on the selection of discount rate. In fact, the smallest system continues to yield positive net benefits using a discount rate of 15 percent.

Other uncertainties—such as the offset of high demand charges discussed earlier—may conceivably detract from profitability. However, increases in the price of electricity charged by Detroit Edison or paid by Detroit Edison for surplus energy could increase net benefits substantially. So too would a project life that extends beyond twenty-five years, which appears reasonable in view of the life expectancy of generating equipment. On balance, the existence of net benefits is far less uncertain than the magnitude of net benefits.

Environmental Impacts

Positive environmental impacts resulting from the reactivation of the Barton site appear to outweigh any negative impacts foreseen in this analysis. A stable ecological equilibrium has been established at Barton, and this should not be affected by power production at the site. The operation of the dam would generally remain unchanged, except that water now flowing freely through the powerhouse would be harnessed by turbines for power generation.

Since reactivation of the Barton site would require a thorough dam and powerhouse structural review (and possibly minor refurbishment), dam safety would be improved and the likelihood of continued structural deterioration greatly diminished. Dam management and operation skills would improve, which would tend to increase flood control ability and reduce potential flood damages.

The recommended flow management is based on "run of the river" operation and should therefore have no adverse effects on lake level or shoreline property owners. Thus shoreline and pond use by such groups as the Barton Sailing Club should not be adversely affected. Impoundment management (erosion and siltation) could have positive environmental consequences at Barton relative to the present management, which calls for two feet or more variation in lake level between winter and summer. The recommended management is to keep the pond at a "normal full pond" level except in anticipation of floods, and in winter months (until after ice breakup) when an eight-to-twelve-inch decrease in level is called for.

The option of building a city aquarium in the lower parts of the powerhouse would probably be foregone if reactivation took place. Plans for the city aquarium are not firm, however, and the likelihood of establishing the aquarium seems small, even with no reactivation.[32] The municipal water supply intake pipe would need to be rerouted from its present location for reactivation to take place. This should not impose serious complications or costs.

The construction phase of reactivating the site will have the greatest environmental impacts, but these will be temporary in nature. The Barton Hills area may experience traffic and noise levels above normal during construction. Interim flow control of the river required for installation of new turbines and structural modifications will have a temporary impact on river use downstream.

The greatest social environmental impact of reactivation is associated with the educational costs or benefits to accrue in relation to plans for a museum at the site. Reactivation of the Barton facility clearly has a direct effect on alternative uses of the site and power-house. The Washtenaw County Historical Society is implementing plans for a museum at the site, but has recently decided that a building in addition to the present powerhouse is necessary. "Costs" (relative to the plans for a museum) of redeveloping the hydroelectric capacity at Barton would be realized in terms of the usable space lost inside the powerhouse and delays to museum opening which could occur due to construction. It is projected that the hydro facility could be completely operable within twenty-one to twenty-seven months of project authorization.

Many possibilities exist for resolving the potential conflicts of both developing a museum and renewing hydroelectric generation. Construction could progress on both projects simultaneously, reducing the potential delays to museum opening due to recommissioning activities. The museum could also remain open while reactivation of the site was in progress (once any dangerous dam and building renovation was complete) thus expanding the educational benefits of the site to include *how* such reactivation takes place, giving a unique view of work in progress.

An operating hydroelectric facility at the site would clearly make the museum a more exciting and appealing place to visit. It would also broaden the range of historical and educational issues which the museum could credibly emphasize. Reactivation would offer an exclusive experience for visitors actually to see an important energy technology of the past in action.[33] Tours could be given, or public viewing areas could be designed into the powerhouse rehabilitation plans. (Not *all* the space in the powerhouse would be required for power generating equipment.) Electricity produced at the dam could be used to power lights and displays at the museum, allowing the museum also to cover such topics as electrical distribution and historical rural electrification.

Intergovernmental Aspects

The primary regulatory barrier to reactivation of the Barton site is the historically long and complex process of acquiring the necessary permits and licenses from the Federal Energy Regulatory Commission. However, the Department of Energy, under the authority of the Public Utilities Regulatory Policies Act of 1978, has begun to simplify regulations covering "minor" projects with an installed capacity of 15,000 kw or less.[34] The Barton site would qualify for a "minor" license, although the time required is uncertain. Under the state constitution, Michigan municipalities are authorized to own and operate electric utilities and to finance their acquisition and operation.

The Public Utilities Regulatory Policies Act of 1978 also provides for loans of up to ten years to municipalities to defray up to 90 percent of the cost of small hydroelectric projects at existing dams. The costs of feasibility studies, preparing an application, and administrative proceedings are allowable costs. If the project turns out to be technically or economically infeasible, the secretary of energy may cancel the unpaid balance and any accrued interest.[35] A project to reactivate the Barton site would qualify for such a loan. An "Applicant's Information Kit" is available.[36] It includes an application form, a guide for small hydroelectric site evaluation, a list of hydropower equipment, manufacturers, and suppliers, a list of firms with an expressed interest in designing such projects, contacts for further information, and instructions.

Conclusions and Recommendations

Based on this analysis, it appears that reactivation of the Barton site would be financially feasible and profitable, and that there are no significant environmental or regulatory obstacles to reactivation. This is a tentative conclusion pending further study by a professional engineer.

It is recommended that the city of Ann Arbor commission a full-scale feasibility study of reactivating the Barton site. The other city-owned dam sites might also be included since some of the costs of simultaneous reactivation might fall relative to increased generating potential.[37] It is further recommended that the city apply for a loan to defray the costs of the feasibility study and survey the potential for additional financial aid from the state and federal governments. Finally, in order to insure that the project is consistent with the broader interests of the community, the city should work closely with the Washtenaw County Historical Society, and should continue "run of the river" operation of the dams. As discussed earlier, impoundment management for the purpose of peak power production would be disruptive of other uses of the Huron.

NOTES

This paper was written in June, 1979. It was revised in May, 1980, although the original analysis remains basically unchanged. The author wishes to thank Donald W. Lystra of Ayres, Lewis, Norris, and May, Inc., and Wayne H. Abbott and Harvey J. Mieske of the Ann Arbor Utilities Department. Responsibility is the author's alone.

1. William J. Lanouette, "Rising Oil and Gas Prices Are Making Hydropower Look Better Every Day," *National Journal,* April 26, 1980, pp. 685–89. David E. Lilienthal, former chairman of the Tennessee Valley Authority and of the Atomic Energy Commission, clarifies the "other considerations":

> We were persuaded to accept the fashionable idea that great new generating stations and huge, regionalized transmission systems would deliver electric energy more efficiently at lower cost to the public than small, local, decentralized ones. . . . Many of those older units were shut down simply because hydropower was no longer 'fashionable.'

He is quoted by Dick Kirschten, "Hydropower—Turning to Water to Turn the Wheels," *National Journal,* April 29, 1978, p. 674.

2. Lanouette, "Rising Oil and Gas Prices," pp. 685 and 689.

3. U.S. Army Corps of Engineers, *Feasibility Studies for Small Scale Hydropower Additions,* vol. 1 (Davis, Calif.: Hydrologic Engineering Center, 1979), pp. 1–5.

4. Lanouette, "Rising Oil and Gas Prices," p. 686.

5. Massachusetts Electric Company and Northeast Utilities Service Company, "A Feasibility Study of the Erving Paper Mills Site," mimeographed (Greenfield, Mass.: Franklin County Energy Conservation Task Force, 1978), p. 1. The plant formerly located at the Barton site in Ann Arbor was retired in relatively good condition after forty-five years of operation.

6. U.S. Army, *Feasibility Studies,* p. 2-2. Lilienthal in Kirschten, "Hydropower," p. 674, estimates that "some abandoned hydro sites might be brought back into operation within eight to fourteen months." One feasibility study estimates the "total time required from authorization to putting power on-line is projected to be twenty-seven months." See Ayres, Lewis, Norris, and

May, Inc., "Assessment of the Feasibility of Recommissioning the French Landing Hydroelectric Facility in Van Buren Township, Michigan," mimeographed (Ann Arbor: City of Ann Arbor, 1979), p. 9.

7. U.S. Army, *Feasibility Studies,* pp. 1–5.

8. The Michigan Department of Natural Resources conducted a statewide dam inventory and inspection program in 1971–72. John Parsons of Ferris State College is engaged in a state-sponsored program to determine ownership of the small dams in Michigan.

9. Detroit Edison Company, "The Hydro-Electric Plants of the Detroit Edison Company," mimeographed (Detroit: Detroit Edison, 1951), fig. 10 (hereafter cited as Detroit Edison, "Hydro-Electric Plants").

10. Lilienthal in Kirschten, "Hydropower," p. 674.

11. U.S., Department of Energy, Idaho Operations Office, *A Guide for Small Hydroelectric Development* outlines a simple procedure. The Operations Office can be contacted at 550 Second Street, Idaho Falls, Idaho 83401 or 208-526-9180. The six volumes bound together in U.S. Army, *Feasibility Studies* present very much more detail. The Hydrologic Engineering Study which publishes it can be contacted at 609 2nd Street, Davis, Calif. 95616. Useful information can also be found in EG&G Idaho, Inc., *Executive Summaries, Small/Low-Head Hydropower PRDA-1706 Feasibility Assessments* (Idaho Falls, Idaho: U.S. Department of Energy, Idaho Operations Office, 1979).

12. Detroit Edison, "Hydro-Electric Plants," p. 4. The historical role of the Huron River in relation to Ann Arbor is discussed in a small pamphlet that serves as a guidebook to the bikepath that follows the river from Argo Dam to Dixboro Road. See Jane Cohen, *Ann Arbor and the Huron River Valley; Take a Closer Look* (Ann Arbor: Huron River Watershed Council, 1979).

13. Phone conversation with Harvey Mieske, Water Treatment Plant Supervisor, April 16, 1979.

14. The author was accompanied by Mr. Mieske, who provided information on the structures and their operation.

15. Phone conversations with Hazel Proctor, Chairperson of the Museum Committee, Washtenaw County Historical Society, January 16, 1979; and with George Owers, City Parks Director, April 18, 1979.

16. Ayres, Lewis, Norris, and May, Inc., "Assessment of the Feasibility of Recommissioning the French Landing Hydroelectric Facility." Don Lystra, the project director, gave immeasurable assistance to the author, and granted permission to use cost data, figures, and tables which had been developed for the French Landing project. The French Landing site, located on the Huron near Belleville, downriver from Ann Arbor, is very similar to the Barton site. A more detailed study of the Barton site would find some costs higher and some lower, but the total costs are not expected to change substantially.

17. Detroit Edison, "Hydro-Electric Plants," p. 10, and the Huron River Watershed Council, 415 W. Washington, Ann Arbor, personal communication.

18. The U.S. Geological Survey can often provide a flow duration curve for a specific site on request, or the curve can be derived from historic water flow records as in this study.

19. To avoid complicating figure 3 even further, this diagrammatic presentation assumes that only one turbine accounts for the installed capacity at each of the three levels, 830, 1000, and 1660 kw. The 1000 kw and 1660 kw alternatives actually would have much more flexibility than shown here, since the two turbines in each system could be run simultaneously or separately, depending on river flow.

The relationship among capacity (C) in kw, stream flow (Q) in feet per second, and net head (H) in feet is:

$$C = \frac{Q \times H}{8.82}(0.746).$$

(The constant 0.746 converts horsepower into kilowatts.) Because the Barton dam has a net head of 25.8 ft, capacity is 2.18 kw per cfs. The net head figure is given in Detroit Edison, "Hydro-Electric Plants," p. 10.

20. The Michigan Department of Natural Resources discourages impoundment management for peak demand capacity for environmental reasons.

21. See note 19.

22. Annual figures are given in Detroit Edison, "Hydro-Electric Plants," fig. 9.

23. Detroit Edison, *Rate Book for Electric Service* (1978), Primary Pumping Rate E-4.

24. Phone conversation with Harvey Mieske, August 2, 1979.

25. See the discussion of theoretical average demand capacity in the previous section.

26. As a rough approximation, the demand shortfall was multiplied by the number of hours per month and valued at the average charge per kwh in table 4. For August, this is 352 kw × 744 hrs. × $.0241 per kwh, or about $6,310.

27. Detroit Edison letter to Ayres, Lewis, Norris, and May, Inc., January 11, 1979.

28. Detroit Edison, *Rate Book for Electric Service*, Contract Rider No. 3, Standby or Partial Service.

29. In 1979, Sylvester Murray, then the city administrator of Ann Arbor, estimated that the interest on a city revenue bond would be in the 6 to 7 percent range, and noted that twenty-five years was the maximum bond life. No taxes are included based on ownership by a tax-exempt municipality.

30. This rate was determined as the "real" rate of interest by adjusting the 1979 corporate interest rate (9.5 percent) for inflation (7 percent). The corporate rate was used as a base on the assumption that money paid for municipal bonds displaces local corporate investment. The analysis also as-

sumes that all construction costs occur in the first two years of the project (see note 6).

31. The following methodology was used to calculate the net present value of benefits summarized in table 8:

Annual net benefits were calculated from the data presented in table 7, and were discounted according to the formula:

$$\text{Total net benefits} = B_0 + \frac{B_1}{(1 + r)^1} + \frac{B_2}{(1 + r)^2} + \cdots \frac{B_n}{(1 + r)^n}$$

where B_n is equal to the net benefits realized in year n.

It was assumed that construction would take place in the first two years of the project and that 10 percent of the total construction costs (line 1 of table 8) would be incurred in year zero and 90 percent in year one. Since the facility would not be fully operational until year two, annual net benefits in years zero and one are negative.

Present value benefits for years two through twenty-six were computed by discounting the net annual benefits (line 4 of table 8) for each of the twenty-five years of operation and summing these values.

The resulting equation for design 1 is therefore (all dollar values × 1,000):

$$B_{total} = (-\$582.0)(0.1) + \frac{(-\$582.0)(0.9)}{(1.025)}$$

$$+ \frac{(\$109.2)}{(1.025)^2} + \frac{(\$109.2)}{(1.025)^3} + \cdots \frac{(\$109.2)}{(1.025)^{26}}$$

A table summarizing the net present value of benefits in the first six years of the project for each of the three systems looks like this:

	Alternative System		
Year	1–830 kw	2–500 kw	2–830 kw
0	−58.2	−107.7	−102.7
1	−511.0	−945.0	−901.8
2	103.9	106.4	113.0
3	101.4	103.8	110.2
4	98.9	101.3	107.5
5	96.5	98.8	104.9
6	94.2	96.4	102.4

If these calculations are carried out over the full twenty-five year operating period (i.e., through year twenty-six), and cumulative total of net present value benefits is kept, it becomes a simple matter to determine the year in which present value benefits exceed present value costs.

32. In a phone conversation on April 19, 1979, George Owers, the city parks director, said movement on the aquarium project was very unlikely because funds were not available.

33. The research of Marshall McLennan and Andrew Nazzaro, Associate Professors of Geography at Eastern Michigan University in Ypsilanti, would contribute to the same purpose. Under a grant from the Michigan History Division of the Michigan Department of State, they have begun to survey "historic water-oriented industrial sites" along the Huron and relate their significance to the evolution of the nineteenth- and early twentieth-century economic landscape. See "Huron: 'Stream of Energy'," *Ann Arbor News,* December 9, 1978.

34. Recent steps are listed in U.S., Department of Energy, "Loans for Small Hydroelectric Power Project Feasibility Studies and Related Licensing," *Federal Register,* January 17, 1980, note 4 on p. 3539.

35. For final rules see Ibid., pp. 3538–49.

36. Contact the Idaho Operations Office of the Department of Energy at the address given in note 11.

37. Operation and maintenance costs are especially likely to decrease per kw of capacity as more dams are added, since it could take nearly the same number of man-hours to operate one dam as it could for two. The Geddes dam is a likely candidate since it was recently rebuilt and has another pumping station located nearby.

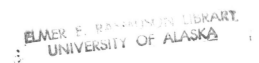

4 Resource Recovery: An Evaluation of Its Revenue and Energy Potentials for Washtenaw County

Robin Sandenburgh

Over the past decade, the term *resource recovery* has become a popular one, used to describe a wide range of human activities and technological systems, from Boy Scout newspaper drives and local recycling centers to mandatory beverage container deposits and sophisticated facilities which utilize refuse as a fuel source. All reflect a common and growing realization—that natural resources are not unlimited, and that material once considered waste can be recycled and reprocessed to provide extended or additional uses.

Of particular appeal from the perspective of locally controlled energy sources has been the development of various energy technologies that produce energy from municipal and county solid waste. Interest in such systems began in the early 1970s, as a handful of municipalities adapted steam-generating boiler facilities to allow them to burn processed solid waste instead of or in addition to fossil fuels.[1] In so doing, they were able to alleviate a growing problem facing communities across the country—acquisition of enough sanitary landfill areas to handle their constituents' refuse. The problem was severe and widespread: a nationwide survey of municipal officials in 1974 cited waste disposal as the most critical issue facing U.S. cities.[2] Using garbage to fire municipal boiler systems provided a simple and effective solution, since garbage that was burned did not have to be landfilled.

By the mid-1970s there was an additional impetus for garbage-to-fuel facilities. As prices for petroleum and other fuels began to increase, solid waste was viewed as one of many renewable energy resources that might provide an alternative to conventional fuels. With the support of the U.S. Environmental Protection Agency (EPA), research was undertaken to find ways of improving garbage as a fuel. Various technologies were developed by both private and public sector researchers, in an effort to convert raw refuse into a more uniform, reliable energy source.

None of the approaches has been problem-free. However, the failures are frequently more dramatic than the successes,[3] and are thus more likely to be reported. Of late, even the advocates of energy recovery systems have encouraged municipalities to conduct an extensive evaluation of key factors before embarking on such a project.

For many of the same reasons that have turned out to be important elsewhere, resource recovery has been under consideration in the city of Ann Arbor since at least 1974. The purpose of this chapter is to summarize, update, and extend the analysis of the issue in Ann Arbor, with special attention to the production of refuse-derived fuel. The paper draws heavily on the extensive and rather mixed results of resource recovery initiatives in other communities.

The next section reviews the recent history of resource recovery and refuse-derived fuel as policy options in Ann Arbor and Washtenaw County. This is followed by discussion of the three main options based on experience elsewhere: (1) source separation of recyclables; (2) direct production of energy through combustion of waste after recyclables are removed; and (3) the production of refuse-derived fuel. The last option, including source separation of recyclables, is then examined from the standpoint of financial feasibility. Key uncertainties in the financial analysis are focused on, and the study concludes with a set of recommendations.

In summary, the principal results are that a refuse-derived fuel facility appears to be financially feasible, but caution is warranted in view of operating difficulties experienced with the technology in other communities and of the limitations of local data currently available. It is recommended that the city begin immediate efforts toward implementing a source separation program. Such programs are relatively low-cost and generally pay for themselves within a few years. Analysis suggests that conditions in Ann Arbor are favorable for a community-wide source separation project. Moreover, the project would generate important operating data on the actual volume of recyclables, citizen participation in home source separation, and the market value of the recovered materials. These results will provide valuable indicators as to what, if any, additional resource and energy recovery activities should be undertaken.

It is further recommended that the city retain a qualified consultant to assemble the information needed to decide whether to go ahead with a full-scale energy recovery facility. The consultant's findings, together with the operating data from the source separation program, will reduce significantly the multiple uncertainties which characteristically plague resource recovery systems.

Finally, it is recommended that the city consider carefully the question of where to locate a resource recovery facility if one is approved. Important concerns are proximity to markets where the waste heat can be utilized for space heating or steam generation. Attention to these locational issues will further enhance the facility's viability.

Background to the Ann Arbor Evaluation

Various resource recovery options have been considered over the past several years both by the city of Ann Arbor and by Washtenaw County. The interest in resource recovery reflected initially the worsening landfill situation, though recently concern for recycling and energy production have been evidenced as well.

The dimensions of the waste disposal problem in Washtenaw County can be summarized briefly. Total solid waste generation is growing at an annual rate greater than the rate of population growth in the county; in other words, per capita waste is increasing. Moreover, the Ann Arbor municipal landfill, which serves several other communities in addition to the city of Ann Arbor, is rapidly approaching capacity. Finally, in the last few years it has become apparent that sanitary landfill may not be an environmentally sound alternative. Several recent studies have shown that existing regulations designed to ensure adequate management of sanitary landfills have not been successful in preventing leachate (liquid which drains through solid waste and mixes with compounds that may harm the environment), vector problems (rodents, flies, and other pests), and other unsanitary conditions.[4] As a result, the state has mandated more stringent regulations in terms of the depth of both the clay lining and daily cover required in all landfills, thereby reducing the capacity per acre of land.[5] These developments, in conjunction with soaring land prices, opened discussion as to whether the sanitary landfill method is, in fact, the most desirable disposal option for either Ann Arbor or the county as a whole.

The first important attempt to assess the viability of resource recovery for the area came in 1974, when the Department of Public Works (DPW) of Washtenaw County commissioned an engineering consulting firm, Jones and Henry (J & H) of Toledo, to evaluate the feasibility of several waste management alternatives, on a countywide basis. The final J & H report, completed in May, 1975, concluded that a facility to produce fuel from municipal waste *was* a feasible option for the county to consider.[6] There appears to have been considerable interest in the project on the part of several county officials at that time, yet no immediate steps were taken toward implementing the J & H conclusions.[7]

In 1977, the Ann Arbor City Council designated an ad hoc committee on solid waste to study the refuse problem. The major area of concern was the municipal landfill site, which was within five years of reaching capacity. Over a period of several months, members of the committee visited a number of municipalities that had adopted various resource and energy recovery strategies. The committee's final report overwhelmingly recommended that the city purchase a solid waste shredder which, by processing the waste into a more compact form, would make it possible to dispose of more refuse per acre of landfill, thereby extending the life of the existing landfill by five to eight years.[8] Moreover, the committee concluded that a shredder would be adaptable to a resource and energy recovery facility, should the city decide to construct one at a later date. Later that year, a consulting firm hired by the city—Henningson, Durham, and Richardson (HDR) of Omaha—confirmed the ad hoc committee's recommendation to acquire a shredder.[9]

Two years later, on April 2, 1979, voters in Ann Arbor approved a $2.825 million bond proposal to finance construction of a solid waste shredding facility.[10] The proposal had become a controversial issue in the months preceding the referendum, with members of the ad hoc committee and the county DPW favoring purchase of a shredder, and the city Department of Solid Waste opposing it on the grounds that it would be less expensive to purchase additional landfill.[11]

The controversy continued after the referendum and, in the fall of 1979, the city council voted to table the shredder proposal until further studies of its feasibility could be completed.[12] Among other things, the council felt it should investigate implementing a more comprehensive resource recovery program before committing the city to a shredder-based system.

Most recently, the city Engineering Department, in cooperation with the University of Michigan, has submitted a grant proposal to the U.S. Department of Energy (DOE) to obtain funding for the study of, among other things, the feasibility of a resource recovery facility to be operated by the city and to supply energy to the university.

Amid all this activity in the public sector, the Ann Arbor Ecology Center has for several years operated a nonprofit, voluntary recycling program. The center maintains a single recycling station, staffed by volunteers, which collects three colors of glass, bimetal and steel cans, motor oil, newspaper, and high-grade paper. The recycling program has been in operation since 1970, and the Ecology Center estimates that it receives roughly 20 to 30 percent of Ann Arbor's recyclables annually.[13] From the inception of the recycling program, the Ecology Center has viewed its role as a temporary one: helping to get the project off the ground and then turning it over either to a private organization or to the city itself.[14] Any recycling effort initiated by the city would thus be able to incorporate the successes already achieved by the Ecology Center's program.

In summary, all of these initiatives suggest that local decision makers, while very much interested in implementing some form of resource recovery, are not yet certain which if any of the many systems will provide the greatest benefits to the community. The next section of this study examines the array of options open to the Ann Arbor/Washtenaw County area and to other municipalities as well.

An Overview of the Options

In broad terms, the selection of a local resource recovery system comes down to three possible choices: (1) a source separation program; (2) a facility which combusts unprocessed refuse to produce energy directly; or (3) a facility that processes waste into a uniform fuel which may be used on site or transported for use elsewhere.[15] A solid waste shredder, such as the one recently approved by referendum in Ann Arbor, is compatible with all three of these systems. Were the city to opt for a recycling program, for example, the shredder could still be used to dispose of the remaining refuse in a way that makes more efficient use of landfill areas. Moreover, both the second and third options could utilize a shredding operation as a precombustion processing stage. Thus, construction of a shredder would not preclude future adoption of any of these strategies, though either of the energy recovery systems would require some retrofitting expenses to fully incorporate the shredder into the new system.

Source Separation

Of the three systems, source separation requires the least capital investment and hence the least amount of risk. Newspapers, glass, aluminum, ferrous metals, and other materials are separated by householders and either delivered to local recycling stations or collected periodically by municipally funded carriers. The collected items are then sold to appropriate materials dealers, often under long-term contracts between the dealers and the municipality.

There are usually three types of problems faced by communities that choose this option. The first is the inherent instability of markets for recyclables. Prices are extremely sensitive to economic fluctuations generally, and to the price and availability of virgin substitutes in particular. Communities cannot, therefore, rely completely on revenue from the sale of recyclables to finance their source separation program.

A second problem concerns citizen participation. Programs that use recycling stations are apt to have a lower rate of participation than will curbside collection (for obvious reasons), yet neither is likely to elicit the level of participation its backers might hope for. Several municipal governments have responded by enacting ordinances that mandate separation at the source, though such mechanisms are effective only with curbside programs.[16]

Scavenging—the removal by unauthorized persons of materials that have been set out for curbside pickup—is a third problem. Here again, the response by many communities has been to adopt local ordinances making scavenging punishable by fine.

Expenses for source separation programs include, at minimum, the cost of the "drop boxes" located around the town, to which residents bring their recyclables. More comprehensive systems may involve additional garbage pickups or special compartmentalized trucks.

Communities choosing to impose mandatory separation or antiscavenging ordinances may incur added enforcement expenses. These costs are quite small, however, relative to those of the other options. Potential benefits include a reduction in the amount of refuse that must be landfilled, and revenues from the sale of the recyclables. Thus, to have a source separation program that is economically viable, the revenues from the sale of the recyclables must exceed the extra costs incurred by their collection.

Many communities apparently are finding source separation to be a financially viable option. A November, 1979, EPA publication listed 177 source separation programs currently operating in the United States.[17] Two programs described in detail in the report are the Boca Raton, Florida, and Marblehead, Massachusetts, operations.[18] While these projects illustrate the dimensions of the revenue and cost trade-off, it should not be concluded that they are "average" or "representative" in any way, since the experiences of other communities are likely to differ markedly.

Boca Raton collects only newspaper and spends approximately $1,100 per month to cover the rental of a collection truck and the hiring of additional labor for the program. Annual costs are therefore about $13,200. However, revenues from selling the newspaper have ranged from twenty-two to forty dollars per ton and, in addition, the city saves eleven dollars for every ton diverted from the landfill it uses. Thus, assuming revenues on the low end of the range, the city must collect 400 tons per year to break even, not an unreasonable goal for a community of 58,000.[19] As a result, the program has proven to be economically feasible since its start-up in August of 1977.

The Marblehead program is part of an EPA demonstration project, funded partially by the town and partially by EPA.[20] Marblehead residents are required to separate their refuse into three categories: (1) paper, (2) clear glass, and (3) mixed brown and green glass. Cans may be put in either of the last two. These three components are collected by a compartmentalized truck once a week. The remaining refuse is collected by standard collection vehicles. The program began in January of 1976 and has received revenues for the recyclables ranging from ten to twenty dollars per ton. Like Boca Raton, Marblehead avoids a dumping charge for each ton diverted from the landfill equal to nineteen dollars per ton. Because the project has proven successful in regularly channeling 25 percent of the waste stream into recovery, in April of 1977 Marblehead was able to eliminate one of its two regular refuse collections. The town now collects garbage once a week and the separated recyclables once a week.

Facilities to Produce Energy Directly
The second type of system makes use of existing boiler technologies, such as waterwall or modular combustion, to produce steam for space heating or generating electricity.[21] Both waterwall and modular combustion incinerators are common, highly reliable, and widely used technologies, which can be run on conventional fuels (such as oil, natural gas, or coal) or combustible refuse. Under this system, either the boiler facility is constructed at the landfill site, or refuse is delivered to existing local boilers. In the former case, the municipality may produce steam and electricity on the site, or it may produce steam alone and transport it across short distances to local electric generating plants. Generally, some form of source separation takes place prior to combustion, to remove the heavy industrial and construction refuse from the waste stream. Additional separation may be undertaken to recover recyclables such as glass or ferrous metals.

Typical difficulties experienced with such systems center around the waste products generated. Because the refuse being burned is essentially untreated or unprocessed, boiler emissions contain various pollutants that require some degree of abatement before the facility can be granted an operating permit. In regions of the country where air quality is already below EPA's National Ambient Air Quality Standards (NAAQS), reducing emissions to an acceptable level can be a significant and potentially expensive undertaking.[22]

A second waste-related concern is the ash residue produced when refuse is burned. It is the ash factor that restricts the number of boiler types which can be used to burn unprocessed refuse, since only certain designs are able to handle ash—and even these may experience malfunctions caused by the accumulation of residues from burning untreated refuse.[23]

A final problem concerns the variability of waste as a fuel. No community's refuse is of a consistent quality; composition is affected by changes in weather, seasonal fluctuations, population shifts, and other exogenous variables. As an energy source it is therefore not wholly reliable, and at times may have to be supplemented by conventional sources such as coal.

Major expenses incurred by this type of resource recovery system are for equipment acquisition and modification. Existing boilers must be modified to handle refuse combustion and resulting residues, or new boilers must be constructed. Municipalities choosing not to construct or operate their own facilities must negotiate an agreement with a private generating facility, and finance the transportation of either the actual refuse or of steam produced at the disposal site. Total costs will vary depending on the specific arrangement chosen and the extent and quality of existing facilities. Table 1 provides an indication of the wide range of costs which may be incurred by facilities of this type, and demonstrates that costs are not simply a function of plant size but of other community characteristics as well.[24]

While the costs of constructing and maintaining energy-producing recovery systems are higher than those of simple source separation programs, the potential benefits are also greater. Because a much larger fraction of the waste stream has been recovered, these systems extend considerably the lifetime for existing disposal sites and forestall the need to acquire additional landfill. This factor is of particular importance for communities in densely populated regions, which already may find it difficult to acquire enough suitable landfill to keep pace with a growing waste supply.

Reduced energy costs are an obvious and especially visible benefit. Whether the refuse is used to generate electricity in a municipally owned facility, used to produce steam that is sold to a private generator, or sold directly to a private user, net community reliance on increasingly expensive fossil fuels is diminished. Moreover, replacing these conventional fuels with a renewable source generates long-term benefits that can only increase over time.

Many energy-producing systems include a provision for material separation and recycling of some kind, either at the source or through a mechanized process at the landfill site. Sale of the recovered materials—generally glass and metals—may provide an additional source of revenue.

Facilities to Convert Refuse to Fuel
A number of highly mechanized systems have been developed over the past decade which process raw refuse into a uniform combustible fuel,

TABLE 1. Facilities Currently Operating in the United States to Produce Energy Directly from Refuse

Location	Combustion Type	Design Capacity (tpd)[a]	Products	Start-up Date	Facility Cost (in dollars)[b]
Braintree, Mass.	Waterwall	384	Steam	1971	$2,500,000 (1970)
Chicago, Ill.	Waterwall	1,600	Steam, ferrous metals	1971	23,000,000 (1970)
Groveton, N.H.	Modular	30	Steam	1975	250,000 (1975)
Norfolk, Va.	Waterwall	360	Steam	1967	2,200,000 (1967)
					1,100,000 (1976)
					200,000 (1978)
North Little Rock, Ark.	Modular	100	Steam	1977	1,450,000 (1977)
Portsmouth, Va.	Waterwall	160	Steam	1976	4,500,000 (1975)
Salem, Va.	Modular	100	Steam	1979	1,900,000 (1978)
Saugus, Mass.	Waterwall	1,500	Steam, ferrous metals	1976	43,000,000 (1974)
Siloam Springs, Ark.	Modular	—	Steam	1975	377,000 (1974)

Source: EPA, Resource Recovery and Waste Reduction Activities: A Nationwide Survey (1979).
a. Capacity given in tons (of refuse) per day (tpd).
b. Year in parentheses indicates year in which costs incurred.

known as "refuse-derived fuel" or RDF. While these facilities differ in their details, all are of the same basic design. Municipal refuse is collected and delivered to the processing facility, frequently situated adjacent to the local landfill. The refuse is then separated by a complex classification system that sorts it according to density into combustible and noncombustible components. Some plants include a second sorting phase that extracts glass and ferrous metals from the waste stream. The remaining combustible fraction is shredded, compacted, and formed into a substance that can be burned in any boiler system equipped to handle ash.

While this option, in many respects, appears to be quite similar to the system just described, the problems experienced by the two are quite different. Whereas the previous approach faced waste-related concerns, RDF systems are plagued primarily by technological and mechanical difficulties. The technologies in question are less than a decade old, with a number of bugs yet to be worked out. As a result, the percentage of downtime for most plants has been much higher than initially forecast.[25] In addition, there have been unanticipated complications: unpleasant odors emitted from the plants, inability of the machinery to handle certain materials without malfunctioning, and difficulties in developing safe and dependable methods for storing various forms of RDF for later use.[26]

These technological impediments take on added importance in the context of a benefit/cost evaluation of the project. The capital cost of most RDF facilities is quite high—in the several millions of dollars— and is significantly greater than the cost of the other two options. Beyond the front-end expenditures on facility construction and equipment acquisition, however, annual operation and maintenance (O & M) charges are generally the next largest cost factor. A higher-than-anticipated rate of equipment breakdowns is apt to inflate this factor further, and to make the entire project less economically feasible.

One benefit of processing the refuse before it is fired is the mitigation of waste-related impacts associated with combusting unprocessed garbage. Because the refuse goes through more complete sorting and other processing before it is burned, substances that are major contributors to air pollution can be removed to create a cleaner fuel. A further improvement over energy produced from unprocessed refuse is RDF's greater reliability and constancy. Unlike unprocessed waste,

RDFs are of a fairly uniform consistency and Btu content, and are therefore a more acceptable replacement for conventional fossil fuels.[27] Table 2 lists several RDF facilities currently in operation in the United States.

In the early 1970s RDF facilities were hailed as the answer to a three-pronged problem facing many municipalities: the increasing scarcity and rising price of land suitable for sanitary landfill, a waste supply that was growing on a per capita as well as a total basis, and energy costs that had already begun their upward spiral. In the enthusiastic rush to bring these facilities on line, the fact that the technologies were still in their infancy tended to be ignored or forgotten. When actual operation commenced and mechanical and other problems began to be recognized, many of those involved in developing and implementing the technologies were forced to reassess their feasibility. Re-

TABLE 2. Facilities to Produce RDF Currently Operating in the United States

Location	Design Capacity (tpd)[a]	Products	Start-up Date	Facility Cost (in dollars)[b]
Ames, Iowa	400	RDF, ferrous metals, aluminum	1975	$6,200,000 (1974)
Baltimore County, Md.	1,200	RDF, ferrous metals	1976	10,000,000 (1975)
Chicago, Ill.	1,000	RDF, ferrous metals	1977	16,000,000 (1975)
East Bridgewater, Mass.	160	RDF	1977	12,000,000 (1976)
Hempstead, N.Y.	2,000	Electricity, glass, ferrous metals, aluminum	1979	90,000,000 (1977)
Lane County, Oreg.	500	RDF, ferrous metals	1979	2,100,000 (1978)
Madison, Wis.	400	RDF, ferrous metals	1979	2,400,000 (1978)
Milwaukee, Wis.	1,200	RDF, ferrous metals, glass, aluminum	1977	25,000,000 (1976)

Source: EPA, *Resource Recovery and Waste Reduction Activities: A Nationwide Survey* (1979).
a. Capacity given in tons (of refuse) per day (tpd).
b. Year in parentheses indicates year costs incurred.

cent analyses of resource recovery systems conclude that communities considering resource recovery must pay greater attention to the pre-construction analysis of such projects.

Feasibility Study of a Resource Recovery Program for Washtenaw County

As the foregoing discussion has indicated, a community considering a resource/energy recovery system must analyze the relative benefits and costs of the three major alternatives in light of its own particular needs. A comprehensive feasibility study is especially crucial for the third option—an RDF facility—since in addition to its greater benefit potential it entails greater risk. Because it is so important to conduct a detailed examination of these projects, and because both the city of Ann Arbor and Washtenaw County have been considering such a project, it was decided to assess the feasibility of a single specific type of RDF facility.

At the outset of this analysis a note of caution is in order. Though resource recovery systems have been in use for over a decade now, sufficient uncertainty continues to surround several factors critical to an individual facility's success or failure. To facilitate the feasibility study procedure, a number of qualifying assumptions have been made, based on data and other information currently available. The analysis is thus dependent on these assumptions which suggest probable, though not certain, outcomes. Results of the analysis should be considered in this light, and interpreted as preliminary findings rather than confirmed facts.

Process Description
The array of resource and energy systems from which to choose is a wide one. Moreover, it must be reemphasized that many of the technologies in question are still in experimental phases of design. As a result, several of the pilot facilities have been plagued by higher costs than originally forecast, an inordinately high percentage of downtime and, in a few cases, have been forced to shut down altogether.[28] While it is clear that resource recovery technologies are not the panacea they were originally perceived to be, an examination of those components that have succeeded can be tremendously instructive to other commu-

nities attempting to determine the optimal solution to their own waste disposal needs.

With respect to the Ann Arbor area, this sort of critical appraisal leads to several initial remarks. For one, engineers generally agree that resource recovery systems have a better chance of success as the volume of solid waste increases.[29] Recent estimates show that Ann Arbor currently generates approximately 350 to 400 tons per day (tpd), a moderate amount, while the county as a whole produces about 850 tpd. A volume of 850 tpd, while not large by municipal standards, is enough to ensure continuous operation of the facility, as well as elevating the project to a size where economies of scale become an important factor in reducing overall costs. For these reasons, a facility designed to serve the entire county appears to be the most viable jurisdictional alternative.

This feasibility study focuses on a process that combines some of the most technologically reliable and environmentally tenable components developed to date. In arriving at this decision, the following objectives were considered:

1. Maximization of the fraction of the waste stream which is recycled, thereby conserving scarce natural resources as well as generating revenue from the sale of these materials;
2. Construction of a facility which, while abating the contamination caused by landfilling (i.e., leachate), would not offset this effect by contributing to other forms of pollution;
3. Design of a comprehensive facility with an eye toward future needs rather than simply on current costs.

On the basis of these considerations, this study considers a resource recovery facility with these components:

1. Separation at the source (household, institution, or firm) of recyclable materials (glass, ferrous metals, paper), with periodic (biweekly or monthly) collection of these components, in addition to regular collection of the remaining waste portion.[30]
2. Shredding and compacting of this remaining portion, which would be marketed as RDF.

This type of waste disposal/resource recovery strategy has been advocated by M. Wentworth of the Environmental Action Foundation.[31]

For this reason, and to simplify future references to the process, it will be referred to simply as the "Wentworth system."

In its broad concept, this process is not dissimilar to the facility proposed by J & H in their 1975 report, "A Washtenaw County Plan for the Management of Solid Waste." The primary difference is the provision for home separation—a feature that was included for several reasons. For one, separation *after* shredding produces recyclables of lower quality than does prior separation, due to contamination from other elements in the waste stream—a problem that shredding compounds.[32] Second, the equipment necessary for postshredding separation—air classifiers and magnetic separators—is both expensive and far from perfected. The combination of the two factors results in higher capital costs, lower annual benefits, and a system that is less ecologically efficient.[33] Home separation, on the other hand, is a low-cost, high-benefit option, producing high-quality recyclables and correspondingly high revenues.[34]

Costs of the Project

Because of the similarity between the Wentworth system and the alternative proposed by J & H, it was possible to rely on many of the cost estimates contained in their final report, with the following modifications:

1. All costs, given in 1976 prices, have been escalated to 1979 prices by a factor of 1.236, the national rate of inflation from January, 1976, through December, 1978.
2. Land prices have been adjusted to reflect a relative increase in land values, particularly those in the southeast region of the county. The recent purchase of 108 acres for additional landfill use, made by the city Department of Solid Waste, was at a price of six thousand dollars per acre,[35] the figure used in the calculations.
3. The J & H cost calculations were based on the presumption that the facility would receive 3,680 tons per week and operate eight hours a day, five days a week. Because of projected increases in waste volume, which will be discussed in the "Benefits" section, it has been assumed that a second eight-

hour shift will be needed, as of 1990, and labor costs have been adjusted accordingly.

4. Certain types of equipment, not included in the J & H estimates, nonetheless appear to be essential to the operation of such a facility.[36] Comparable estimates were obtained from other sources and are so noted.

The breakdown of initial and annual facility costs is given in table 3.

The figures reflect, with the exception of the changes described above, the detailed equipment and facility expenses given by J & H. As both the subtotal and total figures indicate, the initial or "fixed" cost component represents the largest fraction of total costs—$7.67 million versus only $0.47 million in annual costs. The difference reflects the high cost of the processing equipment and facility construction—expenses that are incurred before the facility is operating—and the relatively low operation and maintenance costs incurred after the facility is in use.

Table 4 presents the annual cost flow estimates for the facility over a period of twenty-one years (1980–2000). Columns 4 and 5 give the annual cost of densifying the RDF, a process that makes it easier to handle than if simply compacted, as well as making it a more consistent and marketable energy source. Since densifying is a relatively new process, equipment costs were more difficult to obtain. The only specific estimate available gave the cost per ton of densifying to be approximately $5.00 in 1977.[37] This cost was inflated to 1979 dollars by a factor 1.178 (the appropriate national rate of inflation), to $5.90, and multiplied by the annual total of tons suitable for processing into RDF.[38] Because densifying would not be necessary until the fuel was to be actively marketed, these costs are included beginning in 1990— again, for reasons to be explained in the discussion of benefits of the project. The difference between columns 4 and 5 is the assumed rate of participation in home separation activities. Column 4 gives the annual cost assuming 40 percent of the recyclables are removed prior to processing; the figures in column 5 were calculated on the assumption that only 20 percent are removed. The basis for these "best" and "worst" case assumptions is explained in greater detail in the next section, where the significance is more apparent.

TABLE 3. Facility Costs of a Wentworth Type Resource Recovery System, in 1979 Dollars

Item	Initial	Annual
Facility		
Land	$ 60,000	
Site preparation	24,720	
Site development	376,980	6,180
Building	1,557,360	30,410
Design/legal fees (15%)	302,860	
Contingencies (20%)	403,810	
Subtotal	$2,725,730	$36,590
Processing Equipment		
Receiving conveyor (2)	$155,740	$11,740
Shredder (2)	1,483,200	111,240
Front loader*	145,850	14,820
Misc. tools and equipment*	30,900	3,210
Engineering/legal fees		
(15%—omits* items)	272,350	
Contingencies (20%—omits* items)	363,140	
Storage bin[a]	1,767,000	
Subtotal	$4,218,180	$141,010
Labor[b]		$220,500
Transportation Equipment		
Conveyor (2)	$155,740	$11,740
Compactor (2)	102,340	7,680
Tractor and trailer	281,070	41,780
Rolloff unit*	37,080	12,100
Engineering/legal		
(15%—omits* items)	38,710	
Contingencies (20%)	115,250	
Subtotal	$730,190	$73,300
Total	$7,674,100	$471,400

Source: Jones and Henry (February, 1975).
Note: % = percent of total; omits* = asterisked items not included in total from which percent is drawn
a. The price of a storage bin was not included in the Jones and Henry estimates. The cost given here was taken from the 1977 estimate in Henningson, Durham, and Richardson, *Interim Report on Technology Evaluation.*
b. Annual salaries and benefits for a superintendent, two clerks, two loader operators, scale attendant, shredder operator, welder, mechanic, and two laborers.

TABLE 4. Total Annual Costs, 1980–2000, in 1979 Dollars

Year	Initial (1)	Plant O&M (2)	Labor (3)	Densify (40%) (4)	Densify (20%) (5)	Total (40%) (6)	Total (20%) (7)
1980	$7,674,100					$7,674,100	$7,674,100
1981		$250,900	$220,500			471,400	471,400
1982							
1983							
1984							
1985							
1986							
1987							
1988							
1989			441,000				
1990				$1,668,600	$1,747,500	2,360,500	2,439,400
1991				1,975,200	2,068,600	2,667,100	2,760,500
1992				1,999,900	2,094,400	2,690,900	2,786,300
1993				2,024,000	2,119,700	2,715,900	2,811,600
1994				2,049,200	2,146,100	2,741,100	2,838,000
1995				2,074,400	2,172,500	2,766,300	2,864,400
1996				2,334,800	2,445,200	3,026,700	2,137,100
1997				2,357,500	2,469,000	3,049,400	3,160,900
1998				2,381,400	2,494,000	3,073,300	3,185,900
1999				2,404,900	2,518,600	3,096,800	3,210,500
2000				2,429,000	2,543,900	3,120,900	3,235,800

Note: Arrows indicate that the number remains the same.

Finally, it may appear surprising that no calculation has been made to determine the additional cost of separate collection for the various recyclable components. The reason for this is that in almost all instances where home separation/separate collection programs have been implemented, average collection costs have *declined* rather than increased—in one case by as much as 23 percent.[39] This seemingly paradoxical tendency is explained by the improved efficiency of separate source collection. Because recyclables are picked up once or twice a month, the remaining portion of refuse is reduced by the amount of the recyclables and is more quickly and easily handled on regular collection days. In other words, the total amount of waste has not changed, but the collection process has been divided into more efficient and less time-consuming subtasks, which can result in significant cost reduction.[40] Total costs assuming 40 percent participation are given in column 6, and total costs assuming 20 percent participation in column 7.

Benefits of the Project

The benefits to be derived from implementation of a Wentworth-type system break down into three general categories: (1) relatively straightforward accounting benefits—i.e., revenues realized from the sale of recyclables and, eventually, from the sale of RDF; (2) foregone cost benefits, of which the most important is the increasingly expensive landfill acreage that will not have to be purchased; and (3) "intangible benefits"—adoption of a disposal method that recovers increasingly scarce resources, in an environmentally sound manner, as well as making the county less dependent on nonlocal energy sources. Each of these categories will be considered separately and the total present value benefits will then be compared with the present value of costs from the previous section.

The revenue benefits can be calculated with relative ease, once accurate projections about total annual waste are determined. A considerable amount of effort was devoted to arriving at these annual totals, as it was felt that other projections were too dated to be completely accurate. With respect to these estimates, two important points should be noted. First, base (1980) estimates for the various types of refuse were drawn from J & H estimates, including the total amount of waste produced in the county, the portion of this total that would be received for disposal at a county disposal site, and the fraction of the received total suitable for processing. Second, it appears likely, particularly in light of recent legislation,[41] that some sort of coordinated countywide disposal program will be developed in the near future. As a result, there is no reason why the percentage of total waste received at a county disposal site cannot be increased considerably in the future. Indeed, local public works officials agree that this will be one goal of any proposed system.[42] Given the emphasis on designing as comprehensive a system as possible, the calculations are based on this assumption. The method used to calculate the growth rates of the various sources of refuse entails the following assumptions:

1. Residential/commercial figures have been adjusted to conform to more recent population projections than the ones used by J & H. They have also been altered to reflect the most recent EPA estimates of per capita postconsumer solid waste, estimates that are generally accepted by local solid waste officials: 3.98 lbs/day in 1980, 4.34 lbs/day in 1985, and 4.65 lbs/day in 1990. For the ten years beyond 1990 the figure is assumed to hold constant at 4.65 lbs/day.

2. Annual industrial waste is calculated on the basis of the J & H estimates, extrapolating at a constant rate of increase (1.3 percent) from 1995 to 2000. The same methodology has been used to compute waste from construction activities. Demolition waste, expected to decrease over the next twenty years, is calculated according to the constant rate of decline used by J & H.

3. Annual totals for other sources of waste (hospital, recreational, educational, street, and "bulky and special"), which appear to be relatively constant over time, are taken straight from the J & H report. Even if these figures are somewhat inaccurate, they represent a small enough percentage of total waste (6 to 9 percent) that their impact would be minimal.

4. The model used by J & H estimated that, of the total waste generated within the county, only a certain fraction of each type would be received for disposal at a county-owned landfill site. Their estimates for the various types of waste were:

Residential/commercial	70%
Industrial	40
Hospital	5

Educational	50
Recreational	66
Construction	50
Demolition	50
Bulky and special	10

5. Since local waste authorities agree that these percentages are likely to increase over the next several years (see note 42), they have been adjusted according to the following assumptions:

	1980–85	1986–90	1991–95	1996–2000
Res/Com	70%	75%	80%	85%
Ind	40	50	60	70
Educ	50	60	65	70
Const	50	60	70	80
Demol	50	50	50	50
Bulky	10	25	40	50

Because they represent such a small percentage of total waste, assumptions about increases for hospital or recreational waste were not made. Furthermore, a constant rate over five-year periods has been used, to reflect the fact that increases would come as the result of expiration of contracts with other sites and private landfills gradually going out of business, rather than at a steady annual rate.

Final estimates of total waste received for disposal, and received for disposal and suitable for processing are given in tables 5 and 6. Composition estimates for the local waste stream were drawn from EPA averages and figures supplied by the city Department of Solid Waste,[43] with one modification. The city estimate of the glass fraction (8 to 10 percent) was based on pre–bottle bill data. EPA estimates, however, that returnables comprise about two-thirds of all glass in the waste stream.[44] The estimated glass fraction, therefore, has been reduced to 3 percent. The compositional breakdown of annual refuse received and suitable for processing appears in table 7. The pricing of the recyclables is based on current prices received by the Ecology Center at its recycling station: thirty dollars per ton for glass, twenty dollars per ton for ferrous metals (Fe), six dollars per ton for newsprint, and fifty dollars per ton for high-grade (office) paper.[45] Annual revenues were calculated first by multiplying the price per ton by the

TABLE 5. Total Waste Received for Disposal, 1980–2000, in Tons per Week

Year	Residential and Commercial	Industrial	Hospital	Educational	Recreational	Construction	Demolition	Street Cleaning	Bulky and Special	Total
1980	2,635	508	8	63	2	260	345	59	393	4,273
1981	2,745	515	→	→	→	262	334	→	→	4,381
1982	2,859	522	→	→	→	264	324	→	→	4,494
1983	2,979	529	→	→	→	266	314	→	→	4,613
1984	3,104	536	→	→	→	268	304	→	→	4,738
1985	3,233	543	→	→	→	270	294	→	→	4,867
1986	3,464	687	→	75	→	328	286	→	983	5,892
1987	3,714	697	→	→	→	332	277	→	→	6,147
1988	3,846	706	→	→	→	334	268	→	→	6,281
1989	3,982	715	→	→	→	336	260	→	→	6,420
1990	4,123	725	→	→	→	340	252	→	→	6,567
1991	4,474	882	→	82	→	398	244	→	1,572	7,721
1992	4,552	893	→	→	→	404	236	→	→	7,808
1993	4,630	905	→	→	→	406	229	→	→	7,893
1994	4,711	918	→	→	→	410	222	→	→	7,984
1995	4,793	930	→	88	→	412	215	→	→	8,073
1996	5,162	1,100	→	→	→	476	208	→	1,965	9,068
1997	5,233	1,114	→	→	→	480	202	→	→	9,151
1998	5,306	1,129	→	→	→	484	196	→	→	9,237
1999	5,379	1,144	→	→	→	488	190	→	→	9,323
2000	5,454	1,159	→	→	→	492	184	→	→	9,411

Note: Arrows indicate that the number remains the same.

TABLE 6. Total Waste Received for Disposal and Suitable for Processing, 1980–2000, in Tons per Week

Year	Residential and Commercial	Industrial	Hospital	Educational	Recreational	Construction	Demolition	Street Cleaning	Bulky and Special	Total
1980	2,635	381	8	63	2	130	69	0	393	3,681
1981	2,745	386				131	67			3,795
1982	2,859	391				132	65			3,913
1983	2,979	397				133	63			4,038
1984	3,104	402				134	61			4,167
1985	3,233	407		75		135	59			4,300
1986	3,464	515				164	58		983	5,269
1987	3,714	523				166	56			5,527
1988	3,846	529				167	54			5,664
1989	3,982	536				168	52			5,806
1990	4,123	544				170	50			5,955
1991	4,474	661		82		199	48		1,572	7,046
1992	4,552	670				202	47			7,135
1993	4,630	679				203	45			7,221
1994	4,711	688				205	44			7,312
1995	4,793	697		88		206	42			7,402
1996	5,162	825				238	41		1,965	8,329
1997	5,233	835				240	40			8,411
1998	5,306	847				242	38			8,496
1999	5,379	858				244	37			8,581
2000	5,454	869				246	35			8,667

Note: Arrows indicate that the number remains the same.

TABLE 7. Composition of Waste Received and Suitable for Processing, 1980–2000, in Tons per Year

Year	Suitable	Fe—8%	Glass—3%	News—5%	Office—4%	RDF—0.98 × 80%[a]
1980						
1981	197,340	15,790	5,920	9,867	7,894	154,710
1982	203,480	16,280	6,104	10,174	8,139	159,530
1983	209,980	16,800	6,299	10,499	8,399	164,620
1984	216,680	17,330	6,500	10,834	8,667	169,880
1985	223,600	17,890	6,708	11,180	8,944	175,300
1986	273,940	21,920	8,218	13,697	10,958	214,770
1987	287,300	22,980	8,619	14,365	11,492	225,240
1988	294,420	23,560	8,833	14,721	11,777	230,830
1989	301,810	24,140	9,054	15,090	12,072	236,620
1990	309,560	24,770	9,287	15,478	12,382	242,690
1991	366,440	29,310	10,993	18,322	14,658	287,290
1992	271,020	29,680	11,131	18,551	14,841	290,880
1993	375,490	30,040	11,265	18,774	15,020	294,380
1994	280,170	30,410	11,405	19,008	15,207	298,050
1995	384,850	30,790	11,545	19,242	14,394	301,720
1996	433,160	34,650	12,995	21,658	17,326	339,600
1997	437,370	34,990	13,121	21,868	17,495	342,900
1998	441,790	35,340	13,254	22,089	17,672	346,360
1999	446,160	35,690	13,385	22,308	17,846	349,790
2000	450,630	36,050	13,519	22,531	18,025	353,290

a. If recyclable components are removed from the waste stream, it has been estimated (Wentworth, *Resource Recovery*, p. 58) that the remaining portion is 98 percent RDF. It is for this reason that the remaining fraction (80 percent) has been multiplied by 0.98.

total number of tons of each particular component received for disposal. This figure was then multiplied by the population fraction that could be assumed to participate in home separation, for clearly this factor would be an important determinant of the successes of the recycling phase of the process—and hence the revenues generated. To account for this uncertainty both a low and a high estimate of revenues has been computed (tables 8 and 9). The figures in table 8 are based on a countywide participation rate of 20 percent. This rate was determined by considering the Ecology Center's estimate that its recycling station currently handles about 30 percent of Ann Arbor's recyclables.[46] Since Ann Arbor residents account for roughly 40 percent of the county's population (and correspondingly about the same fraction of its refuse), approximately 12 percent participation would be

TABLE 8. Total Annual Revenues and Other Benefits, 1980–2000, Assuming a Recycling Participation Rate of 20 Percent, in 1979 Dollars

Year	Fe (1)	Glass (2)	Newspaper (3)	Office Paper (4)	RDF (5)	Landfill Foregone (6)	Total A (7)	Total B (8)	Total C (9)
1981	$63,160	$35,520	$11,840	$78,940			$189,500		
1982	65,120	36,620	12,210	81,390			195,300		
1983	67,200	37,790	12,600	83,990			201,600		
1984	69,320	39,000	13,000	86,670			208,000		
1985	77,560	40,250	13,410	89,440		A $ 900,000 B 1,148,650 C 1,449,460	1,120,700	$1,369,300	$1,670,100
1986	87,860	49,310	16,430	109,580			263,200		
1987	91,920	51,710	17,240	114,920			275,800		
1988	94,240	53,000	17,660	117,770			282,700		
1989	96,560	54,320	18,110	120,720			289,700		
1990	99,080	55,720	18,570	123,820	$3,057,890	A 900,000 B 1,466,000 C 2,334,370	4,422,200	4,988,200	5,856,600
1991	117,240	65,960	21,980	146,580	3,619,850		3,971,600		
1992	118,720	66,780	22,260	148,410	3,665,090		4,021,300		
1993	120,160	67,590	22,530	150,200	3,709,190		4,069,700		
1994	121,640	68,430	22,810	152,070	3,755,430		4,120,400		
1995	123,160	69,270	23,090	153,940	3,801,670	A 900,000 B 1,871,040 C 3,759,520	5,071,100	6,042,200	7,930,700
1996	138,600	77,970	25,990	173,260	4,278,960		4,694,800		
1997	139,960	78,720	26,240	174,950	4,320,540		4,740,400		
1998	141,360	79,520	26,510	176,720	4,364,130		4,788,200		
1999	142,910	80,310	26,770	178,460	4,407,350		4,835,800		
2000	144,200	81,110	27,040	181,250	4,451,450		4,885,100		

Note: A = real prices stable; B = real prices increase annually by 5%; C = real prices increase annually by 10%. All total columns rounded to the nearest hundred.

TABLE 9. Total Annual Revenues and Other Benefits, 1980–2000, Assuming a Recycling Participation Rate of 40 Percent, in 1979 Dollars

Year									
1980									
1981	$126,320	$71,040	$23,680	$157,880			$378,900		
1982	130,240	73,250	24,420	162,780			390,700		
1983	134,400	75,590	25,200	167,980			403,200		
1984	138,640	78,000	26,000	173,340			416,000		
1985	155,120	80,500	26,830	178,880		A $900,000 B 1,148,650 C 1,449,460	1,341,300	$1,590,000	$1,890,800
1986	175,360	98,620	32,870	219,160			526,000		
1987	183,840	103,430	34,480	229,840			551,600		
1988	188,480	106,000	35,330	235,540			565,400		
1989	193,120	108,650	36,220	241,440			579,400		
1990	198,160	111,440	37,150	247,640	$3,057,890	A 900,000 B 1,466,000 C 2,334,370	4,552,300	5,118,300	5,986,700
1991	234,480	131,920	43,970	293,160	3,619,850		4,323,400		
1992	237,440	133,570	44,520	296,820	3,665,090		4,377,400		
1993	240,320	135,180	45,060	300,400	3,709,190		4,430,200		
1994	243,280	136,860	45,620	304,140	3,755,430		4,485,300		
1995	246,320	138,540	46,180	307,880	3,801,670	A 900,000 B 1,871,040 C 3,759,520	5,440,600	6,411,600	8,300,100
1996	277,200	155,940	51,980	346,520	4,278,960		5,110,600		
1997	279,920	157,450	52,480	349,900	4,320,540		5,160,300		
1998	282,720	159,050	53,020	353,440	4,364,130		5,212,400		
1999	285,820	160,620	53,540	356,920	4,407,350		5,264,300		
2000	288,400	162,230	54,080	362,500	4,451,450		5,318,700		

Note: A = real prices stable; B = real prices increase annually by 5%; C = real prices increase annually by 10%. All total columns are rounded to the nearest hundred.

achieved even if *no* additional recycling took place outside the city as a result of the new program. It is highly unlikely that this would happen, particularly since home collection greatly facilitates the entire recycling process. This line of reasoning led to the estimate that 20 percent represents the minimum participation rate that could be achieved.

The "best case" rate of participation is reflected in the revenue estimates in table 9. Here a 40 percent participation rate has been used, a percentage that EPA estimates is not an unreasonable goal for such operations—World War II recycling efforts recovered scarce materials at about this same rate.[47] Moreover, the county might consider, as have other communities, a county ordinance mandating home separation, a step that certainly would assure higher participation.[48]

The second potential source of revenue is RDF. Earlier reports dismissed RDF production as unfeasible in Washtenaw County due to the lack of markets for the fuel, since most boilers cannot handle the ash produced by firing RDF. However, while there currently may be no markets within Washtenaw County, it is possible that markets would develop if the fuel were available. In particular, by 1990 the University of Michigan must convert to coal-burning boilers, in order to meet federal requirements.[49] Since coal firing also produces ash, it is conceivable that, at least by 1990, a market would have developed. On this basis, potential revenues from RDF have been calculated beginning in 1990. Because RDF is a relatively new commodity, a relevant market price was difficult to obtain. It was therefore necessary to impute an appropriate shadow price for the fuel, which was done by equating the energy potential of RDF with that of coal. The average real price of coal has been estimated to be $1.37 (in 1979 dollars) per million Btus by 1990.[50] One ton of processed refuse produces 9.2 million Btus; a fair price estimate for RDF is therefore 9.2 × $1.37 = $12.60 per ton. Annual revenue is given in column 5 of tables 8 and 9. Here, again, the assumptions use conservative estimates of revenues, particularly in the case of denying the existence of RDF markets prior to 1990. For while no markets may exist within Washtenaw County at this time, markets currently exist in nearby counties. Figure 1 gives the location of supplementary fuel (RDF) markets in 1977, a market that, given the scarcity and price of other sources, may well expand in coming years.

Turning to the foregone cost category (column 6 in tables 8 and

□ Approximate location of
individual establishments

FIG. 1.   Supplemental fuel (RDF) market locations, Michigan
energy and materials recovery state plan.(Courtesy of
Henningson, Durham, and Richardson.)

9), these estimates reflect the dollar value of land that would not
have to be purchased if this project were undertaken. Assessing the
exact number of acres which otherwise would be required is a highly
speculative process and, rather than overstate the benefits, conservative estimates of future land requirements have been used. The estimates are based on figures calculated by Chen in an analysis of the
Ann Arbor shredder proposal.[51] Here it was estimated that a shred-
der/landfill system would require 650 acres between 1981 and 2000,
while a Wentworth-type process would use only 100. These estimates
are based on total waste projections that are considerably lower than
those developed in this feasibility study, particularly if the percentage

received at a central site does increase over the next two decades, as assumed here. These figures have been used, however, to compare the relative magnitude of land required by the two processes. Moreover, since approximately 65 acres remain to be filled at the existing landfill site and 108 have recently been approved for purchase, the approximately 200 acres have been subtracted from the 650 total. The remaining 450, it has been projected, would be purchased at five-year intervals in 150-acre parcels. With respect to the acreage needed by the Wentworth system, it has been assumed that the 108 plus 65 acres would be sufficient to meet these needs and that, while perhaps *more* land than necessary, the unused portion would be used as backup landfill and would not be sold off.

Following Chen,[52] it is further assumed that, until such time as an active market for RDF is developed, the fuel would be made available at no cost: in other words, simply given to any firm willing to transport it. As a result, there is no need to calculate the amount of land that might be needed to dispose of the RDF between 1980 and 1989. In addition, this arrangement provides a means by which local firms and institutions may be introduced to what is still considered a rather novel fuel source—a process that could further aid in the development of a market for RDF.

To compute the price per acre, three alternative assumptions have been proposed: that land prices remain stable (in real terms) over the next twenty years (fig. A in col. 6 of table 8); that real prices increase at an annual rate of 5 percent (fig. B); and that real prices increase by 10 percent annually (fig. C). To put these figures in perspective, it should be noted that the price paid for land at the Platt and Ellsworth landfill site has increased by 11 percent a year over the last three years from thirty-eight hundred dollars per acre in 1976 to six thousand dollars in 1979.[53] While this trend may not continue, it cannot be ruled out entirely, either.

Total dollar costs are given in columns 7–9 of tables 8 and 9. Column 7 gives the totals assuming stable real land prices, column 8 the 5 percent real price increase, and column 9 the 10 percent real increase.

Before computing the net present benefits, the final category of benefits should be considered briefly, though no attempt will be made to quantify these. There is much to be said for forward-looking projects that not only address existing problems but attempt to anticipate future needs as well. Clearly, the system outlined here accomplishes both of these ends—providing a potential solution to the current waste disposal problem while contributing to future local energy self-reliance. The latter benefit becomes all the more important in light of recent price increases in conventional energy sources, as well as the threat of possible fuel shortages. The more energy that is produced locally, the less seriously will any national crisis affect Washtenaw County. While no dollar figure can be attached to these benefits, they are important ones, nonetheless, and should be taken into account when evaluating a project of this nature.

Finally, the environmental benefits of a comprehensive system such as the one described here are considerable. For one, home separation has proven to be an effective strategy for encouraging widespread participation in recycling efforts. The only other scheme that has elicited very high participation rates is the mandatory beverage container deposits, which only provide incentives for the recycling of glass and aluminum. Added to this resource conservation benefit are the pollution reduction benefits achieved by decreasing the county's reliance on landfilling. As mentioned earlier, the environmental problems generated by this type of waste disposal are significant—including not only aesthetic considerations but health and welfare criteria as well. Lastly, the system frees a valuable resource—land—from a relatively inefficient use and allows it to be diverted to more productive functions. For all of these reasons, comprehensive resource and energy recovery systems provide an environmentally superior alternative to landfilling.

Results

The net benefit of the project (i.e., benefits less costs) are presented in tables 10 and 11. Because the calculations presented in tables 4, 8, and 9 reflect a range of possible assumptions—to account for obvious uncertainties about future land prices and participation in source separation—four possible scenarios have been defined.

Table 10 presents the "best" and "worst" case scenarios or, in other words, the sets of events that would result in the highest and lowest possible net benefits. The best case (cols. 1 and 2 in table 10) assumes public participation in source separation at an average rate of

TABLE 10.   Net Benefits under Best and Worst Case Scenarios

Year	Best Case[a]		Worst Case[b]	
	Net Annual Benefits (1)	Present Value[c] (2)	Net Annual Benefits (3)	Present Value[c] (4)
0	$-7,674,100	$-7,674,100	$-7,674,100	$-7,674,100
1	− 92,500	− 90,200	− 281,900	− 275,000
2	− 80,700	− 76,800	− 276,100	− 262,800
3	− 68,200	− 73,400	− 269,800	− 250,500
4	− 55,400	− 50,200	− 263,400	− 290,700
5	1,419,400	1,254,500	649,300	573,900
6	54,600	47,100	− 208,200	− 179,500
7	80,200	67,500	− 195,600	− 164,600
8	94,000	77,200	− 188,700	− 154,900
9	108,000	86,500	− 181,700	− 145,500
10	3,626,200	2,832,800	1,987,800	1,549,000
11	1,656,300	1,267,300	1,211,100	923,000
12	1,686,500	1,254,000	1,235,000	918,300
13	1,714,300	1,243,600	1,258,100	912,700
14	1,744,200	1,234,400	1,282,400	907,600
15	5,544,800	3,820,900	2,206,700	1,523,700
16	2,083,900	1,403,800	1,557,700	1,049,300
17	2,110,900	1,387,300	1,579,500	1,038,000
18	2,139,100	1,371,500	1,602,300	1,027,300
19	2,167,500	1,355,800	1,625,300	1,016,700
20	2,197,800	1,341,300	1,649,300	1,006,500
Totals		12,075,800		3,048,400

a. Best case assumes costs at 40 percent participation (col. 6 of table 4) and benefits at 40 percent participation, with real land prices increasing annually by 10 percent (col. 9 of table 9).
b. Worst case assumes costs at 20 percent participation (col. 7 of table 4) and benefits at 20 percent participation.
c. Net annual benefits are discounted by 2.5 percent annually.

40 percent, and land prices that increase at a real annual rate of 10 percent. The worst case (cols. 3 and 4) assumes 20 percent public participation in source separation activities, on average, and land prices that remain stable, in real terms, over the twenty-year period of the project.

The present value figures (cols. 2 and 4) represent annual net benefits discounted to account for the fact that a dollar held today is more valuable than a dollar held at some future time t. Specifically, the dollar held today is worth one dollar *plus* the amount of interest it could earn by time *t*. Therefore, a dollar must be *discounted* by the rate of interest, to arrive at an amount which, if held at time zero (today) would yield one dollar in time *t*. The interest rate used is thus known as a *discount rate*. The annual discount rate used to calculate the present value of benefits was 2.5 percent and was arrived at by subtracting the long-term projected rate of inflation (7 percent) from the current rate of return on corporate investments (9.5 percent), or the opportunity cost of the capital.[54] The rate of 2.5 percent thus represents the *real* opportunity cost, and assumes a relatively inelastic supply of capital available for local investment projects. Total net present value benefits were computed by summing the discounted net annual benefits of the project over its twenty-one year life.

Under the best case scenario, the project yields $12,075,800 in total present value benefits, and under the worst case scenario, $3,048,400. Thus, even under the least favorable assumptions, the project appears to be profitable.

To narrow the range of the expected value of the project, table 11 presents two "most likely" scenarios. The "most likely" designation refers to the question of land prices. Based on recent trends in land prices in the Washtenaw County area (see note 53), the expectation of a real annual increase of 5 percent is reasonable.

The "optimistic" and "pessimistic" characterization refers to expected rate of participation in source separation: 40 percent may be somewhat optimistic, yet 20 percent is likely to be overly pessimistic (see note 47). Here, as in table 10, the present value figures (cols. 2 and 4) have been discounted at an annual rate of 2.5 percent.

Under these "most likely" scenarios, net present value benefits range from a low of $4,380,700 to a high of $9,827,700, suggesting that the actual figure would be apt to fall within these parameters.

In sum, the evaluation suggests that, under a wide range of assumptions about future events, the project appears to be economically feasible. Clearly these results are dependent on assumptions made throughout the evaluation process, and were these assumptions to be varied the results could change significantly. However, it should be reiterated that where such assumptions have entered into the eval-

TABLE 11. Net Benefits under Most Likely Case Scenario

Year	Optimistic Case[a]		Pessimistic Case[b]	
	Net Annual Benefits (1)	Present Value[c] (2)	Net Annual Benefits (3)	Present Value[c] (4)
0	$−7,674,100	$−7,674,100	$7,674,100	$−7,674,100
1	− 92,500	− 90,200	− 281,900	− 275,000
2	− 80,700	− 76,800	− 276,100	− 262,800
3	− 68,200	− 73,400	− 269,800	− 250,500
4	− 55,400	− 50,200	− 263,400	− 290,700
5	1,118,600	988,700	897,900	793,600
6	54,600	47,100	− 208,200	− 179,500
7	80,200	67,500	− 195,600	− 164,600
8	94,000	77,200	− 188,700	− 154,900
9	108,000	86,500	− 181,700	− 145,500
10	2,757,800	2,154,400	1,987,800	1,991,100
11	1,656,300	1,267,300	1,211,100	923,000
12	1,686,500	1,254,000	1,235,000	918,300
13	1,714,300	1,243,600	1,258,100	912,700
14	1,744,200	1,234,400	1,282,400	907,600
15	3,645,300	2,517,000	3,177,800	2,194,200
16	2,083,900	1,403,800	1,557,700	1,049,300
17	2,110,900	1,387,300	1,579,500	1,038,000
18	2,139,100	1,371,500	1,602,300	1,027,300
19	2,167,500	1,355,800	1,625,300	1,016,700
20	2,197,800	1,341,300	1,649,300	1,006,500
Total		9,827,700		4,380,700

a. Optimistic case assumes costs at 40 percent participation (col. 6 of table 4) and benefits at 40 percent participation with real land prices increasing annually by 5 percent (col. 8 of table 9).
b. Pessimistic case assumes costs at 20 percent participation (col. 7 of table 4) and benefits at 20 percent participation with real land prices increasing annually by 5 percent (col. 8 of table 8).
c. Net annual benefits are discounted by 2.5 percent annually.

uation methodology, care has been taken to insure that they favor conservative estimations. Moreover, the attraction of RDF as an alternative energy source improves with every price increase for conventional fuels. Finally, though these calculations represent only a first approximation of the benefits and costs of this particular resource recovery system, it is clear that, at the very least, the project merits further serious attention.

Conclusions and Recommendations

The results of the feasibility analysis in the previous section should be interpreted with caution. While the project studied appears to be economically feasible, it would be unwise either to accept these indications as final conclusions or to neglect the consideration of other possible energy recovery approaches. Indeed, above all else the study indicates the need to address the inherent uncertainties surrounding projects of this type so as to minimize the risk associated with whichever options are chosen.

The results suggest three specific recommendations. First, it is recommended that the city implement a source separation program for recovery of recyclable glass, metals, and paper. The costs of such a program are not prohibitive—certainly much lower than those of either type of energy recovery system. Moreover, because of the ten-year effort of the Ecology Center, the city enjoys the benefits of a citizenry already familiar with source separation/recycling, as well as the expertise of the Ecology Center staff. Finally, last year's approval of the shredder referendum suggests that Ann Arbor residents are aware of the waste disposal problem and willing to do something to help alleviate it. For all of these reasons, participation in the program may be sufficiently high even without enacting an ordinance mandating separation at the source, though such an option should not be ruled out.

Moreover, implementing a source separation program can be the first phase in adopting a comprehensive waste disposal system. There are two benefits of this phased-in approach. For one, the source separation program will provide actual data on the volume of recyclables, the rate of citizen participation, and the market value of various recyclable materials, reducing some of the uncertainties about a more comprehensive facility. Secondly, the program would sustain both official activity and citizen interest in resource recovery, giving the city additional time to investigate larger and more expensive projects before making a financial commitment.

A second recommendation is for the city to hire a qualified consultant familiar with resource recovery to produce an up-to-date report on the technological options available, as well as to gather additional information relevant to conditions in Ann Arbor. Specifically, the report should address the following key factors:

Equipment costs. While efforts have been made in this feasibility study to update the equipment and facility costs provided in the J & H report, the fact remains that the original estimates are now almost six years old. Much has changed in the resource recovery field during this period, and these developments may suggest alternative systems that are more reliable and more cost-effective. For this reason, the consultant should be required to produce detailed and up-to-date cost estimates for the two or three RDF designs best suited to the Washtenaw County area.

Waste stream analysis. Here again, the estimates presented here of city and county solid waste were derived from earlier projections and updated to reflect recent population trends. Thus, even the revised estimates depend to a certain extent on the validity of the earlier projections on which they are based. An accurate estimate of the quantity of a community's solid waste is extremely important. In the past, facilities designed on the basis of inaccurate or insufficient waste stream data were often larger and more expensive than needed. In addition, seasonal fluctuations in the waste stream must be analyzed to obtain an accurate picture of the pattern of energy potential that can be expected.

In addition to assessing the *quantity* of solid waste, the *quality* of Washtenaw County refuse should also be tested. While the Btu content of all municipal refuse will fall somewhere in a specified range, each community's waste will differ in this regard.[55] Moreover, it is impossible to provide a reliable and accurate measure of the energy benefits of a system without analyzing the heat potential of the refuse. For example, the city of Burlington, Vermont, conducted lab tests on a sample of its solid waste and found the Btu content to be higher than average.[56] Engineers have concluded that Vermont's mandatory beverage container deposit, which removes a high percentage of glass and aluminum from the waste stream, is largely responsible for this unexpected effect. The point here is that it is not enough for a community to assume the thermal content of its solid waste, since inaccuracies can lead to critical misestimations.

Some of this uncertainty should be alleviated in the near future. The city of Ann Arbor recently commissioned a consultant to conduct a waste stream analysis of the refuse delivered to the municipal landfill site.[57] Their findings should be communicated to others brought in to assess the feasibility of such a project.

Obtaining markets. In the last year or two, the market factor has taken on increased importance. The study presented here assumed, as have others,[58] that a market for RDF could be found once the fuel was being produced. However, this presumption is not being borne out by recent experience. Moreover, a primary element in the financial failure of RDF projects is to *assume* that markets will develop, and to construct the plant without a guaranteed customer for its products. As a result, EPA is now advising communities considering energy recovery systems not to take any steps beyond a preliminary feasibility study *until and unless a market for the facility's products* (steam, RDF, recyclables) *has been located, and the terms of the agreement have been finalized.*[59] The city or county should obtain a formal commitment from the University of Michigan, or the consultant should be required to identify alternative customers, before additional resources are committed to the project.

Specifying details of the facility. Certain important facility details have been considered only briefly, if at all, in the analysis up to this point. While such treatment is sufficient for a first-cut analysis, these details should be addressed and resolved before the project progresses further.

One issue is plant size. The importance of designing a facility compatible with the quality and quantity of the community's waste stream already has been discussed. It should be reemphasized, however, that bigger is not necessarily better in this instance, and excess capacity results in higher—and avoidable—costs.

Pollution from the facility presents another problem to consider. Once again, the emissions produced by different communities' refuse will vary widely, and the consultants should be required to test the emission potential of Ann Arbor's refuse. Neglecting to consider possible emission violations, or to determine the level of acceptable emission in one's air quality region, is to risk constructing a facility that cannot obtain a license to operate or that requires extensive and expensive pollution abatement retrofitting.

Finally, it is recommended that Ann Arbor officials and interested residents consider carefully and thoroughly the decision of where to locate an energy recovery facility, should one be approved. Once a confirmed market is located, a site should be chosen that minimizes the cost of transporting the refuse, the RDF, or the steam that is produced on site. Moreover, the location should be selected so that waste heat from the plant can be utilized for space heating or steam production in another facility nearby.

Attention to these locational issues has additional long-term benefits. As the price of conventional liquid fuels continues to increase, the cost of spread-out, suburbanized land use patterns rises as well and, at some point, may well become prohibitively expensive. Future exigencies are likely to require a transition to more compact, energy-efficient urban design.[60] Such a shift in land use would permit less wasteful energy usage, by employing the cogeneration methods described above, and make the community less dependent on shrinking supplies of nonrenewable fuels. The location decision for an energy recovery system will provide the city of Ann Arbor with a timely opportunity to begin addressing these concerns.

NOTES

This paper was written in April, 1979. It was revised in June, 1980, although the original analysis remains basically unchanged. The author wishes to thank especially Harry Butler of the U.S. Environmental Protection Agency; Guy Larcom, former city administrator of Ann Arbor; and Richard C. Porter of the University of Michigan Department of Economics for their helpful comments.

1. Bradford J. Max, *Resource Recovery and Waste Reduction Activities: A Nationwide Survey* (Washington, D.C.: U.S. Environmental Protection Agency, 1979), p. 20. Max's work contains the most current listing of resource recovery facilities in the United States, including the earliest ones and those that are temporarily or indefinitely shut down. Among the very first such facilities were an EPA demonstration plant that processed solid waste into refuse-derived fuel (RDF) in St. Louis, Missouri (1972), a waterwall combustion incinerator producing steam in Braintree, Massachusetts (1971), and a waterwall incinerator producing steam and recovering ferrous metals in Chicago, Illinois (1971). The first commercial RDF facility built in the United States was a 400-ton-per-day (tpd) plant constructed in Ames, Iowa, in 1975.

2. See National League of Cities and U.S. Conference of Mayors, *Cities*

and the Nation's Disposal Crisis (Washington, D.C.: National League of Cities, 1973).

3. Marchant Wentworth, *Resource Recovery: Truth and Consequences* (Washington, D.C.: Environmental Action Foundation, 1977), and Office of Technology Assessment, *Materials and Energy From Municipal Waste* (Washington, D.C.: Government Printing Office, 1979). Wentworth's book provides an overview of the major types of problems and the most widely known failures. The Office of Technology Assessment (OTA) report provides a more in-depth review of the entire resource recovery field, both successes and failures. Often-cited problems are those experienced by the St. Louis demonstration project, where burning RDF with coal resulted in doubling the particulate emissions from the facility; the Baltimore pyrolysis plant, where spontaneous combustion occurred in a bin in which shredded fuel was being stored; and the Nashville waterwall combustion facility, which was plagued by noxious odors, air pollution problems, and inconsistent production of steam, and eventually was closed down.

4. The environmental problems associated with sanitary landfill have been widely discussed in print. Among the references most useful for general overview purposes are *The Resource Recovery Industry: A Survey of the Industry and its Capacity* (U.S. Environmental Protection Agency publication SW-501c, 1976); and U.S Environmental Protection Agency, *Resource Recovery and Source Reduction, Fourth Report to Congress* (Washington, D.C.: U.S. Environmental Protection Agency, 1977). Valuable information related to the specific conditions in Michigan may be found in State of Michigan, Seventy-ninth Legislature, *The Solid Waste Management Act* (Act 641 of the Public Acts of 1978); Henningson, Durham, and Richardson, "State of Michigan: Interim Report on Quantities and Composition of Solid Waste" (Omaha: Henningson, Durham, and Richardson, 1977); and Jones and Henry Engineers, Ltd., "A Washtenaw County Plan for the Management of Solid Waste. Final Report" (Toledo: Jones and Henry, 1975).

5. Ann Arbor Department of Solid Waste, "Solid Waste Disposal in Ann Arbor: An Evaluation and Recommendation," mimeographed (Ann Arbor: Department of Solid Waste, 1979). The report includes a letter from officials with the state Department of Natural Resources which refers to the new requirements. The mandate hits particularly hard at the Ann Arbor landfill site because, until recently, it has been permitted to operate with "variances"—i.e., with clay linings and daily cover less deep than actually required—because of the superior quality of the area as a landfill site. Recent samples have determined that newly acquired areas are not as ideally suited, geologically, for landfill purposes, necessitating that these areas not be allowed to operate with variances.

6. Jones and Henry, "A Washtenaw County Plan," pp. 3–8.

7. Telephone conversations with present and former members of the Washtenaw County Department of Public Works, in February, 1979, suggest

that one reason the project never went any further was the failure to get a formal commitment from the University of Michigan to use the RDF. While other possible buyers had been considered, the university had been seen as the most feasible market.

8. Ann Arbor Ad Hoc Committee on Solid Waste Disposal, "Final Report to Ann Arbor City Council," mimeographed (May 17, 1977).

9. Henningson, Durham, and Richardson, "Feasibility Study of Solid Waste Shredding Facilities for the City of Ann Arbor, Michigan" (Omaha: Henningson, Durham, and Richardson, 1978).

10. "Voters Approve Shredder Proposal," Ann Arbor News, April 3, 1979.

11. Ann Arbor Department of Solid Waste, "Solid Waste Disposal in Ann Arbor," pp. 7–9.

12. "Council Clogs Shredder Plans," Ann Arbor News, November 14, 1979.

13. Telephone conversation with Steve McCargar, Coordinator, Ann Arbor Ecology Center, on March 16, 1979.

14. Ibid.

15. A detailed description of various resource recovery technologies can be found in Michael B. Bever, et al., Analysis of Technological Options for Solid Waste Disposal and Resource Recovery (Cambridge, Mass.: MIT Environmental Impact Project, 1978) and U.S. Environmental Protection Agency, Resource Recovery Plant Implementation: Guides for Municipal Officials (Washington, D.C.: U.S. Environmental Protection Agency, 1976).

16. See Max, Resource Recovery, p. 6.

17. Ibid.

18. Ibid., pp. 8–9.

19. Citizen's Advisory Committee on Environmental Quality, Energy in Solid Waste: A Citizen's Guide to Saving (Washington, D.C.: Government Printing Office, 1974), pp. 4–14. The report estimated annual U.S. production of refuse to be 3.2 lbs per person per day in 1974. Of this, 31.3 percent is paper of some type. A town with a population of 58,000 thus produces 67,744,000 lbs of refuse per year (3.2 × 58,000 × 365) or 30,240 tons. The paper component is 0.313 × 30,240 or 9,466 tons. Thus, even if citizen participation in the collection program were only 5 percent, more than 400 tons of paper could be collected annually.

20. See U.S. Environmental Protection Agency, Source Separation: The Community Awareness Program in Somerville and Marblehead, Massachusetts (Washington, D.C.: U.S. Environmental Protection Agency, 1976).

21. U.S. Environmental Protection Agency, Resource Recovery Plant Implementation: Guides for Municipal Officials provides a complete explanation of these combustion systems. Briefly, modular combustion units are small, self-contained incinerators designed to handle only small quantities of waste. Several units or "modules" may be used in one facility to achieve the needed

plant size. A waterwall incinerator is constructed with walls of welded steel tubes, through which water is circulated to absorb the heat created by combustion. The heated water may then be used to produce steam.

22. Office of Technology Assessment, *Materials and Energy*, pp. 103–16.

23. Ibid., pp. 105–6.

24. These estimates are from Max, *Resource Recovery*, which contained the most current listing at the time of publication.

25. Office of Technology Assessment, *Materials and Energy*, chapter 5 and especially pp. 102–7.

26. Ibid.

27. In addition, because the fuel is of a more uniform density and Btu content, combustion is more complete and less ash and lower emissions in general are produced.

28. See note 3 above.

29. U.S. Environmental Protection Agency, *Resource Recovery Plant Implementation: Guides for Municipal Officials* (Washington, D.C.: U.S. Environmental Protection Agency, 1976). The *Implementation Guides* are an eight-volume series, containing an excellent treatment of the minimum criteria which should be met before undertaking a resource recovery facility. The most recent and comprehensive discussion of the subject is U.S. Environmental Protection Agency, *Resource Recovery Management Model* (Washington, D.C.: U.S. Environmental Protection Agency, 1979).

30. U.S. Environmental Protection Agency, *Resource Recovery and Source Reduction*.

31. Wentworth, *Resource Recovery*, pp. 57–59.

32. Ibid., and Dan Knapp, Tom Brandt, and Don Corson, "Mine the Trash Cans, Not the Land," in *Rain*, November, 1978, pp. 4–8. Both discuss the inefficiency of postshredding separation.

33. Wentworth, *Resource Recovery*, pp. 56–59.

34. Ibid.

35. Ann Arbor Department of Solid Waste, "Solid Waste Disposal in Ann Arbor."

36. Specially designed bins are necessary for storing RDF between processing and transportation or combustion. This cost was neglected by the Jones and Henry study.

37. Henningson, Durham, and Richardson, "State of Michigan: Interim Report on Technology Evaluation" (Omaha: Henningson, Durham, and Richardson, 1979), p. X-9.

38. This annual figure was derived by adding the total refuse suitable for processing into RDF (col. 6 of table 5) to the amount of other components not recycled. That is to say, assuming 40 percent participation, column 6 was added to $(1 - .4) \times$ (col. 1 − col. 6). In the case of 20 percent participation, the calculation became $(1 - .2) \times$ (col. 1 − col. 6) plus column 6.

39. Wentworth, *Resource Recovery,* p. 52.

40. The situation in Marblehead, Massachusetts, is a case in point. See note 20 above and Max, *Resource Recovery,* p. 8.

41. State of Michigan, *The Solid Waste Management Act.*

42. Telephone conversation with Joseph Price, Director, Washtenaw County Department of Public Works, on April 6, 1971.

43. EPA averages were obtained from U.S. Environmental Protection Agency, *Resource Recovery and Source Reduction.* Figures on the composition of waste going to the Ann Arbor municipal landfill are from a telephone conversation with Richard Garay of the Ann Arbor Department of Solid Waste, on February 6, 1979.

44. U.S. Environmental Protection Agency, *Resource Recovery and Source Reduction.* The Michigan mandatory beverage container deposit legislation (Michigan's "bottle bill") went into effect in December, 1978. A mandatory deposit of five or ten cents (depending on the size and type of the container) is charged on all beer and soft drink containers, refundable when the container is returned to an establishment which sells such beverages.

45. Telephone conversation with Steve McCargar of the Ecology Center, March 21, 1979.

46. Ibid.

47. U.S. Environmental Protection Agency, *Resource Recovery and Source Reduction,* pp. 37–38.

48. See Max, *Resource Recovery,* pp. 10–17.

49. Telephone conversation with M. VanDerKooy of the University of Michigan Department of Physical Properties on March 28, 1979.

50. This estimate is from ICF, Incorporated, a Washington, D.C. consulting firm that does energy forecasting.

51. Kan Chen et al., "Value Oriented Social Decision Analysis: Enhancing Mutual Understanding to Resolve Public Policy Issues," mimeographed (April, 1979).

52. Ibid.

53. Telephone conversation with Richard Garay, Ann Arbor Department of Solid Waste, on January 30, 1979.

54. To test the sensitivity of the results to the choice of discount rate, the net present value of benefits for the two most likely cases (see table 11) was calculated using a 5 percent discount rate, or double that used in the actual analysis. With a 5 percent discount rate, total net present value benefits for the "optimistic" scenario are $4,762,200 and for the "pessimistic" scenario, $1,148,400. The choice of discount rates thus has a definite effect on net benefits, yet both scenarios continue to yield positive total net benefits.

55. Wentworth, *Resource Recovery,* discusses the Btu content of refuse, as does Office of Technology Assessment, *Materials and Energy,* especially pp. 100–101.

56. Telephone conversation with Jim Ogden, project manager for the proposed Burlington, Vermont, facility on April 8, 1979.

57. Interview with Dan Hanlon of the City of Ann Arbor Engineering Department on May 20, 1980.

58. See notes 38 and 39 above.

59. U.S. Environmental Protection Agency, *Resource Recovery Management Model,* emphasizes the importance of securing a market prior to taking further implementation steps.

60. See Herman E. Koenig and Lawrence M. Sommers, eds., *Energy and the Adaptation of Human Settlements: A Prototype Process in Genesee County, Michigan.* (East Lansing: Michigan State University Center for Environmental Quality, 1980).

5   Solar Applications at City Parks

Dale S. Johnson and Gary Woodard

Sunlight is a distributed energy resource. It is available in modest quantities everywhere from time to time, but is not concentrated anywhere in large amounts.[1] Efficient utilization of energy from the sun depends upon capturing and using it at a particular site, rather than concentrating it at a large facility and transporting it to the end user. Each solar application constitutes only a very small proportion of a community's energy budget. If successful, however, each application can be a step toward further applications at other comparable sites. And a large number of applications can eventually displace a significant amount of increasingly scarce fossil fuels that would otherwise be used for heating and other purposes.

This study focuses on conservation and solar applications at the Veterans Park pool in Ann Arbor: a pool cover, a solar heating system for pool water, and a solar-assisted hot water system for the shower house. Although water heating is only a small component in the city's energy budget, it is an appropriate starting point for an investigation of the solar potential in Ann Arbor after conservation measures have been considered. Water heating is widely regarded as the easiest solar application for various technical and economic reasons. In addition, Veterans Park is an appropriate location for a demonstration project. It is located within sight of the busy intersection of Jackson Road and Stadium Boulevard–Maple Road. Any solar collectors installed would be visible from Jackson Road. The pool is visited twenty-three thousand times each summer, largely by young people who will live most of their lives in the new energy era. For these reasons, Veterans Park is a promising site for a solar demonstration project, which, if developed, would attract the attention of all parts of the community and particularly young people.

The Veterans Park pool facility is a special case, but so in some respect is every other potential site. An analysis of Veterans Park is

142

relevant to other sites in Ann Arbor because the methodology, cost considerations, and other factors can be adapted. In selecting one highly visible site for analysis and possible construction of a demonstration project, the city can identify some of the opportunities and problems that will arise elsewhere and begin to learn how to address them. A working example at Veterans Park, accompanied by periodic reports on its actual performance, would help others in the city assess additional sites in the residential and commercial sectors on a more informed and realistic basis. It is important to avoid both continued reliance on fossil fuels where solar applications are appropriate, and premature commitments where solar applications are not.[2] Thus, an analysis of Veterans Park can serve as an important first step toward clarification of the solar role in Ann Arbor's energy future.

The first two sections of this analysis provide background on Ann Arbor's municipal swimming pools, with emphasis on current heating costs at Veterans Park. The next three sections focus on the benefits and costs of pool covers, a solar pool heating system, and a solar-assisted hot water system, respectively. The following section emphasizes the significance of a solar demonstration beyond the direct financial implications. The concluding section clarifies the objectives of a solar policy for the city of Ann Arbor, and recommends several steps to begin implementation.

Municipal Pool Facilities

In 1966 Ann Arbor voters approved a $2.5 million bond issue for recreational facilities. One million dollars of this amount was added to $0.8 million of federal matching grants to buy 400 acres of land for new parks. The remainder of the bond issue was used to finance three major recreational facilities at the Buhr, Fuller Road, and Veterans parks.

At Buhr and Fuller Road parks, tennis courts were built with refrigeration coils under the surface so that the courts can be flooded and used as ice skating rinks in the winter. Veterans Park has an indoor, year-round ice arena. Quarter-million-gallon heated swimming pools were built at Buhr and Veterans Parks, each with a separate toddler's wading pool. The Fuller Road pool is nearly twice the size of the other two. Each of the three outdoor pool facilities includes a shower house.

All three pools are good candidates for energy savings through conservation and solar applications. They are outdoor, heated pools, exposed to the weather, with unshaded roof areas nearby where solar collectors could be mounted. This study focuses on the Veterans Park facility because of its layout and location.

As shown in figure 1, the Veterans Park ice arena, located next to the pool's pump house, has a large sloping roof with a southern exposure. The roof is easily seen from Jackson Road near the busy Jackson Road–Stadium Boulevard–Maple Road intersection. Collectors mounted on this roof would offer a constant visual reminder of the solar option in Ann Arbor to motorists on Jackson Road.

The pool shares a year-round, full-time manager with the adjoining ice arena, and temporary help is hired through the swimming and ice skating seasons. Like the other outdoor municipal pools, Veterans Park pool is open from Memorial Day to Labor Day each year. The temperature of the pool is kept between 76° and 78° F because "if you let it fall just two or three degrees below that you get a lot of complaints real fast," according to Brian Durham, assistant manager at Veterans Park. A natural gas–fired boiler rated at 1.467 million Btu per

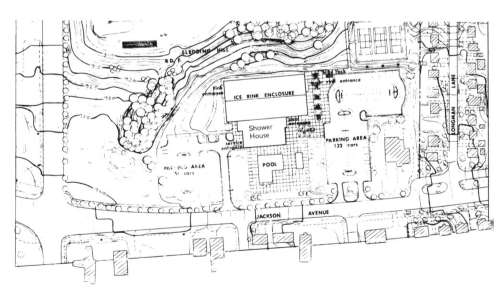

FIG. 1.   Site plan of the Veterans Park pool facility and ice arena. (Courtesy of the City of Ann Arbor.)

hour input and 1.117 million Btu per hour output is used to heat the pool. Mr. Durham estimates that the pool heater is turned on eight hours a day for about five days when the pool is first filled to bring it up to the desired temperature. During May and June the boiler operates only an hour or two per day; during July and August the sun keeps the pool warm and the gas heater is hardly used at all.[3] A second boiler supplies hot water that is used for showers and space heating in the shower house, and a third boiler is used exclusively for heating the ice arena. All three boilers are fed through a single meter.

Approximate operating costs of the three outdoor pools as reported in the city administrator's proposed 1980–81 budget are given in table 1. For each object of expenditure, the 1979–80 estimate is given above the 1978–79 expenditure. Such figures are to be used with caution. They vary in part as a result of budget carry-overs between fiscal years. For instance, the $800 entry for chemicals at Veterans Park for 1979–80 probably understates chemical usage since the actual expenditure was $1,145 in the previous year and $2,033 in the year before that. Moreover, for Veterans Park, the city keeps two recreational accounts, one for the pool facility (including the pool and the shower house) and one for the ice arena. Utility bills for Veterans Park as a whole are administratively apportioned between the two accounts by the Parks and Recreation Department.

Lacking separate natural gas meters and bills for each of the three boilers at Veterans Park, the annual costs of heating the pool and of heating the shower house are not directly known. These annual costs are estimated in the next section. The annual heating cost apportioned to the pool facility (pool plus shower house) at Veterans Park for 1979–80, as shown in table 1, is $2,250. This figure appears to be low relative to the $3,800 estimated heating cost at Buhr Park, which has a similar pool facility but no indoor ice arena. It also appears low relative to another estimate of $3,942, based on an analysis of the monthly costs of natural gas at Veterans Park in 1979.[4] Thus, $3,800 to $4,000 is probably a more accurate estimate of 1979–80 pool facility heating costs at Veterans Park. The total 1979–80 heating bill for Veterans Park is about $13,000.

Despite these gaps and ambiguities, the figures in table 1 do indicate that heating costs are relatively modest. Total heating costs comprise less than 4 percent of expenditures for the three outdoor

TABLE 1. Ann Arbor Outdoor Pool Expenditures, 1978–79[a] and 1979–80[b]

Expenditure	Buhr Park		Fuller Road Park		Veterans Park[c]	
	Dollar Amount	Percentage	Dollar Amount	Percentage	Dollar Amount	Percentage
Natural Gas						
1979–80	$3,800	3.5%	$4,000	3.1%	$2,250	4.1%
1978–79	3,616	4.0	3,942	2.7	2,921	5.5
Electricity						
1979–80	10,800	10.0	14,500	11.3	3,600	6.6
1978–79	10,740	11.8	14,130	9.8	9,812	18.4
Water						
1979–80	5,500	5.1	12,900	10.0	3,800	7.0
1978–79	4,808	5.3	12,398	8.6	4,025	7.6
Chemicals						
1979–80	1,750	1.6	1,900	1.5	800	1.5
1978–79	632	0.7	3,537	2.5	1,145	2.2
Labor						
1979–80	57,600	53.4	70,940	55.2	32,969	60.4
1978–79	53,502	58.5	86,448	60.2	25,796	48.5
Other						
1979–80	28,370	26.3	24,350	18.9	11,158	20.4
1978–79	18,098	19.8	23,108	16.1	9,508	17.9
Totals						
1979–80	$107,820	100.0	$128,590	100.0	$54,604	100.0
1978–79	91,396	100.0	143,563	100.0	53,207	100.0

Source: City of Ann Arbor
a. Actual expenditures
b. Estimated expenditures
c. The city keeps two accounts for Veterans Park, one for the pool facility (shown here) and one for the ice arena. Only one account is kept for recreational facilities at Buhr and Fuller Road parks.

pools and only 25 percent of the overall energy costs at the facilities. Three times the amount spent on natural gas was spent on electricity, used largely to freeze the ice rinks,[5] and the chemical bills for a pool facility are often half as large as the total heating bills.

Heating Costs at the Pool Facility

The potential financial benefits to the city of conservation and solar applications stem from the avoidance of future costs. The chemical costs that might be avoided are reasonably well known, because they are a line item in the budget and directly attributable to the pool itself. The natural gas costs that might be avoided are much more difficult to estimate because the pool boiler and the shower house boiler do not have separate meters. This section estimates the cost of heating the pool with natural gas for the reference year 1979–80, and estimates the cost of shower water and space heating in the shower house as the remainder of pool facility heating costs.

Alternative Estimates

One method of estimating the annual cost of pool heating at Veterans Park relies on the hours of operation of the boiler used for pool heating. From the description of Mr. Durham, as previously noted, the boiler operates about ninety hours each summer from the initial heating period in May until July, when heating is no longer necessary. Using the rate of thirty-five cents per hundred cubic feet of natural gas (or ccf) and the pool boiler rating of 1.467 million Btu per hour input, the cost can be calculated as

$$90 \text{ hrs} \times \frac{1,467,000 \text{ Btu}}{1 \text{ hr}} \times \frac{1 \text{ ccf}}{103,200 \text{ Btu}} \times \frac{\$0.35}{1 \text{ ccf}} = \$448.00$$

Another method of estimating annual pool heating costs is by a theoretical analysis of heat transfer. The relevant equations require solar incidence and degree-day measurements that are available for Ann Arbor from the University of Michigan Department of Atmospheric and Oceanic Science. The equations require some assumptions about the thermal characteristics of the pool and wind incidence at the pool surface. Although complicated, the equations are within the competence of heating systems engineers.

Simpler calculations may also be used, however, to provide the necessary estimate. Since a gallon of water weighs about 8.6 pounds, the weight of the 222,440 gallons of water in Veterans Park pool is about 1,912,984 pounds. Assuming this water comes out of the city water supply at about 50° F and must be raised at least 25° F by the boiler, then the amount of heat required to raise the temperature of the pool is 47,824,600 Btu. (One Btu is defined as the amount of heat required to raise the temperature of one pound of water one degree Fahrenheit.) Using the pool boiler input and output ratings, the *initial cost* of heating the entire pool once would be:

$$47,824,600 \text{ Btu} \times \frac{1,467,000 \text{ Btu/hr input}}{1,117,000 \text{ Btu/hr output}}$$

$$\times \frac{1 \text{ ccf}}{103,200 \text{ Btu}} \times \frac{\$0.35}{1 \text{ ccf}} = \$213.00$$

This calculation ignores the sun's heat falling on the pool and heat losses during filling and initial heating. If, as Mr. Durham's estimate implies, the ratio of subsequent heating to initial heating is 5 to 4, the cost of *subsequent heating* is:

$$\$213 \times \frac{50 \text{ hrs subsequent heating}}{40 \text{ hrs initial heating}} = \$266$$

Taking the estimates of initial and subsequent heating costs together, the total cost of heating the pool for a season is $479.

A third rough method of estimating the cost of heating the pool at Veterans Park is to examine the heating cost of other pools in southeastern Michigan. The Willoway Day Camp pool in nearby Wixom has a natural gas–fired pool heater with its own meter and, consequently, a reliable basis for determining pool heating costs. The pool is used about three weeks less than Veterans Park pool each season, but it is kept about 6° F warmer. The owner reports that before the camp purchased a solar pool heater in 1975, the pool heating bills were $600 to $800 a year, or about $1,555 to $2,074 in 1980 dollars adjusted for inflation in local natural gas prices.[6] Assuming the two pools have the same average depth, Veterans Park pool is one-fourth the size of the Willoway pool in both surface area and volume. (Heating losses are proportional to surface area; heating load, apart from losses, is proportional to volume.) Consequently, Veterans Park pool can be expected to have one-fourth the heating costs, or approximately $389 to $518.

Some Implications

A range of $389 to $518 for pool heating at Veterans Park in 1979–80 is much lower than most pool analysts expected the pool would require.[7] Yet the first estimate of $448 and the second estimate of $479 fall within this range. These estimates are based on simplified assumptions about the amount of gas input to the pool boiler and the amount of heat required for the pool, respectively; and such key factors as hours of operation and pool boiler ratings may be more or less inaccurate. A 10 percent error in either the hours of operation or the input rating would affect the first estimate by 10 percent. A 10 percent error in the *ratio* of input to output ratings or the *ratio* of initial to subsequent heating hours would affect the second estimate by 10 percent. Nevertheless, lacking a direct measure of pool heating costs or a much more detailed theoretical analysis, this study uses the second estimate of $479—$213 to heat the pool initially, $266 to heat the pool during the remainder of May and June, and a negligible amount to heat the pool for July and August—in the benefit/cost analysis that follows. The estimate is near the high end of the range; a higher estimate more consistent with the expectations of pool analysts would tend to enhance the potential financial benefits of conservation and solar alternatives.

If the cost of heating the pool in 1979–80 is roughly $500 and the cost of heating the pool facility is about $3,800 to $4,000, then the cost of shower heating and space heating in the shower house would be about $3,300 to $3,500, and the cost of heating the ice arena would be about $9,500 to $9,700—to account for the known total of about $13,000 in annual heating costs at the Veterans Park facility as a whole.

Separate Monitoring

Separate monitoring of the gas consumed at the pool boiler is the most reliable way of resolving the issue. Probably the simplest alternative for the city would be to have the Michigan Consolidated Gas Company install a separate meter and open a separate account for the pool heater. Because the company reads meters only at two-month intervals, it would be·necessary for city employees to read the meter themselves, in between the scheduled company readings. This alternative is costly, however. In addition to an initial installation fee there is an eight-dollar monthly service charge which amounts to ninety-six dollars per meter on an annual basis.

A less expensive alternative could be implemented by the city itself. Since natural gas–fired boilers are controlled by electric thermostats or switches, the amount of time that a boiler operates can easily be measured by connecting an elapsed-time clock to the circuitry. Operation of the boiler would advance the elapsed-time clock. The amount of gas consumed could then be calculated from the time elapsed over a given period, assuming the Btu/hr input rating of the boiler is accurate. Elapsed-time clocks are advertised in solar equipment catalogs for about eight to ten dollars each.

Pool Covers

Conservation measures are normally worth investigation before solar applications. Swimming pool heat can be conserved in basically three ways. The temperature of the pool can be lowered, although this is highly unpopular with swimmers. The pool could be used for a shorter season, but even the traditional Memorial Day to Labor Day season is barely fifteen weeks, and reducing the season further would reduce the total benefits of the pool to the community. The third and frequently most appropriate method of conservation is installation of a pool cover, used by about 1 percent of the pools in the country.[8]

When a pool is left uncovered, water, heat, and chemicals are lost at the surface. The primary purpose of a pool cover is to reduce these losses at night or when the pool is not in use, by trapping the water, heat, and chemicals that would otherwise escape. Moreover, if the cover is translucent and left in place during the day, it works like a greenhouse to trap more solar energy than would an uncovered pool.

Both homemade and commercially made covers are constructed from soft plastic. The simplest design uses mylar sheets stretched over a frame of hollow plastic tubing. The tubing floats in the pool and breaks into sections for storage. Another kind consists of a double layer of plastic with air bubbles sealed in between—basically a stronger version of the plastic bubble sheets used in airmail packaging. These sheets float easily on the pool surface and can be rolled up or folded for storage. A variant of this design consists of the plastic bubble material cut into hexagonal pads three or four feet across. The pads are easily thrown on the surface where they arrange themselves into a honeycomb pattern. While they are easier to put on when the pool is closed, they are a little more difficult to catch and remove when the pool is opened up again. (Covering a pool tightly or completely is generally not considered worth the extra effort. If only 95 percent of a pool is covered, the cover will reduce losses of water, heat, and chemicals at the surface by nearly 95 percent while it is in place.)

Covers are best suited to backyard pools that are used only a few hours per day or per week, because the covers save and collect more energy the longer they remain in place. Covers also impose obvious costs. In addition to the initial purchase price, they must be removed before the pool is used and replaced later. In the case of a municipal pool, both tasks would have to be done each day during the swimming season by a city employee. The covers are also short-lived. They are usually warranted for only three or four years because over time ultraviolet radiation from the sun, exposure to pool chemicals, and repeated handling destroys the plastic material. When not in the pool, they must be protected from the sun and from swimmers as well.

This section assesses the financial savings and costs of a pool cover at Veterans Park under three possible operating assumptions: the use of a pool cover during the initial heating period, through the first half of the season, and through the full season.

Annual Savings

We have been unable to find serious research on the savings from use of pool covers, although one pool cover manufacturer supplies a list of testimonials. However, rough estimates can be made of costs avoided in initial heating, subsequent heating, and chemical use. (The costs avoided in replacing water are negligible and therefore ignored.)

Operating experience at the Willoway Camp pool sheds some light on the proportion of initial heating costs avoided. The solar collectors used there supply enough heat to bring the pool from ground temperature to swimming temperature in only four to six days, even though the surface area of the collectors is only 40 percent of the surface area of the pool.[9] Presently, the Veterans pool is filled a week or so before the swimming season starts, and the pool is heated over several days using the gas boiler. If the pool were filled two or three weeks before the start of the season and covered with a translucent cover, the water could be heated by the sun alone to near the desired temperature. This simple change would save essentially all of the initial heating costs of $213, the figure used below as an estimate of the first-year savings in initial heating costs through use of a pool cover.

Advertising claims suggest that a pool covered over most of its surface area most of the time could realize a 75 percent savings in subsequent heating requirements.[10] Heat losses through evaporation (as well as radiation and conductance) are proportional to the surface area of the pool and the length of time evaporation takes place. For a municipal pool that is in use twelve or more hours a day these savings are more likely to be about half the maximum, or 38 percent. The analysis is complicated, however, by the fact that the pool cover during the swimming season would be in place in the colder, nighttime hours—the time when heat losses would be highest. As a rough estimate, as much as 55 percent of heat losses might be prevented by a pool cover. Fifty-five percent of the previous estimate of $266 for subsequent pool heating amounts to a first-year savings of $146. These savings would be realized after the initial heating period but before the last half of the swimming season, when gas heating is no longer required.

The pool cover promotional literature also makes casual reference to savings on chemicals from using a pool cover. Discussions with a pool chemical salesman, a chemistry professor, and a city engineer all suggest that the savings for a pool with the characteristics of Veterans Park would be on the order of 25 percent to 35 percent. The 1980–81 budget estimates chemical expenditures at Veterans Park at $800. As noted earlier, however, this is an underestimate of actual use since chemical expenditures were $2,033 and $1,145 in the two previous years, and the Buhr Park pool, identical in size, was estimated to use $1,750 in chemicals in the summer of 1980. Using an estimate of 30 percent savings from evaporation losses avoided, a low estimate of $800 and a high estimate of $1,750 in annual chemical costs, the expected savings in the first-year chemical costs if the cover were used for a full season range from $240 to $525. The expected savings would be half these amounts if the cover were used for the first half of the season, and negligible if used only during the initial heating period.

Initial and Annual Costs

Pool cover prices are quoted on the basis of the number of square feet of material required. For the 5,913 square feet of pool area at Veterans Park, the salespeople contacted for this study chose to quote in terms of 6,000 square feet. The price per square foot depends upon the type of cover, the manufacturer, and the dealer. Covers often sell for sixty to seventy cents per square foot. Salespeople for solar heating firms have quoted forty-six to sixty cents per square foot, and a Detroit manufacturing firm offered to supply a cover at thirty-five cents per square foot. The latter estimate, the cheapest, results in a total cost of $2,100 to purchase a cover for Veterans Park pool.

Rha Talwar of the Mid-American Solar Energy Center suggested another option based on the experience of Cocoa Beach, Florida. The maintenance staff made pool covers for the city by stretching 6 mil polyethylene over hollow, one-and-one-half-inch plastic pipe. These covers cost about four cents per square foot, including labor;[11] at this rate the initial cost for a cover for Veterans Park would be about $240.

In addition to the initial cost, the city would have to pay for covering the pool and removing the cover prior to use of the pool. If each operation required about twenty minutes of labor[12] from each of two workers at a cost of $6 per hour,[13] the cost would be $8 each time the cover is used. If each operation required thirty minutes from each worker at the same hourly rate, the cost would be $12 per use. It is assumed that the cover would be put in place and removed only once per year during the initial heating period; a total of 52 times per year during the initial heating period and the first half of the 102-day swimming season; and 103 times per year from the initial period through the entire swimming season. Consequently, labor costs for the three options, respectively, would range from $8 to $12; $416 to $624; and $824 to $1,236; on an annual basis. These are real costs, but they would not show up as increased operating expenses. Operating a pool cover would simply displace some other activity already included in the pool budget.

Financial Evaluation

Financial evaluation of a project to cover Veterans Park pool can be expressed in terms of the present value, defined as the sum of project costs and benefits appropriately discounted over time. The costs of the project are the initial cost of the pool cover and the labor costs of putting it in place and removing it each day. The economic benefits are the heating costs and chemical costs avoided by using a pool cover. The discount rate reflects the real rate of return that could be earned through alternative investments. It is roughly the amount by which the prime interest rate exceeds the general rate of inflation. This difference is fairly constant, and taken here to be 2.5 percent. In addition, natural gas prices are rising more rapidly than prices generally, so that the real value of a unit of natural gas saved next year will be greater than the value of the same amount saved today. This fact is incorporated through a parameter g, which is the difference between the natural gas price inflation rate and the general inflation rate.

The relationship among these factors is summarized in the equation

$$PV = -C_O + \sum_{t=0}^{n} \left[-C_i + S_c + S_h(1 + g)^t \right] \left(\frac{1}{1 + r} \right)^t$$

where PV is the cumulative present value of the project through year n, and where

C_O = the initial cost of the pool cover,
C_i = the annual cost of labor,
S_c = the annual savings in chemicals,
S_h = the annual savings in heating,
r = the discount rate,
g = the rate of gas price inflation less the general inflation rate, and
t = the year, with $t = 0$ taken as 1980.

We have opted against the commercial pool cover because of the very high initial cost, and focused instead on the evaluation of the inexpensive homemade cover under three alternative scenarios: (1) use during the initial heating period only, (2) use during the initial heating period and through the first half of the season, and (3) use during the initial period and through the full season. Each option, in turn, has been evaluated under optimistic and pessimistic assumptions to accommodate uncertainty. The high estimates of savings, the low estimates of costs, and a real rate of natural gas price increases of 10 percent per year are included in the optimistic assumptions. The pessimistic assumptions use the low estimates of savings, high estimates of costs, and a real rate of natural gas price increases of 3 percent per year.

As shown in tables 2 and 3, a homemade pool cover used only

TABLE 2.   Present Value (in dollars) of a Homemade Pool Cover Used during Initial Heating under Optimistic Assumptions

| | Labor Costs | | Annual Savings | | | | |
Year	Initial	Annual	Chem.	Heat	Net Benefit	Discounted	Present Value
1980	$240	$8	$0	$213	$-35	$-35	$-35
1981	0	8	0	234	226	221	186
1982	0	8	0	258	250	238	423
1983	0	8	0	284	276	256	629
1984	0	8	0	312	304	275	955
1985	0	8	0	343	335	296	1,251
1986	0	8	0	377	369	318	1,569

Note: These estimates refer to the scenario termed Option 1. Optimistic assumptions include the high estimates of savings, low estimates of costs, and a real rate of natural gas price increases of 10 percent per year.

TABLE 3.   Present Value (in dollars) of a Homemade Pool Cover Used during Initial Heating under Pessimistic Assumptions

| | Labor Costs | | Annual Savings | | | | |
Year	Initial	Annual	Chem.	Heat	Net Benefit	Discounted	Present Value
1980	$240	$12	$0	$213	$-39	$-39	$-39
1981	0	12	0	219	207	202	163
1982	0	12	0	226	214	204	367
1983	0	12	0	233	221	205	572
1984	0	12	0	240	228	206	778
1985	0	12	0	247	235	208	986
1986	0	12	0	254	242	209	1,195

Note: These estimates refer to the scenario termed Option 1. Pessimistic assumptions include the low estimates of savings and high estimates of costs, and a real rate of natural gas price increases of 3 percent per year.

during the initial heating period (option 1) would pay for itself in the second year. The present value in the second year is $186 under optimistic assumptions and $163 under pessimistic assumptions. This difference grows over time largely as a function of the different rates of natural gas prices assumed. The difference of $4 in annual labor costs is relatively insignificant.

A homemade pool cover used during the initial heating period and the first half of the season (option 2) would pay for itself in two years under optimistic assumptions, but would not pay for itself at all under pessimistic assumptions. In other words, this option is risky. If labor costs turned out to be at the high end of the range ($624 as opposed to $416 per year), chemical savings turned out to be at the low end of the range ($120 as opposed to $263 per year), and gas prices increased at a real rate of only 3 percent per year, this option would not be a worthwhile investment.

The third option entails even greater risk. A homemade cover used for initial heating and the entire heating season would pay for itself in the third year under optimistic assumptions, and would not pay for itself at all under pessimistic assumptions. The full-season option is less attractive than the half-season option because the annual labor costs exceed the annual savings in chemicals and because the savings in natural gas consumed are the same, under either set of assumptions.

On grounds of a shorter payback period and less financial risk, the use of the homemade cover during the initial heating period only is the most attractive option. The positive present value could be increased to an unknown degree by painting the pool a dark blue.[14] This would increase the amount of heat absorbed from the sun throughout the season and would not add to costs provided the dark blue paint were applied only after present stocks of light blue-green paint are used up. Moreover, the use of the cover only during the initial heating period would extend the useful life of the cover. Relative to other options, the exposure to sunlight and chemicals would be minimized and handling would be reduced to putting the cover in place and removing it for storage only once per year. Under these circumstances, the cover would last well beyond the three to five years projected for use each day during the full season.

Active Solar Pool Heating System

Ann Arbor's three outdoor municipal pools, like most others, are equipped with pumps and filters to keep the pool water clean, and include a gas boiler to heat the pool water. To convert to an active solar pool heater, the minimum necessary addition to such a system is a bank of solar collectors mounted on the roof of a nearby building. Each collector is a series of small tubes of stainless steel or black polyethylene plastic. Sunlight heats these tubes, and this heat is transferred to the pool water pumped through them, in what might be called a "garden hose" effect. The water leaves the collectors only one or two degrees warmer than when it entered, but this constant flow of heat is sufficient to raise the temperature of the pool to 80° F or more.[15] Figure 2 shows a typical active solar pool heating system, together with water flows.

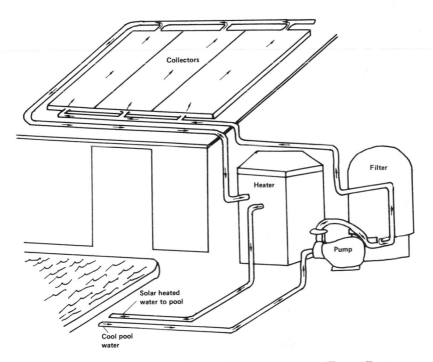

FIG. 2.   A typical active solar pool heating system. (From "Factsheet: Solar Swimming Pool Heaters" [Rockville, Md.: National Solar Heating and Cooling Information Center, 1978].)

The collector area needed to heat a specific pool depends on a number of factors including the desired temperature of the pool, the type of collectors used, and the local climate. The size of the pump required to lift the water to the collectors depends upon their height and distance from the pool. Systems may be improved with temperature sensors and simple control units that pump the water through the collectors only when the sunlight is sufficiently bright. Systems designed for demonstration purposes may include simple recorders documenting just how much energy and money the new pool heater is saving each season. The systems are normally developed by solar equipment retailers, who size and design a customer's system according to extremely detailed instructions provided by the pool equipment manufacturers. Some of the manufacturers provide their retailers with computerized analyses for individual pools.

Active solar collectors appear to be largely maintenance-free. Small leaks do occur infrequently, but these are easily fixed. If mounted flat on a roof, collectors must be removed each fall and remounted each spring, to prevent damage caused by freezing. Usually, however, collectors are mounted at an angle and need only be drained for the winter. One source reports that black plastic collectors bleach to a dull gray after a few years and must be turned over to maintain full effectiveness,[16] but most collectors are warranted for ten years without reinstallation.

Financial analysis of an active solar pool heating system is comparatively simple because there are no ongoing labor costs (maintenance is negligible) and because the ongoing savings are entirely from heat (the system does not save chemicals). Three main factors are important to the analysis: first, the price of the system; second, the projected annual savings on natural gas that would otherwise be used to heat the pool; and third, a discount factor that represents considerations such as the cost of money and the rate of energy inflation. The more expensive it is to borrow money, the more expensive such a capital-intensive system will be. High rates of energy inflation, on the other hand, increase the value of future savings in heating costs, and hence increase the value of an active solar pool heating system.

Purchase Price
The price quoted by a dealer reflects in a single number both the size of the proposed system and the per-unit materials and labor costs of

building the system. Since most of the costs of a system are proportional to the number of collectors mounted, the total price can reasonably be expressed as a product of the square feet of collector area and the price per square foot of collector area. Estimates for a system sufficiently large to provide heat for Veterans Park pool (excluding the shower house) during its fifteen-week season were requested by the authors from three dealers in the Ann Arbor area. The estimates summarized in table 4 were provided on the basis of good will and the possibility of future business, but without the direct incentive of an impending purchase order.

There are striking differences among the three sets of estimates. The most obvious is that the least expensive system costs less than a fifth as much as the most expensive system designed to do the same job. The price per square foot of collector varies by nearly a factor of two, and the number of collector panels recommended varies by nearly a factor of three. Only dealer C provided estimates for different mounting configurations.

In addition to these differences, the information provided contains certain gaps. When dealer B was asked how use of a pool cover would affect the system, he replied that it would be a desirable way of keeping the pool warm in the morning, but he was unable to suggest what size active solar system would produce the same result. None of the dealers was able to provide useful guidance on the gas heating costs that would be avoided by the recommended system. In addition, none estimated the "solar fraction" that would minimize pool heating costs. (The solar fraction is the proportion of total heating require-

TABLE 4. Recommended Solar Systems and Cost Estimates for Veterans Park Pool

Dealer	Number of 4 × 10 ft. Panels	Collector Area (in sq. ft.)	% of Pool Surface Area	Price (per sq. ft.)^2	Total Initial Cost
A	88	3,520	60%	$11.64	$41,000
B	84	3,360	57	8.04	27,000
C	44 lying flat	1,760	30	6.06	10,680
	35 on sloped racks	1,400	24	6.75	9,450
	30 on sloped roof	1,200	20	6.37	7,650

Source: Ann Arbor area solar equipment dealers

ments supplied by a solar heater, with the remainder supplied by a backup heater.) When a backup heater is already in place, a solar fraction approaching 1.0 tends to be less cost-effective because increased capital costs generally exceed additional fuel savings. Since Veterans Park already has a gas boiler that could be kept as a backup heater, the optimal system is most likely a solar heater assisted by the gas boiler on exceptionally cold days.[17]

It is impossible to determine from the estimates provided just how much of the gas costs each "full-sized" system can be expected to displace, much less what solar fraction is optimal for a gas-assisted solar pool heater in this part of the country. The optimal size of a pool heater is not known to the consumer prior to a purchase order, and it may not be known afterward, either, until the system is installed and its performance monitored.

Savings

The financial benefits of a solar pool heater are derived entirely from savings in natural gas costs avoided. If the heater is designed to provide only a fraction (i.e., the solar fraction) of the pool's heat, then the savings would be only that fraction of the annual heating bill. As we have seen, the optimal solar fraction is unknown, and the cost estimates were provided for systems purported to be large enough to provide all the pool's heat. For these reasons, and for simplicity, this analysis assumes that a solar pool heater would provide all the pool's heat. Thus, using the previous estimate of annual natural gas costs, the entire financial benefit from a solar pool heater at Veterans Park would be $479 per year, adjusted each year by the real rate of inflation for natural gas. The assumption of a solar fraction of 1.0 tends to bias both system costs and savings upwards, but the bias is greater for costs than for savings.

Discount Rate, Inflation, and Municipal Financing

The discount rate was discussed earlier as the real rate of interest or the real cost of money, calculated for the purpose of this analysis as about 2.5 percent. This rate reflects the cost of private borrowing, or the opportunity cost of *not* investing money. It is appropriate for the financial analysis of pool covers because the capital and operating expenses are small and would not typically be financed by the sale of municipal bonds. However, larger projects financed by the sale of municipal bonds may require a more complicated method of calculating the discount rate because municipal bonds are in effect subsidized by the federal government.

Interest received from municipal bonds is exempt from federal income tax, thereby making them a more attractive investment. If an investor in the 50 percent personal income tax bracket invests money at 12 percent interest, half of the income received on that investment is taxed away, leaving the investor with an effective return of 6 percent. If investors buy municipal bonds paying only 6 percent, they keep the entire interest and enjoy the same after-tax return as if they had invested in private bonds paying twice the interest rate. Thus, the municipal bond discount rate is equal to half the prime interest rate less the rate of inflation, assuming a 50 percent personal income tax bracket. Some sample calculations are provided in table 5. This tax advantage for cities allows them to finance capital expenditures at about half the interest rate that must be paid by private firms. The exact amount of the advantage depends on the length of the investment and the inflation rate, but it can be substantial.[18]

For normal transactions by prime borrowers, the 2.5 percent discount rate is appropriate. But for a city with a class A bond rating financing capital projects, the 2.5 percent discount rate is quite conservative, and a negative discount rate may, in fact, be more appropriate.

TABLE 5.   Discount Rates for Projects Financed by Tax-Free Municipal Bonds, in Percentage

Inflation Rate	Expected Prime Interest Rate[a]	Expected Bond Rate	Municipal Bond Discount Rate[b]
8%	10.5%	5.25%	−2.75%
10	12.5	6.25	−3.75
12	14.5	7.25	−4.75
14	16.5	8.25	−5.75
16	18.5	9.25	−6.75

a. The expected prime interest rate is assumed to exceed the rate of inflation by 2.5 percent.
b. The municipal bond discount rate is about half the prime interest rate less the rate of inflation, because tax-free bonds are a reasonable investment only for investors in high (e.g., 50 percent) tax brackets.

Evaluation of an Active Solar Pool Heater
The relationship among the various factors that have a bearing on the financial evaluation of an active solar pool heater are summarized in the equation

$$PV = -C_O + \sum_{t=0}^{n} S_h(1 + r_e)^t \left(\frac{1}{1 + r_b}\right)^t$$

where *PV* is the cumulative present value of the project through year *n*, and where

C_O = the initial cost of the pool heater
S_h = the annual savings in heating
r_e = the annual rate of real energy inflation
r_b = the appropriate discount rate with bonds
n = the number of years the heater is used, and
t = the year, with $t = 0$ taken as 1980.

The present value of an active solar pool heater is thus sensitive to initial costs, first-year savings in gas costs, the rate of real energy inflation, and the discount rate.

The nature of this sensitivity, in terms of payback period rather than present value, is displayed for a wide range of cases in figure 3. The vertical scale gives the payback period in years. The horizontal scale represents a composite discount factor r, which incorporates the effects of general and energy inflation. Under the assumption of financing with municipal bonds, $r = r_b - r_e$. An r of -15.75 percent, for example, can be interpreted as a negative municipal bond rate of -5.75 percent less a real energy inflation rate of 10 percent. A negative municipal bond rate of -5.75 percent, in turn, can be interpreted as the difference between an expected prime interest rate of 16.5 percent and an expected bond rate of 8.25 percent at a general inflation rate of 14 percent (see table 5). Under the assumption of financing without municipal bonds, r can be interpreted as the real cost of money (the prime interest rate less the general rate of inflation, or about 2.5 percent) less the real rate of energy inflation.

The numbers in the figure give the ratio of initial system cost to 1980 heat savings (C_O/S_h) required to achieve payback in a given number of years at various composite rates. For example, a system costing

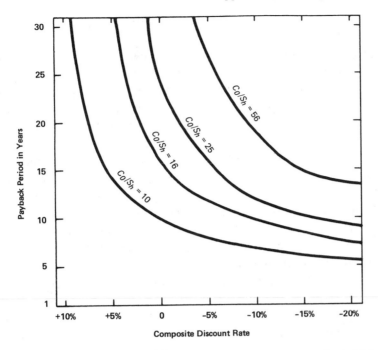

FIG. 3.   Payback periods of solar pool heating systems, by initial cost/savings ratios and composite discount rates. C_O/S_h is the ratio of initial system cost to first-year savings in gas heating costs. The composite discount rate is the municipal bond rate less the real energy inflation rate.

twenty-five times its 1980 fuel bill could pay for itself in ten years at a −16 percent composite rate; in fifteen years at a −7 percent composite rate; or in twenty-five years at a 0 percent composite interest rate. The curve labeled twenty-five thus represents the payback period of a system costing twenty-five times its first-year annual savings for any composite rate between about +1 percent and −20 percent.

Two other systems, each based on previous cost and savings estimates, are similarly represented by curves in figure 3. On the low side is a system that assumed the $7,650 initial cost estimate of dealer C (table 4) and $479 in 1980 fuel savings. The C_O/S_h ratio is thus $7,650/$479, or about 16. On the high side is a system that assumes the $27,000 initial cost estimate of dealer B and the same 1980 savings of $479. The C_O/S_h ratio is thus 56. The shaded area highlights the range of potential systems that fall between these two extreme cases in terms of initial cost.

Two significant conclusions can be drawn from figure 3. The first is that if the C_o/S_h ratio cannot be reduced below 16, then the system cannot pay for itself in less than about eight years *regardless of the general inflation, energy inflation, or discount rates used.* As the composite rate becomes more favorable to the right of the figure, the C_o/S_h = 16 curve flattens out too rapidly to ever drop much below eight years. The ratio could be reduced if a cheaper system were found, if it were discovered that the 1980 equivalent heat savings were greater than $479, or if some other government agency paid part of the cost, effectively making the system cheaper to local government. But as long as the $7,650 cost and the $479 savings are fixed, there is no bond rate or energy inflation rate that would allow the system to pay for itself much before its ten-year warranty elapsed.

The second conclusion is that if longer payback periods are allowed, then several of these systems can be cost effective. If the $7,650 system lasts nine years, it would just pay for itself under the most favorable assumption of −5.75 percent discount rate with bonds and a real energy inflation rate of 10 percent (i.e., a composite rate of −15.75 percent). If the system lasts fifteen years, it would pay for itself *and* return a net profit of $6,000 under the moderate assumption of a −7 percent composite rate. If it lasts sixteen years, it would pay for itself even under the very conservative assumption of a zero composite rate.[19]

In conclusion, an active solar pool heater at Veterans Park could be a good investment for Ann Arbor, but the investment appears to be marginal on economic grounds alone. (Additional grounds are explored in a later section of this chapter.) Assuming an expected life of ten years and a composite discount rate less than −9 percent, the $7,650 system proposed by dealer C could pay for itself and return a small profit.

Active Solar-Assisted Hot Water Heating System

Shower water and the shower building at Veterans Park are currently heated by a gas-fired boiler system, which includes a large reservoir to store hot water in the building. This hot water heating system could become solar-assisted through the installation of glazed solar collectors. In the summer, the collectors would be used primarily to help heat shower water. In the winter, they would help heat the building, which serves as a changing house for the adjoining ice arena.

A solar-assisted hot water heating system based on technology developed for domestic applications is a more sophisticated alternative to a pool heating system.[20] The collectors would be installed on the roof, but they would be more durable to be able to withstand year-around use, and covered with glass to produce higher temperatures. Depending on whether they are made of metal or plastic, and depending on the configuration of tubes, glazed solar collector panels weigh from ten to twenty pounds per square foot. It would thus be necessary to confirm that the roof of the ice arena at Veterans Park would support this extra weight.[21] Although hot water collectors produce higher-temperature water, they are less efficient. The existing gas-fired system, including the storage reservoir, would have to be retained to provide auxiliary heat when needed.

The economics of a solar-assisted hot water heating system may well be more attractive than a pool heating system. Recall that while pool heat cost only about $500 in the reference year, heating of the shower water and shower house cost an estimated $3,300 to $3,500 in that year. Thus the maximum potential savings of a solar-assisted hot water system are greater by a factor of six or seven. The fraction of the maximum potential savings that could actually be realized by a particular design, and whether the initial costs would increase in proportion to savings, are not known. The range of uncertainty could be reduced by another round of proposed designs and cost estimates from local dealers; and the model used in the previous section, together with the results presented in figure 3, could be used to make a rough estimate of the financial implications. However, in view of the uncertainties that would inevitably remain, it is more appropriate at this point to emphasize the indirect consequences of a solar demonstration project.

The Significance of a Demonstration Project

As we have seen in table 1, heating costs and potential benefits at Veterans Park are small relative to both energy costs and total costs.

Moreover, without minimizing the financial uncertainties involved, a solar pool heater is a relatively small investment that would probably pay for itself over its useful life. A solar-assisted hot water system would probably do the same, although the investment is somewhat larger. Thus, on grounds of energy and dollar savings alone, a solar application at Veterans Park would be, by itself, only a very modest step into the energy future.

Under these circumstances, the most significant consequences are indirect. A solar project could serve primarily as a demonstration to encourage other solar applications throughout the city as they become economical. Solar energy will only begin to make a substantial difference in Ann Arbor, financially and as an alternative energy source, as the number of applications increases through a process of diffusion and adoption. A solar demonstration project at Veterans Park would facilitate this process in at least three ways.

First, the installation of collectors would be a constant reminder of the solar alternative to the thousands of motorists who drive by Veterans Park each day. For swimmers, this reminder would be reinforced by the tangible sensation of warmth in utilizing the pool or the showers and shower house. For the community as a whole, it would be reinforced by periodic reports through local media on the performance of the system. Sustained exposure to the solar alternative on the part of a large number of people is necessary to stimulate the interest of those relative few who are willing and able to invest in solar energy in the short run.

Second, reliable performance data generated by a demonstration project at Veterans Park would address the uncertainties of those who are considering an investment in solar energy devices. As this study has demonstrated, a considerable expenditure of effort to evaluate solar applications at a single site in Ann Arbor nevertheless leaves a number of uncertainties. These uncertainties could be reduced through more detailed a priori analysis, but only at a substantial fraction of the cost of the system itself.[22] This a priori analysis makes sense for a project (like reactivation of the Barton dam[23]) that entails substantial capital costs and few opportunities for replication. For a project that has modest capital costs and many opportunities for replication, it makes more sense to initiate the process of diffusion and adoption through a demonstration project. In this case, the city can facilitate the process and reduce the uncertainties by assuming a modest financial risk on behalf of the community, making a small investment in a demonstration project, and monitoring and publicizing the results.

Finally, the results of a demonstration project at Veterans Park would be relevant to decisions about other potential solar applications in the city. On the one hand, what was learned at Veterans Park could be readily applied at Buhr and Fuller Road parks. More importantly, the results could be applied to the thousands of domestic hot water systems throughout the city. In this connection, a solar-assisted hot water system based on hardware developed for domestic applications has a distinct advantage over a pool heater.[24] On the other hand, there is no adequate substitute for locally generated performance data on solar applications, even if the demonstration project is a pool heater. The results of the project would reflect the local climate as well as the capability of at least one local dealer and the reliability of the hardware he or she sells, installs, and services. Given the differences between one locality and the next in these respects, information about other solar applications in the sunbelt or the nation generally is much less useful.

The efficiency of the market, in both theory and practice, depends upon a flow of relevant and reliable information. By improving the information available to Ann Arborites, a solar demonstration project would help them to avoid premature investments in solar energy hardware where it is not economical, and to realize the benefits of solar energy where it is.

Conclusion and Recommendations

The major conclusion of this study is that each solar application considered by the city government should be viewed primarily as a demonstration project, and designed accordingly to produce relevant and reliable information to support other decisions about when and when not to invest in solar energy. In view of this policy objective and the preceding analysis, several steps can be recommended.

First, the city engineer should install elapsed-time clocks or other metering devices on all the gas-fired boilers located at Veterans, Buhr, and Fuller Road parks. Better information on the range of natural gas consumption among boilers and over time will improve a priori estimates of the potential savings of any solar application. More importantly, the evaluation of a pool cover or an active solar heating system at a particular site requires a comparison of gas consumption before and after installation, and gas consumption at comparable sites without such applications.

Second, further a priori analysis should focus on a solar-assisted hot water system at Veterans Park. This solar application as a demonstration project has the most direct relevance to thousands of future decisions about solar-assisted domestic hot water systems. If either the size of the initial investment is too large or the payback period is too long, a solar pool heater could be considered as an alternative that would realize some of the purposes of a demonstration project with modest risks and initial costs. It is important to emphasize, however, that a priori analysis becomes increasingly expensive in relation to system costs as the range of uncertainty is reduced. It soon becomes more economical for the city to assume the modest financial risk on behalf of the community and to make a small investment in order to generate reliable information on the solar potential in Ann Arbor.

Third, passive solar and conservation techniques—dark blue paint and a homemade pool cover for the initial heating period each season—should.be implemented at one or more of the three municipal pools after baseline levels of natural gas consumption in the pool-heating boilers have been established. These techniques are compatible with a solar-assisted hot water system since the latter would provide heat for the showers and the shower building, but not the pool, and are competitive with an active solar pool heater.

Solar applications at city parks provide relatively low-cost, low-risk opportunities for the city government to demonstrate its intention to provide leadership in local energy policy for the community and the Midwest.[25]

NOTES

This paper was written in May, 1980, and revised in September, 1980, and April, 1981. The authors wish to thank Dan Hanlon of the Engineering Department, city of Ann Arbor, for his assistance. Responsibility is the authors' alone.

1. See U.S., Department of Energy, Assistant Secretary for Environment, Office of Technology Impacts, *Distributed Energy Systems in California's Future: Interim Report,* vols. 1 and 2, HCP/P7405-01 and 02 (Washington, D.C.: Government Printing Office, 1978).

2. "Error signals" proliferate in proportion to the number of premature commitments in a community. The resulting expectation that solar energy applications don't work—that they are unreliable or uneconomical, for example—tends to persist after it is no longer true. The net effect of premature commitments is to postpone rather than to accelerate the diffusion and adoption of the technology.

3. Telephone conversation with Brian Durham, assistant manager at Veterans Park, April 23, 1980.

4. About 31 percent of the total annual gas bill at Veterans Park in the calendar year 1979 was incurred from mid-May, when pool heating begins, through early September, when the swimming season ends. Since the ice arena was not used for summer skating in 1979 (and the cost of heating the arena building in the summer is negligible in any case), it is reasonable to attribute all of the 31 percent, or $3,952, to the pool and shower house. This figure underestimates the annual pool facility heating bill because the shower house is heated in the winter when it is used as a changing room for skaters. However, the showers are not used in the winter.

5. The outdoor rinks at Buhr and Fuller Road parks are no longer frozen by artificial means.

6. Telephone conversation with Mr. Mel Seidman, owner of the Willoway Day Camp, May 5, 1980. The adjustment for inflation is based on 13.5¢ per ccf in 1975 and 35¢ per ccf in the summer of 1980.

7. None of the pool analysts advised of these results had done an analysis of natural gas costs at Veterans Park.

8. *Solar Heating and Cooling,* June, 1978, p. 10.

9. Telephone conversation with Mr. Mel Seidman, May 5, 1980.

10. Sealed Air Corporation advertises that their cover "cuts heating costs up to 75 percent" in *Solar Engineering,* October, 1978. *Solar Heating and Cooling,* June, 1978, p. 10, reports that 70 percent of a pool's heat loss is from evaporation, and that a pool cover can reduce nighttime losses by 60 percent.

11. Telephone conversation with Rha Talwar, April 23, 1980.

12. Mike Morger of Vinyl Fab Industries, pool cover manufacturers, Livonia, Michigan, estimates twenty minutes to cover the pool.

13. A lifeguard paid $3.50 per hour would cost the city about $6.00 per hour in wages, insurance, bookkeeping, etc., according to Dan Hanlon, city engineer.

14. A pool like the Fuller Road pool, which is used for competitive swimming, should be left a light blue-green color or should have only the bottom painted dark blue. Competitive swimmers need a light colored pool or light-dark contrasts in order to detect the side of the pool before banging into it.

15. *Factsheet: Solar Swimming Pool Heaters* (Rockville, Md.: National Solar Heating and Cooling Information Center, 1978).

16. Conversation with Pat Lyons of Sunstructures Inc., Ann Arbor, Mich., March 13, 1980.

17. For a discussion of the solar fraction, see Arthur E. McGarity, *Solar Heating and Cooling: An Economic Assessment* (Washington, D.C.: Government Printing Office, 1977).

18. For example, at 10 percent inflation a ten-year corporate bond paying $3,000 per year would sell for about $17,120. The same bond sold tax-free by a city would bring $22,300, or about 30 percent more.

19. Figure 3 can be used in another way: What is the maximum initial cost/savings ratio at which a system would pay for itself, given a composite discount rate and the expected useful life of the system (or the desired payback period, if less than the useful life)? For example, if the composite rate is believed to be −5 percent and the expected useful life is believed to be ten years, then figure 3 indicates that an initial cost/savings ratio less than or equal to 13.0 is required for the system to pay for itself.

20. It is an alternative in that it would compete for space on the roof to install collectors. However, a hybrid system using glazed collectors and heat exchangers could be designed to provide heat for pool water and for shower water and space heating in the shower house, as needed.

21. According to Dan Hanlon, city engineer.

22. More complete models than the one used here can be found in John A. Clark, "Solar Energy Economics—The *A Priori* Decision," *International Journal of Heat Mass Transfer* 19 (1976):1095–1106. As we have seen, however, the major problem in this case is not a lack of models but a lack of reliable data.

23. See chapter 3.

24. Michigan residents can obtain up to 59 percent rebates on the initial cost of a solar system purchased for private use. The 59 percent includes federal and state income tax credits and the Michigan sales tax exemption for solar equipment. See Michigan Department of Commerce, Energy Administration, *The Michigan Solar Tax Credit Program* (Lansing: Michigan Department of Commerce, 1978).

25. City of Ann Arbor, Office of Community Development, *1980 Energy Plan,* (Ann Arbor: Office of Community Development, 1980).

6 Feedback for Energy Consumers

Ronald D. Brunner

For a number of years now, consumers around the country have been urged to eliminate the unnecessary "fat" in our energy budgets. Conserving energy is something like dieting.[1] Under a supervised program, a dieter uses calorie charts to help decide what foods to eat and perhaps what exercises to try. But a dieter also needs a bathroom scale to keep track of the payoffs (or lack of them) in terms of pounds lost. The system works if the dieter is motivated for any of a number of reasons.

Among the many reasons for eliminating unnecessary energy consumption are pressures on the household budget from rising energy costs and the threat of future energy shortages. Moreover, *Tips for Energy Savers* and similar publications and services for consumers are widely available.[2] Like calorie charts, they can be used to help decide how to cut back energy consumption and what is worth trying. But after some steps have been taken, how can the energy consumer know the consequences? In short, "what is the equivalent of the bathroom scale?"[3]

A variety of devices have been proposed or tested, ranging from simple on-off lights that signal changes in air conditioning requirements to sophisticated digital readout devices located in the kitchen that signal the rate of energy consumption. However effective, they are expensive. The gas or electric meter located in the basement or outside the house entails no additional cost, but most consumers need a good deal of help to learn how to read it and use the results. Such help can be provided on a neighborhood scale.[4]

Monthly utility bills are an inexpensive, community-wide alternative. The gas or electric company already employs meter readers and sends a bill to each consumer each month. Although utility bills are normally designed for company accounting and billing purposes, they can be redesigned to draw attention to the consequences of consumer energy decisions. In particular, they can clarify whether (and to what extent) the consumer has achieved reduced usage and dollar savings goals through attempts to conserve, and which conservation measures work. Carefully controlled experiments indicate that such feedback can result in significant reductions in unnecessary energy consumption under a variety of circumstances. Practical applications suggest that redesign of utility bills for consumer feedback purposes is feasible, inexpensive, and effective.

This paper applies the results of such experiments and practical applications to the task of improving the feedback supplied to Ann Arbor energy consumers through monthly utility bills. It reviews local utility bills from a consumer feedback perspective and proposes an initial design to remedy several deficiencies. It also considers the institutional framework through which local utility bills might be redesigned. Finally, a concluding section recommends the redesign of local utility bills as part of Ann Arbor's emerging energy conservation policy.

The feedback approach complements other approaches to energy conservation in local and national energy policy. *Tips for Energy Savers* and similar publications provide useful but quite general planning suggestions. Feedback, in contrast, provides insight into which suggestions have worked in specific cases. The difference is important to the extent that each household differs from the others in energy-using behavioral and structural characteristics.[5] On-site home "energy audits" by experts are an improvement over consumer publications in terms of specificity. But planning estimates are less reliable and often less persuasive than the results of experience, and only the consumer (not the invited expert) can have the sustained opportunity and interest to monitor results on a household basis. Feedback enables the individual consumer to learn from his or her own experience.[6] Finally, energy price increases are the principle instrument of conservation in national energy policy. But many consumers cannot distinguish cost increases attributable to small, gradual price increases from those attributable to their own energy consumption. Thus, "the knowledge gap may limit energy savings from smaller price increases. Feedback may nicely fill this gap, and in part this may explain the effectiveness of feedback."[7] In short, appropriate feedback improves the effectiveness of price signals.

The Feedback Approach

Feedback works through both motivational and informational effects.[8] First, it can improve performance of a task like energy conservation by drawing attention to any change in the gap between performance and goal. A decrease in the gap tends to reinforce motivation. An increase in the gap tends to motivate a person to try harder or persist longer so long as the goal is maintained. Second, feedback can improve performance not only by signaling *whether* there is a change in the discrepancy, but also *why*. Information that helps a person distinguish and understand the factors affecting performance can be used to adjust behavior to improve performance.

Both motivation and information may be necessary. Without motivation, information about how to improve performance is irrelevant to behavior; but without such information, a motivated person may become frustrated. It is important to recognize that such feedback as a comparison of consumption this month with consumption from the corresponding month a year ago may have both motivational and informational effects; and that feedback provided through monthly utility bills or other means is not the only source of motivation and information. Each consumer has predispositions, including motivations and information, that have a bearing on the effectiveness of feedback and consumer behavior.

A number of experiments in different settings by different researchers have shown that *frequent* (i.e., daily or weekly) feedback consistently helps consumers reduce their energy use as much as 10 or 20 percent. Better results tend to be realized when consumers accept explicit goals reflecting motivation levels and when feedback to the household is understandable and credible.[9] These experiments provide valuable insights into the evaluation and redesign of consumer feedback messages. A few of the major experiments are summarized below for this purpose. But first it is worthwhile to review the evidence that *monthly* feedback through utility bills or similar means can reduce energy consumption at reasonable cost in both experimental settings and practical appplications.

Simple Monthly Feedback: An Experiment
In an experiment conducted in 1976 with the cooperation of the Blackstone Valley Electric Company in Pawtucket, Rhode Island, re-

searchers selected twenty pairs of nonvolunteer households, each matched on a neighborhood basis.[10] The matched pairs were then randomly assigned to control and feedback groups of twenty each. Households in the control group received the normal monthly bill, and the company provided data on their electricity consumption to the researchers. Households in the feedback group received a letter from the company a few days after the normal monthly bill during the intervention period, February through May, 1976. The letter is reproduced in figure 1. It expresses consumption for the most recent month as a percent change relative to a baseline and points out the monetary consequences. For each month, the baseline is the average of the household's consumption for the same month in 1973 and 1974.

The results were expressed as the percent change from the baseline for the feedback and control groups over the preintervention, intervention, and postintervention periods, as summarized in table 1. For the control group, consumption relative to the baseline held rather

---

THIS IS NOT A BILL

Dear Consumer:

   With all the concern over energy conservation, we thought you might like to know whether you are consuming more or less electricity now than in previous years. Based on our records for this address over the last three years, your consumption of electricity this last month was:

____% below previous years. Congratulations! You are saving energy.

____% above previous years.

(For those of you who would like more detail, this last month you consumed ____ kwh of electricity, compared to the previous average of ____ kwh. At today's prices, this means you saved/spent about an extra $____.)

FIG. 1.   A letter for a simple monthly feedback experiment. (From Steven C. Hayes and John D. Cone, "Reduction of Residential Consumption of Electricity Through Simple Monthly Feedback," *Journal of Applied Behavior Analysis* 14, no. 1 [Spring, 1981].)

TABLE 1.   Results of Simple Monthly Feedback Experiment

Group	Period		
	Preintervention[a]	Intervention[b]	Postintervention[c]
Feedback	6.5%	−4.7%	11.3%
Control	2.2	2.3	−0.3
Difference	4.3	7.0	11.6

Source: Adapted from Steven C. Hayes and John D. Cone, "Reduction of Residential Consumption of Electricity Through Simple Monthly Feedback," *Journal of Applied Behavior Analysis* 14, no. 1 (Spring, 1981).

Note: Consumption is expressed as a percent change from baseline consumption (the average over 1973 and 1974) for each combination of group and period.

a. January, 1975, through January, 1976
b. February, 1976, through May, 1976
c. June, 1976, through August, 1976

steady over the three periods with a slight drop in the postintervention period. For the feedback group, consumption dropped sharply in the intervention period. The apparent effect of simple monthly feedback is even more enhanced when the percent change scores of the control group are subtracted from those of the feedback group in order to control for possible climate-related variables. The experimental design controls for the obvious alternatives to the interpretation that the feedback letter resulted in reduced electricity consumption of 4.7 percent to 7.0 percent.

If one assumes that consumption relative to the baseline by the feedback group would have continued at 6.5 percent through the intervention period in the absence of feedback, the dollar savings from reduced electricity consumption was about five times the dollar cost of preparing and mailing the feedback letters. There is no guarantee that results of this magnitude can be replicated elsewhere, since differences in predispositions and other circumstances matter. Moreover, the significance of various parts of the letter, the letter format, and the postintervention increase in feedback group consumption remain unclear. Nevertheless, these results are encouraging as to the costs and benefits of simple monthly feedback.

Simple Monthly Feedback: Practical Applications
A number of utilities have revised bills to improve energy feedback to their customers.[11] Although details are often lacking, these applica-

tions shed further light on the feasibility, costs, and benefits of simple monthly feedback.

The comparative use indicator adopted by the Atlantic City (New Jersey) Electric Company in 1974 is an unusually well documented and instructive case.[12] It consisted of the following message printed by computer on residential customers' bills: YOU USED XX PER CENT LESS [or MORE] ENERGY THAN SAME PERIOD IN 1973. By May, 1974, when the comparative use indicator was fully implemented, 1974 residential consumption of electricity had dropped 4.6 percent below the 1973 level, while consumption nationwide had increased more than 3 percent. In March and April, before implementation, the trends in usage in Atlantic City roughly paralleled the national trends. Introduction of the indicator just after the 1973–74 oil embargo, when prices were increasing and interest was high, seems to have been an important factor in its effectiveness.

Atlantic City Electric estimated the direct cost of its comparative use indicator at about five hundred dollars, mostly for computer programming. More significant, however, were the costs of consumer inquiries and complaints. Because of insufficient prior publicity, the first mailing of bills with the comparative use indicator (about 5 percent of the total) more than doubled the normal number of customer inquiries. These were handled with existing staff using a computerized information system, and the number of inquiries dropped off quickly. More troublesome were consumer complaints. Some customers were concerned about what appeared to be "snooping" by the power company, and six objected so strongly that the message was removed from their bills. Fourteen customers insisted on meter tests to verify increases in consumption. Others were confused and angered by a notice that they had reduced consumption even though dollar costs had increased. This reflected rapid rate increases and the pervasive frustrations of the immediate postembargo period. Customer beliefs that they had been "ripped off" by the company led to cancellation of the comparative use indicator a year later. In 1979, a company spokesman reflected that it was a great idea introduced at the wrong time. Introduced with proper promotional material at any other time, it would have been a success, in his opinion.[13]

Other applications have avoided the operational problems experienced by Atlantic City Electric. For example, according to a staff member of the Michigan Public Service Commission, public response to Detroit Edison's Energy Use Report (which is similar to Atlantic City Electric's) has been favorable.[14] Aside from clarifying feasibility, effectiveness, and cost considerations, the Atlantic City Electric experience underscores the importance of explaining monthly utility bill feedback to customers and the timing of introduction.

Motivation, Information, and Message Design
An experiment during the peak summer cooling season in 1976 demonstrated the importance of the motivational aspect of feedback by inducing conservation goals.[15] One hundred families in a planned unit development in New Jersey were selected and randomly assigned to one of five groups. Families in one pair of groups were asked to adopt the difficult goal of reducing electricity consumption by 20 percent. Families in another pair of groups were asked to adopt the relatively easy goal of a 2 percent reduction. In each of the two pairs of groups, families in one group received feedback three times a week and families in the other did not. The fifth group was a control group; families in it were not asked to set a goal nor did they receive feedback.

The results show that, relative to the control group,

> The 20 percent goal group with feedback used 13 percent less electricity;
> The 2 percent goal group with feedback used 4.5 percent less;
> The 20 percent goal group without feedback used 1.3 percent less; and
> The 2 percent goal group without feedback used 1.2 percent *more* electricity.

The impressive results in the first group were attributed to the joint effect of feedback and a difficult goal to enhance motivation. It is worth noting, however, that the reduction in the second feedback group was 2.5 percent in excess of the easy goal.

The implication is not necessarily that local leaders should attempt to induce difficult goals as a complement to feedback, although this is an option. Some leaders might question whether inducing goals is an appropriate role and, if so, whether the goals would be accepted. The implication is that feedback at a minimum should help consumers formulate their own goals consistent with individual levels of motivation. Judging from this and other studies reviewed above, provision of a comparison against a baseline may produce acceptable if not maximal results.

A related experiment a year later at the same site in New Jersey demonstrated that feedback can be rendered uninformative and therefore ineffective if it is perceived to bear little relationship to consumer behavior.[16] The experiment was designed to test a simple light bulb signaling device as an alternative to feedback in written form. For comparative purposes, feedback was provided to part of the sample in written form alone, updated three times a week, as in the previous experiment. However, the method of calculating written feedback was simplified. Unexpectedly, the written feedback had no significant effect on electricity consumption. According to the investigators,

> Interviews conducted after the experiment revealed that most residents thought the feedback scores jumped around too much to be believable. They reported seeing little relationship between their conservation actions and the feedback scores. Consequently, the feedback was ignored. The credibility of feedback was not an issue in [previous] successful studies.[17]

Feedback was ineffective because the simplified calculations less reliably controlled for the effects of weather changes. It was also ineffective because the mode of presentation, a chart updated three times a week, made the instability of scores obvious.

One survey of these and related experiments summarizes the implications for the design of the feedback message.

> While goal-setting and [household-specific], credible information systems should be part of feedback tactics, the best type of information (kwh, percent change, cost) remains unclear. One guess is that any information that is sensitive to consumer efforts and is credible will probably work.[18]

Review of Local Utility Bills

Although utility bills are designed primarily for company accounting and billing purposes, they can be redesigned for consumer feedback purposes. As a step toward redesign, this section reviews examples of recent bills provided by Michigan Consolidated Gas Company and Detroit Edison, the utilities that serve Ann Arbor, from a consumer feedback perspective.

First, what information is provided to help a consumer assess energy cost reductions with respect to goals? Information that indicates what gas or electricity costs *would have been* without conservation efforts compared with *actual* costs can reinforce successful efforts or signal the need for new ones.[19] A historical baseline can be used to estimate what costs would have been without new conservation efforts, and also can be used by the consumer to clarify goals. Second, what information is provided to help a consumer understand the consequences of his or her actions in holding down energy costs? Information that adjusts for changes in other factors, such as weather and rates, enables the consumer to perceive the relationship between his or her own initiatives and changes in energy costs, and therefore to learn how to conserve more effectively.

The assumption here is that the most important and pervasive interest among energy consumers is to reduce or eliminate unnecessary energy costs. (Some consumers may be primarily interested in energy conservation for environmental, moral, or other reasons, including keeping up with the Joneses.) Energy costs, exclusive of sales tax, depend upon the level of consumption and the applicable rate schedule. The consumer can control the former but not the latter. Consequently, motivational and informational feedback with respect to consumption as well as to costs are considered in the reviews that follow.

Michigan Consolidated Gas Company Bills

Figure 2 provides an example of natural gas bills received each month by residential consumers in Ann Arbor. This May, 1980, bill gives consumption for the most recent service period, April 12 to May 15, as 104 ccf under *Units Used in 100 Cubic Feet*. The bill provides no baseline consumption figure for comparative purposes. Unless the consumer keeps and consults bill stubs from previous months or years, he or she has no reliable way of knowing whether gas use has increased or decreased. The single bill does not reinforce successful efforts nor does it signal the need for more effort.

The company schedules meter readings every other month, with

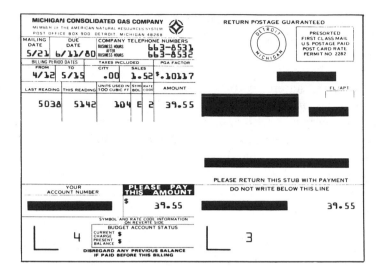

FIG. 2.   A recent example of a Michigan Consolidated Gas Company bill

estimated readings in the intervening months. Consequently, the number of units used on each monthly bill is based on at least one potentially inaccurate estimate. In the example in figure 2, the meter was read by the company when the account was opened in August, 1978, and only one time since, apparently because the meter is located in the basement and no one is normally home to admit the meter reader on work days. Apart from one missing record and five customer-supplied readings, the meter was estimated at the end of all other service periods. Since company estimates are necessarily a function of previous consumption levels at the same location, the relationship between new conservation efforts and subsequent changes in consumption is obscured until the next actual reading. Unless the consumer distinguishes between estimated and actual readings, understands the need to wait until the next actual reading, and has the patience to do so, the consumer's conservation efforts will have no apparent effect on consumption according to the bill, even if the efforts are successful.

The relationship between conservation initiatives and changes in gas consumption is further obscured by the absence of adjustments for complicating factors over which the consumer has no control. The length of the service period reported in the May, 1980, bill in the example is thirty-three days, while the length of the service period reported in the corresponding bill of the previous year was thirty days. If the same number of units were used per day in the two periods, and consumption in the two periods were compared, this factor alone would account for an apparent increase in consumption of 10 percent.

Differences in outdoor temperature also have a direct bearing on gas consumption.[20] Degree-days measure space heating load as a function of outdoor temperature.[21] The number of degree-days per day in the service periods reported in the May, 1980, and May, 1979, bills were 14.4 and 13.2, respectively. Based on records for this account through May, 1980, a difference of one degree-day is equivalent on average to a difference of about 0.16 ccf in gas use. Over a thirty-three day period, the difference in degree-days is about 39.5 and the expected difference in gas use is about 6.3 ccf. In other words, outdoor temperature differences account for an expected increase of about 3.4 percent in gas consumption in the current period over the previous period.[22]

Unless the consumer acquires the necessary data and makes the necessary calculations, effective conservation efforts tend to appear ineffective if the service period lengthens or the heating load increases. Conversely, ineffective efforts may appear to be effective when the service period shortens or the heating load decreases. In either case, the appearance is misleading, and complicates over time any attempt to learn from experience how to adjust consumption levels to consumption goals.

Now consider cost feedback. The cost of current consumption in the example in figure 2 is given as $39.55 under *Amount* and under *Please Pay This Amount*. (The latter is not necessarily the same as the cost of current consumption because it may include a previous balance, service call charges, and refunds.) No baseline is included to help the consumer set cost goals and compare them with current performance. Any feedback to boost motivation is, in effect, left to the consumer to develop.

The relationship between consumer conservation initiatives and changes in gas costs is obscured in part by meter estimates, differences in the length of service periods, and differences in outdoor temperatures. As we have seen, these affect the apparent relationship between conservation initiatives and changes in consumption, which in turn are components of changes in costs. The other components are changes in rates.

It is necessary to describe the current rate structure based on an opinion and order by the Michigan Public Service Commission in November, 1979.[23] The rate structure includes a service charge of $4 per service period, independent of the amount of gas consumed. The rate for the first 100 ccf is 22.491¢ per ccf, and the rate for each additional ccf is 25.491¢, or 3¢ more. This is an inverted block rate structure. It is designed to discourage excess consumption of gas by charging higher rates for higher "blocks" of consumption. (It applies only during the billing months of May through October; from November through April a three-block structure applies.) In addition, the effective rate includes a Purchased Gas Adjustment (or PGA) factor, which varies monthly according to the prices paid by the company to its suppliers. The PGA factor for May, 1980, is 10.177¢ per ccf, as shown in figure 2. In this example, the service charge, the first block of 100 ccf, the additional 4 ccf, and the PGA factor account for 10.5 percent, 59.1 percent, 2.7 percent, and 27.7 percent, respectively, of the total gas cost for May, exclusive of the 4 percent sales tax.

The relationship between consumer conservation initiatives and changes in gas costs tends to be obscured by rate increases. If consumption a year ago had dropped by 39 ccf to the 104 ccf reported in the May, 1980, bill, increases in rates would have been sufficient to cancel any apparent dollar savings.[24] In other words, a 27.3 percent decrease in gas use would make no apparent difference to the consumer who compared the cost of gas on the two bills, unless he or she is aware of changes in rates and adjusts accordingly.

The marginal rate is the component of the rate structure most sensitive to consumer behavior. The marginal rate is the price paid for the last unit of gas used. In May, 1979, the marginal rate consisted of a flat rate of 18.766¢ and a PGA factor of 5.209¢, a total of 23.975¢ per ccf. (Under the flat rate structure then in effect, each unit cost the same; consequently the marginal and average rates per ccf are the same.) In May, 1980, the marginal rate for 104 ccf consists of the 25.491¢ higher block rate and PGA factor of 10.117¢, a total of 35.608¢ per ccf. Marginal rates vary as the consumer moves from a lower to a higher rate block (or vice versa) as a result of changes in consumption; from the warm weather to cold weather rate schedule in

November; from the cold weather to warm weather rate schedule in May; and with occasional surcharges. For example, the Michigan Public Service Commission recently ordered a 0.495¢ surcharge to take effect in July, 1980.[25]

Although the PGA factor and sales tax are always printed on the front of the bill and the rate schedule is occasionally stamped on the back, full information on the price of gas is normally available to the consumer only if he or she writes for it. Natural gas and electricity are among the few products for which the full consumer price is not consistently and prominently displayed.

Detroit Edison Bills

Figure 3 presents an example of the electricity bills received by residential consumers in Ann Arbor in May, 1980. The bill indicates there were 493 kilowatt-hours used in the service period from April 3 to May 5, and that the current bill amounts to $29.16.

From the standpoint of cost feedback, there is little improvement over the gas bill. No baseline is provided to compare with the current

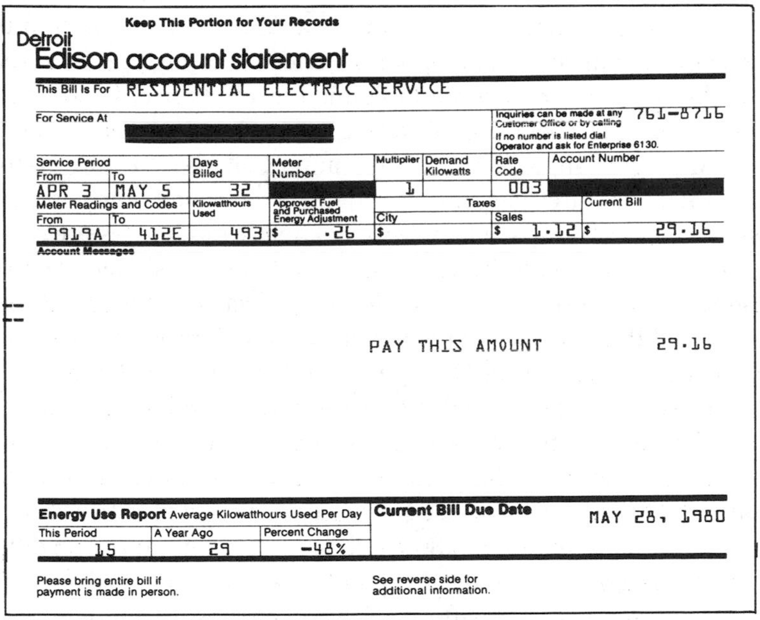

FIG. 3.   A recent example of a Detroit Edison bill

cost. Apart from consumption, there is no information on changes in the other factors which give rise to changes in cost, and which tend to be confounded with deliberate efforts to conserve. The bill received in April noted that new rates went into effect on March 15, but neither the new rates nor the old rates were given. The customer is merely notified each month that the rate code for residential electric service is 003 and (on the reverse side) that rate schedules are available on request. The approved fuel and purchased energy adjustment for the current period is given as twenty-six cents, but the change from the previous period or the corresponding period of the previous year is not.

From the standpoint of consumption feedback, there is a substantial improvement over the gas bill for the same period. Since early 1979 Detroit Edison bills have included an Energy Use Report now located in the lower left corner of the bill. In this example it informs the consumer that an average of 15 kwh per day were used in this period compared to 29 kwh a year ago, a 48 percent reduction. The apparent effect is to reinforce the motivation to conserve by drawing attention to the positive results—at least for those consumers who focus on use rather than cost. Expression of electricity use in kwh per day removes the confounding effects of variation in the length of the billing periods compared. The apparent effect is to highlight the relationship between conservation efforts and electricity use. Pending further research, a temperature adjustment for electricity use in southeastern Michigan appears to be less important than a temperature adjustment for natural gas use. Residential air conditioning is not a necessity and electric space heating is relatively rare in this area.

A closer look reveals, however, that the Energy Use Report can be sufficiently erratic over time to render it ineffective for feedback purposes. (Recall the unexpected results of the New Jersey electricity conservation experiment in 1977, reported above.) The problem can be traced to inaccurate scheduled meter estimates. Table 2 provides the relevant data by month for the periods since the account was opened. For each period over the first year of the account, an extremely high estimate of 900 kwh or more used per service period is followed by an extremely low amount of about 300 kwh or less. Month-to-month differences of this magnitude are not difficult for the consumer to detect, and are easily interpreted as a pattern of overestimates subsequently corrected by actual meter readings. The problem was reflected in the En-

TABLE 2. Example of Energy Use Report Data, 1978–80

| Service Month | 1978–79 | | | | | | 1979–80 | | | | | |
| | Service To | Days Billed | kwh Used | Average kwh Used per Day | | | Service To | Days Billed | kwh Used | Average kwh Used per Day | | |
				This Year	Year Ago	% Change				This Year	Year Ago	% Change
July							8–8	30	A 196	7	—	—
August	9–7	37	E1099				9–5	28	E 596	21	—	—
September	10–6	29	A 306				10–4	29	A 471	16	11	+45
October	11–6	31	E 939				11–2	29	E 499	17	30	−43
November	12–6	30	A 112				12–4	32	A 572	18	—	—
December	1–9	34	E 969				1–7	34	E 609	18	29	−38
January	2–6	28	A 139	5	—	—	2–4	28	A 484	17	—	—
February	3–7	29	E 954	33	29	+14	3–4	29	E 487	17	33	−48
March	4–6	30	A 35	1	—	—	4–3	30	A 549	18	—	—
April	5–8	32	E 928	29	33	−12	5–5	32	E 493	15	29	−48
May	6–7	30	A 27	1	25	−96						
June	7–9	32	E 906	28	—	—						

Source: Data from Detroit Edison bill stubs of household electrical use retained by an Ann Arbor consumer.
Note: The account was not opened until August, 1978. The Energy Use Report was initiated January, 1979. E is an estimated meter reading, A is an actual meter reading. Dashes in "year ago" and "% change" columns indicate no data reported.

ergy Use Report when it was initiated with the bill for January service through February 6, 1979. The computer billing program leaves blanks in the last two fields of the Energy Use Report in about half the bills, apparently because the percent change exceeds plus or minus 100 percent. In the remaining months, the percent change figures are based on two consumption figures, each of which is based on one highly inaccurate estimate. Thus the percent change figures bear little or no relationship to consumer behavior or actual consumption, and are therefore readily discounted as irrelevant by the consumer.

The problem will be remedied soon, however, although it provides an instructive lesson for other utilities. In March, 1980, the Michigan Public Service Commission adopted a proposal from Detroit Edison, supported by the commission staff and an administrative law judge, to provide for monthly meter reading of domestic service.[26] In a related action, the commission adopted a rule for a billing procedure that corrects for the number of days in the service period, which varies from about twenty-eight to thirty-five days.[27] Otherwise, with the inverted block electric rates now in use, the effect of a longer service period would be to move more of the kwh used into higher rate blocks. The result would be to penalize the consumer with higher and unwarranted electricity costs. Inaccurate meter estimates like those reported in table 2 have the same effect.

Summary and Conclusions
With the exception of Detroit Edison's Energy Use Report, the gas and electric bills now received by Ann Arbor households are not well designed for consumer feedback purposes. In terms of consumption feedback, the gas bill lacks a use comparison, an adjustment for changes in the length of the service period, and an adjustment for changes in outdoor temperature. In terms of cost feedback, both the gas and electric bills lack a cost comparison and an adjustment for rate changes that tend to obscure the dollar savings of conservation measures. Full rate information is neither consistently nor conveniently available in either case.

Redesigning Bill Information

In redesigning bill information for consumer feedback purposes, the major trade-off is "between the value of increasing information and the risks of distracting or confusing consumers."[28] The obvious constraints are the limited amount of space left on the bills and limits on the information already retained by the utilities. This section introduces an initial revision of the bills received by Ann Arbor energy consumers, and considers the design from the perspective of feasibility, costs, and benefits.

An Initial Design

A "Consumer Report," identical in form for both gas and electric bills, is suggested in figure 4. Since most Ann Arborites receive a bill from each company each month, the use of an identical form would simplify the process of explaining how to interpret and use the reports, and minimize confusion on the part of consumers.[29] The information specific to each household that would be printed by computer is underscored in figure 4. The figures used here for illustrative purposes are taken from the accounts discussed in the previous section. In effect,

Michigan Consolidated Gas

Consumer Report: Request Booklet for Details			
	This Month	Year Ago	% Change
Use per day in units of 100 cubic feet	3.3	5.6	-43%*
Marginal rate per unit	35.6¢	24.0¢	+48%

At today's rates, the savings resulting from your decrease in units used this month is $29.63.
*Differences in outside temperatures have tended to require about 3.4% more gas for home heating.

Detroit Edison

Consumer Report: Request Booklet for Details			
	This Month	Year Ago	% Change
Units used per day in kilowatt hours	15	29	-48%
Marginal rate per unit	6.32¢	5.36¢	+18%

At today's rates, the savings resulting from your decrease in units used this month is $26.28.

FIG. 4.   An initial design of consumer reports to supplement utility bills. The illustrative statistics are based in part on estimated rather than actual meter readings. (Form adapted in part from Fred D. Baldwin, "Meters, Bills, and the Bathroom Scale," *Public Utilities Fortnightly*, February 3, 1977, p. 15. Statistics derived from utility records retained by an Ann Arbor consumer and from degree-day data provided by the University of Michigan Department of Atmospheric and Oceanic Science.)

the Consumer Reports provide feedback information that could have been included in the sample bills reproduced in figures 2 and 3. Assume for purposes of illustration that the Consumer Reports are based on actual rather than estimated meter readings. Estimates are a problem to which we return later.

For energy consumption feedback, the reports incorporate Detroit Edison's Energy Use Report. In the case of the gas report, the 43 percent reduction in use is based on 104 ccf over thirty-three days in the 1980 service period and 167 ccf over thirty days in the 1979 service period. Adjusted to eliminate the 10 percent change in the length of service periods, the average use per day of 5.6 ccf a year ago works out to 184 ccf for a thirty-three day period. Also, the 3.4 percent increase in space heating load as a result of outdoor temperature differences suggests that the 43 percent reduction in use underestimates the effect of behavioral and structural changes initiated by the consumer.

The Consumer Reports thus adjust units used for variations in the length of service periods, and (in the case of gas) provide a percentage correction for differences in outdoor temperatures. These factors might otherwise obscure the relationship between consumer initiatives and changes in gas or electricity consumption. Moreover, the reductions in gas and electricity use (despite a slight increase in space heating load in the case of gas) provide some reinforcement for the conservation measures implemented. An increase in gas or electricity use, on the other hand, would have signaled a problem requiring action. Whether the effect is reinforcement, the signaling of a problem, or something in between, depends upon the goal the household has implicitly or explicitly set for itself. Feedback information merely helps the household formulate and realize such goals.

For energy cost feedback, the reports go beyond Detroit Edison's Energy Use Report. In the case of natural gas, the marginal rate of a ccf increased 48 percent from the 1979 service period to the 1980 service period. (The components of marginal rates in both periods were described in the previous section.) If gas use this year had dropped from the higher to the lower rate block—from more than 100 ccf to less—the marginal rate would therefore have dropped by three cents per ccf, and the percent change in the marginal rate would have dropped to +36 percent. While the marginal rate can be affected by consumer action, the service charge (which increased from $3.75 to $4.00 per month) cannot.

In addition, the Consumer Reports provide feedback on the dollar value of the change in consumption using current prices. If a consumer achieves a decrease in consumption this year compared to last year, he or she logically realizes savings over the amount that otherwise would have been paid, regardless of rate changes. In the case of natural gas, the 184 ccf used a year ago (adjusted for the difference in length of the service periods) would have cost $69.18 at May, 1980, prices. The decrease of 80 ccf translates into a savings of $29.63 over the actual amount paid for 104 ccf, $39.55. To a consumer unaware of rate changes and differences in the length of service periods, the apparent savings from a comparison of costs on the two bills would have been only $5.85. If the consumer had increased use this year compared to a year ago, the report would have indicated that "At today's prices, the *extra cost* resulting from your *increase* in units used this month is $XX.XX."

The Consumer Reports thus clarify for the consumer the relationship between conservation initiatives and changes in costs. Since the two key determinants of changes in costs—units used and marginal rate—are presented in the same format, the consumer can easily compare changes in their direction and magnitude. The use of marginal rates aggregates and summarizes compactly the relevant part of the rate schedule, monthly rate adjustments, and surcharges, as well as movement from one rate block to another. In addition, the sentence reporting dollar savings (or extra costs) controls for rate changes and highlights the effects of changes in use. Finally, motivational as well as informational effects are enhanced by the Consumer Reports. A message about the dollar savings of decreased use can be expected to reinforce and confirm the value of energy conservation measures; a message about the extra cost of increased use can be expected to signal a financial penalty and perhaps enhance the motivation to conserve. Requests for publications like *Tips for Energy Savers* might increase.

In a highly mobile setting such as Ann Arbor, the Consumer Reports would have more aggregate impact if applied by location or meter rather than by name of customer. Otherwise, the 40 percent of the city's population that moves in or out of town each year, and others who change location within the city, would not receive them.[30] Table 2 indicates that Detroit Edison's Energy Use Report is already applied by location since comparisons are made with the first half of 1978 when the account was in another name. In addition, the Consumer Reports would have more aggregate impact if sent to commercial as well as residential customers. The bill forms are the same in each case.

Estimates and Credibility

The initial design for a Consumer Report assumes that consumption figures are accurate. Otherwise, the feedback may be misleading or so erratic that it bears little relationship to consumer behavior and is therefore ignored. Under these circumstances, any potential payoff in terms of energy conservation would be foregone. The major problem in this connection is the use of scheduled meter estimates every other month by Michigan Consolidated Gas. (Detroit Edison, as we have seen, abandoned scheduled meter estimates in the summer of 1980.)

Doubling the number of gas meter readings per year would clearly be expensive. Nevertheless, a case can be made that the expense is worthwhile. Under the current gas rate schedule, a residential customer who used 100 ccf in each of two consecutive service periods would avoid the higher block rate. However, if the meter estimate between those two periods were either too high or too low, the effect of the estimate would be to push some of the 200 ccf used into the higher rate block. The result is an unwarranted surcharge proportional to the inaccuracy of the estimate.[31] How often this happens, and for how many customers, is an open question. But in the case of Detroit Edison, which has more experience with inverted block rates, the unwarranted surcharge generated customer complaints and was a factor in the Michigan Public Service Commission's decision to order monthly meter readings. It is possible that the additional costs to consumers of monthly meter readings would be repaid by savings from the elimination of the unwarranted surcharge and from use reductions resulting from improved feedback.

Unless or until the commission orders monthly readings of the meters of Michigan Consolidated Gas customers, it would be preferable from a consumer feedback perspective to avoid the loss of credibility. One alternative would be to use a Consumer Report similar in form to the initial design in figure 4 every month. It would cover a two-month period bracketed by consecutive meter readings, and would ignore the intervening estimate. Another alternative would be a Consumer Report radically redesigned to take advantage of the statistical properties of cumulative, year-to-date figures.[32] For example, year-to-date consumption and cost totals could be compared to the corresponding year-to-date totals from the previous year. Inaccurate estimates would thus be corrected every other month when the meter was read, and the magnitude of errors as a proportion of the cumulative total would diminish through the course of the year.

Feasibility, Costs, and Benefits
The initial design is feasible in terms of space constraints and the information available. There is ample space on the present form used by Detroit Edison (see fig. 3). The space remaining on the Michigan Consolidated Gas bill is limited but adequate if the parts of the Consumer Report not specific to a household were printed in small type as part of the form. (Detroit Edison's Energy Use Report was introduced on a form identical in size and similar in layout to the form presently used by Michigan Consolidated Gas.) Current consumption and cost information are of course available for each account since they are necessary for billing purposes. Both utilities keep a thirteen-month record of consumption and cost for each account in computer-readable form to respond to customer inquiries. Outdoor temperature data are collected and used to forecast and analyze variations in demand. In addition, the utilities have the expertise to modify computer programs, and computers to perform the necessary calculations for a single Consumer Report in microseconds. And of course a bill is sent to each customer each month in any case.

A consumer could develop his or her own energy feedback report, if the consumer looked up utility bills from a year ago, acquired the most recent degree-days data, consulted current rate schedules, and knew how to do the calculations. Perhaps some do. But in many cases, the effort required each month might exceed the effort required to prepare a federal income tax return each year. Such a substantial investment in time and expertise is not likely to be widespread, nor is it necessary or efficient given the resources already at the disposal of the utilities.

The additional direct costs of providing a Consumer Report similar to those in figure 4 depend upon details of the billing system in use. However, there are indications that such costs are modest, on the order of a few to several thousand dollars. The additional direct costs to Atlantic City Electric of its comparative use indicator were estimated at about five hundred dollars. According to one informal estimate, Detroit Edison's Energy Use Report required about eighty hours of a programmer's time, plus additional time for debugging the program and staff meetings.[33] A booklet or other explanatory material, which appears prudent in the light of the Atlantic City experience, would add to initial costs. Operating costs would consist primarily of additional computer processing time, assuming customer inquiries could be handled through facilities and personnel already in place. Both initial and operating costs would be borne by customers when included in the utilities' rate bases.

The economic benefits to consumers of providing a monthly feedback report depend upon the amount of unnecessary energy use voluntarily eliminated as a result of the report and the marginal rate. In recent years, residential energy consumers in Ann Arbor have used roughly 40 million ccf of natural gas and 200 million kwh per year.[34] A 1 percent reduction in gas use at the current marginal rate is worth about $142,000 on an annual basis. A 1 percent reduction in electricity use at the current marginal rate is worth about $126,000 on an annual basis. The longer the reduction is maintained, the larger the benefits. Although results obtained from consumer feedback in other settings are not necessarily transferable, the Blackstone Valley Electric experiment, the 1976 New Jersey experiment, and the Atlantic City Electric experience suggest that use reductions of 4 percent to 5 percent are not out of the question. The value of such reductions from the perspective of consumers, local energy self-reliance, national energy independence, and the two utilities that serve Ann Arbor may differ.

Institutional Framework

The city of Ann Arbor has no franchise agreements with Detroit Edison and Michigan Consolidated Gas, although understandings about most of the operations of the two utilities within the city's jurisdiction have been evolved in practice.[35] The matter of energy feedback to consumers has not been clarified simply because it has not come up until recently. The program options recommended for consideration by the Ann Arbor Energy Steering Committee include energy feedback as part of a residential retrofit program.[36]

The Energy Steering Committee, or one of its task forces, provides a forum for discussion of energy feedback options with knowledgeable representatives of the two utilities. Among the important topics that merit input from all parties are the following:

Operating experience regarding the relative frequency of unscheduled (and, for natural gas, scheduled) meter estimates

Improvements in the initial design suggested in figure 4

Expected costs of revising billing systems to provide monthly feedback to gas and electric customers

Expected benefits of providing such feedback

Possible inclusion of the commercial sector as well as the residential sector in a feedback program

If closer inspection confirms present indications that energy consumer feedback is an effective and inexpensive approach to energy conservation, a plan of action in the form of a recommendation to the Michigan Public Service Commission might be worked out and presented to the city council and to company officials.

Under state law, the Public Service Commission has regulatory authority over investor-owned utilities. This includes the specification of information on bills, an area which has been under active consideration by the commission and its staff.[37] In March, 1979, in connection with a Michigan Consolidated Gas rate case, the staff recommended a residential customer information system.

The system should provide the residential gas customer with comparative information on their own gas usage, adjusted for weather variations, and a number they can call to receive expert advice on measures to better control energy usage.

I believe such an information system will result in better understanding by the customer of his consumption and total bill. The system should provide better company/customer relations and in time reduce customer complaints concerning high bills. The Applicant, in my opinion, has the resources and experience to develop and implement such a residential customer information system.[38]

Reference was made to precedents, including Detroit Edison's Energy Use Report. The proposal was apparently rejected without comment in the commission's opinion and order in the case.[39]

In January, 1978, in connection with a Detroit Edison rate case, the staff proposed a revision in bill information similar to that suggested in figure 4. The proposal, as later summarized by the commission, was that Detroit Edison's

> bills to its residential customers be changed so as to state monthly consumption for the same period in the previous year for the same location; what the bill would have been, based on consumption the previous year and the percentage increase in unit electric prices from the previous year.[40]

In lieu of this proposal the commission adopted Detroit Edison's alternative, the Energy Use Report, which, as we have seen, provides consumption but not cost feedback, and no indication of rate changes.

In a subsequent case, the staff reported a favorable customer response to the Energy Use Report and suggested in addition

> that the Company should mail to their customers the rate schedules applicable to them at least once a year or within 60 days of a major rate order. Principal reason for this is to signal the customers the changes in rate design and rate levels on which they can appropriately base their consumption decisions.[41]

The commission agreed that "customers should be made aware periodically, and especially after a rate case, what their rate is and how it is designed in order to plan their consumption."[42] The commission ordered Detroit Edison to submit a sample letter or brochure to the staff for approval.

More generally, the adoption by the commission of higher rates for higher blocks of consumption is one indication of the commission's interest in reducing unnecessary energy use. Improvements in both consumption and cost feedback information and in the provision of rate information is a means of enhancing the effectiveness of such rate designs. Particularly in commission orders affecting Detroit Edison, the record demonstrates the evolutions of improvements in bill information for consumers.

Summary and Recommendation

Utility bills can be redesigned for consumer feedback purposes. In both experimental settings and practical applications, simple monthly feedback has been shown to be a feasible, relatively inexpensive, and effective way of helping consumers eliminate the unnecessary "fat" in their energy budgets.

A review of the gas and electric bills received by Ann Arbor consumers each month indicates several limitations from a feedback standpoint. In terms of energy costs, neither bill helps the consumer set cost goals and assess performance with respect to them; and neither illuminates the relationship between consumer conservation initiatives and changes in energy costs. The electricity bill is a substantial improvement over the gas bill in terms of energy use feedback.

This paper recommends that local utility bills be redesigned for consumer feedback purposes. An initial design for gas and electric Consumer Reports has been suggested as an addition to future bills. Even if such a design helped Ann Arborites reduce gas and electric use by only 1 percent, the dollar savings would exceed the cost of the new feedback many times over.

The Ann Arbor Energy Steering Committee provides a forum for developing the initial alternative in conjunction with representatives of the broader community and the utilities. If closer inspection confirms present indications that consumer feedback is an effective and inexpensive approach to energy conservation, a proposal in the form of a recommendation to the Michigan Public Service Commission might be worked out and presented to city council and company officials.

NOTES

This paper was extensively revised in July, 1980, from a draft written the previous year. Lawrence B. Mohr of the Institute of Public Policy Studies and Harry G. Broadman, now of Resources for the Future, provided helpful comments. Responsibility for statements made here is the author's alone.

1. Fred D. Baldwin, "Meters, Bills, and the Bathroom Scale," *Public Utilities Fortnightly,* February 3, 1977, pp. 11–17.
2. Federal Energy Administration, Office of Energy Conservation and

Environment, *Tips for Energy Savers,* FEA/D-76/513 (Washington, D.C.: Government Printing Office, 1977).

3. Baldwin, "Meters, Bills, and the Bathroom Scale," p. 11.

4. Richard A. Winett, Michael S. Neale, and H. Cannon Grier, "The Effects of Self-Monitoring and Feedback on Residential Electricity Consumption: Winter," *Journal of Applied Behavior Analysis* 12, no. 2 (Summer, 1979):173–84. A group of consumers who received instruction, a training package, recording sheets, a daily note on expected use, and weekly prompting turned out to be reliable and persistent readers of their own meters on a daily basis, and reduced electricity consumption by 7 to 8 percent. Reductions in use persisted after termination of the intervention phase of the experiment. Dr. Winett has kindly given the author a copy of the materials used in this experiment, which could be adapted for use in Ann Arbor by a neighborhood association as a self-help project.

5. Richard A. Winett and Michael S. Neale, "Psychological Framework for Energy Conservation in Buildings," *Energy and Buildings* 2 (1979):101–16. Winett and Neale report that "even when households were matched on occupant demographic characteristics, physical structure, and location (e.g., shade and sun) electricity use could differ two- or three-fold" (p. 109).

6. Winett and Neale, "Psychological Framework," distinguish information antecedent to conservation behavior (such as "tips" and appeals) from information on the consequences of behavior, and observe that "information and appeals seem to be ineffective, while consequence procedures are apparently quite effective" (p. 102).

7. Ibid., p. 109. For the understanding of price effects, the work of Herbert Simon provides a psychological alternative to neoclassical economics. See his Nobel Prize lecture, "Rational Decision Making in Business Organizations," *American Economic Review* 69 (September, 1979):493–513, and "Rationality as Process and as Product of Thought," *American Economic Review* 68 (May, 1978):1–16.

8. See Winett and Neale, "Psychological Framework," on goal setting, credibility, and the knowledge gap in the section on feedback; Paul Stern and Gerald T. Gardner, "A Review and Critique of Energy Research in Psychology," *Social Science Energy Review* 3 (Spring, 1980):1–71, at p. 19; and Lawrence J. Becker, "Joint Effects of Feedback and Goal Setting on Performance: A Field Study of Residential Energy Conservation," *Journal of Applied Psychology* 63 (1978):428–33, at p. 428.

9. Winett and Neale, "Psychological Framework," p. 109.

10. Steven C. Hayes and John D. Cone, "Reduction of Residential Consumption of Electricity Through Simple Monthly Feedback," *Journal of Applied Behavior Analysis* 14, no. 1 (Spring, 1981):81–88.

11. Detroit Edison's Energy Use Report is described in the next section. The Pacific Gas and Electric Company (California) employs a tabular comparative use indicator similar to Detroit Edison's. The Seattle City Light

computer-generated message is more succinct: "XXXX KWH USED YEAR AGO 'USE ENERGY WISELY'." The Connecticut Light and Power Company includes a weather factor: "ENERGY USAGE NOTE [/] YOU USED XX% MORE KWH PER DAY THIS PERIOD THAN IN THE COMPARABLE PERIOD LAST YEAR AND IT WAS YY% COLDER THIS YEAR." The Southern Connecticut Gas Company mails an updated report to each of its customers every four months. The report identifies billing periods over the last year and lists for each the number of days; hundred cubic feet of natural gas used; metering (estimate refers to scheduled estimate; reading refers to actual company reading); and degree-days. It also gives a heating score for the entire period with a note that "If you get a higher score your use will have become more efficient." The Connecticut Light and Power utility bill feedback is evaluated in Marketing Services Company, Inc., "RECIP Program Study," mimeographed (Hartford: Connecticut Light and Power Company, 1979). This is a survey study that does not include data on actual consumption from meter readings.

12. Kurt W. Riegel and Suzanne E. Salomon, "Getting Individual Customers Involved in Energy Conservation: A Printed Comparative Energy Use Indicator on Customer Bills?" *Public Utilities Fortnightly,* November 7, 1974, pp. 29–32.

13. Phone conversation with Matt Custer, head of public relations, Atlantic City Electric Company, January 23, 1979.

14. Dr. Hasso C. Bhatia, Director, Office of Tariff Analysis, Michigan Public Service Commission, in testimony in Detroit Edison's Case No. U-6006, 1979.

15. Becker, "Joint Effects of Feedback and Goal Setting."

16. Lawrence J. Becker and Clive Seligman, "Reducing Air Conditioning Waste by Signalling it is Cool Outside," *Personality and Social Psychology Bulletin* 4 (July, 1978):412–15.

17. Becker and Seligman, "Reducing Air Conditioning Waste," p. 415.

18. Winett and Neale, "Psychological Framework," p. 10.

19. The logic of comparing what did happen with what would have happened is reviewed in Patrick D. Larkey, *Evaluating Public Programs* (Princeton: Princeton University Press, 1979), pp. 28–40.

20. Lawrence S. Mayer and Yoav Benjamini, "Modeling Residential Demand for Natural Gas as a Function of the Coldness of the Month," *Energy and Buildings* 1 (1977/78):301–12.

21. Degree-days are the average of the daily maximum and minimum temperature in degrees Fahrenheit, subtracted from 65° F, and then summed over the days in a given period. If the average of the maximum and minimum temperature for a day is greater than or equal to 65° F, the number of degree-days for that day is zero.

22. That is, 6.3 ccf is 3.4 percent of 184 ccf, the average consumption per day a year ago adjusted to a thirty-three-day service period length. Recall

that the consumption data used here for illustrative purposes are based on estimated rather than actual meter readings.

23. Michigan Public Service Commission, "Opinion and Order, Case No. U-5955," mimeographed (November 6, 1979). The residential rates given in appendix A have since been increased, but the structure remains the same. Current rates are used in the text of this paper.

24. 143 ccf at May, 1979, rates cost the same as 104 ccf at May, 1980, rates.

25. Michigan Public Service Commission, "Order Granting, In Part, Motion for Partial and Immediate Relief, Case No. U-6372," mimeographed (July 1, 1980).

26. Michigan Public Service Commission, "Opinion and Order, Case No. U-6006," mimeographed (March 14, 1980), p. 125.

27. Ibid., pp. 125–27.

28. Baldwin, "Meters, Bills, and the Bathroom Scale," p. 13.

29. According to a recent survey, 73 percent of a probability sample of Ann Arborites reported that their main source of heating fuel is natural gas, and 70 percent reported that they paid directly for their heat and electricity use. See Michigan Department of Commerce, Energy Administration, "PACES: Public Awareness Campaign Evaluation Survey; Report on Survey of Ann Arbor Residents," mimeographed (December, 1979), p. 33.

30. Chong W. Pyen, "Mobility Outdates City Planning Data," *Ann Arbor News,* May 10, 1979.

31. To illustrate the cost implications of inaccurate estimates in the case of electricity, refer to the service periods for December, 1978, and January, 1979, in table 2. The amounts billed for these two months were $51.29 and $8.78, respectively, for a total of $60.07. On the assumption that the two-month consumption of 1108 kwh was equally distributed between the two service periods, the two-month total cost would have been $3.46 (or 5.8 percent) less than the total amount actually paid. Of this $3.46, $1.45 can be attributed to the transfer of more kwh into a higher rate block; $1.88 can be attributed to the difference in the fuel and purchased power adjustment between the two billing periods; and the remaining $.13 is the increased sales tax. This calculation ignores the difference in the length of the two billing periods.

32. For a discussion of this alternative see Baldwin, "Meters, Bills, and the Bathroom Scale," pp. 14–15.

33. From a meeting with three employees of Detroit Edison in its Ann Arbor office, May 7, 1979.

34. From data supplied to the Local Energy Policy Seminar by Michigan Consolidated Gas and Detroit Edison.

35. In the *Ordinances of the City of Ann Arbor,* the city clerk's office could find only two franchise agreements approved June 2, 1884, and October 6, 1884, granting privileges to electric companies that no longer exist.

36. City of Ann Arbor, Office of Community Development, *1980 Energy Plan* (Ann Arbor: Office of Community Development, 1980), p. C-4.

37. Under the Public Utilities Regulatory Policies Act of 1978 (Public Law 95-617), each state regulatory authority is required to conduct hearings on standards of information for utility customers. Michigan Public Service Commission, "Opinion and Order, Case No. U-6006," notes on pp. 130–31 that an act of the state legislature, 1975 PA 317 (MCLA 429.355), "provides for the Commission to require utilities to periodically inform customers of their rates."

38. Mr. Wilbur McNinch of the commission staff in testimony in Michigan Consolidated Gas Case No. U-5955.

39. Michigan Public Service Commission, "Opinion and Order, Case No. U-5955," notes on p. 77 that "all contentions and proposed findings of the parties not herein specifically determined are hereby rejected."

40. Michigan Public Service Commission, "Opinion and Order, Case No. U-5502," mimeographed (September 28, 1978), p. 118.

41. See note 14.

42. Michigan Public Service Commission, "Opinion and Order, Case No. U-6006," p. 132.

7 A Community Energy Report

Ronald D. Brunner and Diane Sable

Households vary widely in levels of energy consumption. Some structures are tighter, better insulated, and more efficiently equipped than others, of course, but the behavior of the occupants also matters. One veteran builder underscored the range of behavioral variation when he reported

> the [personal] experience of having identical townhouses with common walls and seeing the utility bill for exactly the same number of square feet, same amount of windows, facing in the same direction, and the same insulation and the bills differ by a factor of 3 to 1.[1]

Whether structural or behavioral in origin, the existence of such wide variations in energy consumption across similar households suggests that some households use "too much" energy. If household members are unaware of this situation, they have little reason to take the first step toward practical energy conservation measures. The result is that the potential benefits of improved energy efficiency to both the household and the community are postponed or foregone.

The question of how much is "too much" is not only important but also difficult to answer.[2] More informative utility bills might provide the members of the household with a partial answer. Current electricity or natural gas consumption might be found to be too much with respect to the consciences of household members, the household budget, or energy consumption a year ago. But a household might also be satisfied on these grounds and still turn out to be consuming far more than similar households. Community norms are among the relevant answers to the question of how much is "too much." But in Ann Arbor, at least, these norms are largely undefined and known only very approximately (if at all) through conversations with friends and neighbors.

This study develops and recommends a community energy report to provide timely and reliable information on household energy consumption levels in Ann Arbor, and to encourage households to consider periodically whether they are using "too much" energy relative to others in the community. The basic idea is to collect data on the consumption of the main forms of energy—gasoline, electricity, and natural gas[3]—from a sample of Ann Arbor households, and to circulate the results to the rest of the community through monthly articles and updates published in the *Ann Arbor News* and other media.[4] The purpose is to stimulate, inform, and sustain the clarification of community energy consumption norms.

"Social norms are rules for conduct. The norms are the standards by reference to which behavior is judged and approved or disapproved."[5] A report on, say, median consumption of gasoline in Ann Arbor automobiles last month is not a social norm, but a means of developing and clarifying norms. Of course median consumption levels change from month to month and differences in household circumstances are worth taking into account. But a motorist who used more than the median number of gallons might conclude this was "too much" and take steps to cut back. A motorist who used less than the median amount might feel good about it and perhaps tell others. Responses such as these define standards of reduced energy consumption, just as "keeping up with the Joneses" defines standards of conspicuous consumption. Through a community energy report, norms would be shaped by those who volunteer data and those who consider, discuss, and otherwise act on the results. Participation is voluntary.

A community energy report can play a distinctive and useful role in efforts to conserve energy. Like a public relations campaign, a community energy report can generate publicity and, under favorable circumstances, energy awareness. "Don't Be 'Fuelish' " and similar slogans from national sources have not been effective, and have generated some skepticism and resistance.[6] Whether appeals from local sources would be more effective is as yet unclear. In contrast to most conservation slogans, a community energy report relies more on information and education than exhortation. With a report, community leaders need not presume to know what individual households should do about energy consumption, and exhort them to do it. Rather, those households that discover through the report that they are using "too much" energy and wish to reduce excess consumption can turn to existing services for energy conservation information and financing. Such services might otherwise remain underutilized. Encouraging and enabling people to ask the question, "how much is too much?" is a first step toward helping them eliminate whatever unnecessary consumption exists.

Like mandatory standards, the community norms that might arise under favorable circumstances from an energy report could motivate people to reduce energy consumption. In contrast to mandatory standards, however, a community energy report respects the option of households to conserve or not, according to their own assessments of needs and opportunities. Partly for this reason, a report is easier to adopt than mandatory standards in the absence of energy shortages. In the event of an energy shortage, accurate information on community energy consumption provides the basis for the adoption of realistic standards and for widespread compliance.

The next section reviews some reasons why a community energy report is worth consideration as a component of local energy policy. Subsequent sections develop an initial design for an Ann Arbor energy report, and consider how to implement it on a pilot basis. A final section provides conclusions and recommendations.

A Rationale

So far as we can determine, no community has implemented a community energy report of the kind proposed here. The approach, in short, is untested. Nevertheless, a number of indirect considerations suggest that such a report can be an effective instrument of household energy conservation, and how it might be designed to enhance probable effectiveness. Among these considerations are some community experiences of partial relevance, theory, and circumstances in Ann Arbor.

Community norms arising from local publicity and the comparison of household utility bills can be an effective instrument of energy conservation. The 18 percent per capita reduction in residential energy consumption in Davis, California, within several years after 1973 illustrates the point. The Davis achievement cannot be attributed to rising energy prices, since rates paid in Davis were the same as rates paid in nearby communities where per capita residential energy consumption increased over the same period. The achievement is often but erroneously attributed to the direct effects of the Davis energy conservation building code that went into effect in January, 1976. One participant set the record straight in congressional testimony. He noted that

> the publicity that has occurred in Davis that has gotten the citizenry more energy-conscious, has saved most of that 18 percent.
>
> The fact of the matter is that the number of new houses built under the energy code as compared to the total housing in Davis is probably somewhere around 5 percent, so if the new houses used zero [energy], that wouldn't account for anything like 18 percent.
>
> There is a great deal of discussion in the press and among people—there are people in Davis whose favorite recreation is comparing utility bills.[7]

The comparison of utility bills reflects and reinforces the formation of energy consumption norms, as well as their application.

Publicity arising from the controversy that led to the adoption of the ordinance in Davis, rather than the ordinance itself, appears to have stimulated the norm formation process. From a theoretical standpoint, it is significant that the issue as presented to the public focused attention on the direct, immediate implications for households (in contrast to national energy issues); and that the issue engaged informal social groups through spontaneous conversations and organized social groups through scheduled presentations, as well as local news media. Face-to-face contacts are highly influential in most circumstances. The process of norm formation was informed by consumption and cost figures provided through utility bills, which facilitated comparisons across households. A community-wide point of reference for purposes of comparison could have been provided by a community energy report. In the absence of such a report, the theoretical expectation is that cues or reference points were taken from the more respected members of various groups. The norm formation process was sustained over a sufficient period of time by the duration of the controversy. It lasted for more than four years from the introduction of the proposal in May, 1973. What happened in Davis was not an aberration, but a convergence of circumstances that effectively engaged quite general processes of norm formation.[8]

One question is whether the appropriate circumstances exist in other communities. Of major importance is the intensity of motivations. Lower consumption norms are the more specific and socially imperative embodiments of the motivations that sustain the norm formation process. In Davis, these included dollar savings, environmental concerns, and moral injunctions against waste.[9] Communities differ in the intensity of motivations that might be tapped and crystallized in the form of lower energy consumption norms. It should be noted, however, that energy price increases in excess of general price increases have intensified the motivation to save dollars since the Davis experience. All communities have the means to compare energy consumption and costs through the use of utility bills and channels of communication within and among overlapping social groups of various degrees of organization. Communication potential, like intensity of motivation, is a matter of degree.

Another question is whether a community energy report, as a substitute for controversy, can effectively tap whatever potential exists in order to initiate, inform, and sustain the norm formation process. Initial attention can be enhanced by simultaneous introduction through a number of communication channels, including civic groups, and by introducing the report at a time when interest is relatively high. In climates such as southeastern Michigan, interest in space heating costs tends to surge with the first cold spell in the fall. Interest tends to peak during energy shortages. A report can be made more informative by focusing on the consumption levels from which norms can be developed, by being specific about conservation practices, and by presenting this information in an attractive and readable way. Aggregate statistics supplemented by examples sufficiently specific to serve as models for others are means of meeting these requirements. Finally, a report can help sustain the norm formation process by drawing attention to successful examples of household energy conservation and to the net benefits of energy conservation to the community as a whole.[10]

The failure of an energy index suggests an approach to avoid. According to one source,

> Allegheny County [Pennsylvania] had little response to their Daily Energy Index, which compared current consumption to consumption in 1976/77. The county stopped computing the figure when the local news media stopped carrying it, apparently due to lack of interest.[11]

The daily index was an aggregate of several forms of energy expressed in British thermal units, or Btus.[12] As such, it was a radical departure from the ways in which energy consumption is experienced by individual citizens. Most of us experience energy consumption in terms of nondaily purchases of specific fuels: gasoline bought at the pump every week or so, monthly natural gas and electric bills. Interest and comprehension can be enhanced by adapting a community energy report to the prior experience of the audience.

The city of Ann Arbor has received a grant from the Energy Administration of the Michigan Department of Commerce to develop and conduct a Local Energy Conservation Public Awareness Campaign as a model for other Michigan communities. The assumption is that information disseminated to the public can make a difference in energy consumption. Both a conventional public relations campaign and a community energy report would be constrained by the motivational and communication potential existing in the community. As the first phase of the project, the Public Awareness Campaign Evaluation Survey (PACES) conducted in December, 1979, reveals that generally less than a third of the respondents agree on any particular response to most opinion items. In this sense, opinion appears to be largely unstructured despite the volume of official exhortations to conserve since the 1973–74 oil embargo. For the question, "From which *person* or *organization* do you think you can get the *most believable* information about energy?" the response that attracted the highest percentage of respondents, 19 percent, was "Nowhere/No one." The next highest response, 14 percent, was "Private Sources/Individual Organizations."[13] It may be that circumstances are sufficiently favorable to take a chance on a community energy report, based on education rather than exhortation, and on information from households in the community rather than public officials.[14]

As part of the program, a community energy report could be an innovative means of enhancing and sustaining energy awareness, and of reducing unnecessary energy consumption. Those Ann Arborites who discover consumption levels above community norms could be directed to the clearinghouse for energy conservation information, which is already under discussion. Their conservation measures eventually would be reflected in the report as lower consumption levels, encouraging still others to take the first steps. This approach does not require community leaders to presume to tell Ann Arborites in general that they should conserve. Rather, it increases households' incentives and ability to do so according to their own assessments of particular needs and opportunities. If mandatory cutbacks should ever become necessary as a result of energy shortages, a community energy index would provide a foundation of shared information and consent to do so efficiently and effectively.[15] Whether such effects as these would be sufficiently large to repay the effort cannot be reliably known short of implementation on a pilot basis.

An Initial Design

As already noted, the proposed report would be based on household energy records of a sample of Ann Arbor households, with the results circulated to the rest of the community through a monthly update and accompanying article in the *Ann Arbor News* and other media. This section considers, in turn, the development of sample statistics from household energy records; presentation of the results in the form of a graph; and articles to supplement the updated graph each month.

Data and Statistics
The construction of the proposed report begins with the records of individual households. As an illustration, consider the records of a two-person household on the near west side in Ann Arbor. The records for gasoline, electricity, and natural gas for 1978–79 are given in table 1.

The gasoline data are compiled from a log updated by household members each time they purchase gasoline. The end date is the date of the last purchase of the month. Miles is the difference between odometer reading at consecutive end date purchases. Units in gallons and costs in dollars are summed over purchases within the month. As a result of these conventions, the figures are only approximate for any given month. To take the most extreme example, the figures for January, 1979, refer to the period December 26 to January 10. It would be possible to estimate the actual number of units and costs for the calendar month, but only at great increase in data handling costs. As can be seen in table 1, the end dates provide a reasonable approximation to thirty-day periods corresponding to calendar months.

With the exception of degree-days, the electricity and natural gas

TABLE 1. An Example of Household Energy Records, 1978–79

	Gasoline			Electricity				Natural Gas			
Month	Date	End Miles	Units (gal.)	Cost ($)	End Date	Deg. Days	Units (kwh)	Cost ($)	End Date	Deg. Days	Units (ccf)	Cost ($)
July 1978	7–28	489	15.7	9.35	8–8	23	171	9.12	8–9	23	13	5.71
August	8–28	170	5.8	3.55	9–11	2	230	11.12	9–10	2	24	8.12
September	9–26	489	14.7	9.13	10–9	233	168	9.95	10–9	233	39	11.59
October	10–27	228	11.4	7.10	11–7	474	268	15.68	11–9	517	64	18.08
November	11–28	331	14.1	9.00	12–7	917	246	14.07	12–7	874	96	25.14
December	12–26	212	8.4	5.66	1–10	1,459	304	17.37	1–8	1,344	141	30.31
January 1979	1–10	193	8.8	6.10	2–7	1,291	235	12.94	2–8	1,462	128	32.69
February	2–25	64	2.8	2.00	3–9	1,301	186	11.54	3–9	1,246	130	32.84
March	3–23	201	6.6	4.70	4–9	890	248	14.50	4–9	890	81	22.19
April	4–25	206	8.0	6.10	5–9	463	395	23.11	5–8	463	61	19.05
May	5–30	219	7.9	6.35	6–8	207	204	12.59	6–8	207	37	13.25
June	6–27	275	8.8	7.50	7–10	84	718	37.61	7–9	84	28	10.96
July	7–20	247	7.7	7.25	8–8	2	186	12.13	8–9	2	25	10.24
August	8–30	317	11.8	11.44	9–10	69	616	33.09	9–9	69	29	11.64
September	9–20	120	3.8	3.75	10–10	224	236	14.63	10–9	200	24	10.32
October	10–25	314	10.8	10.50	11–12	680	382	21.18	11–8	570	67	23.50
November	11–27	310	12.3	12.35	12–11	809	249	15.09	12–7	822	62	22.82
December	12–22	265	10.0	10.25	1–14	1,254	377	20.09	1–7	1,092	95	32.66

Source: Energy use data supplied by an Ann Arbor consumer. Degree-day data provided by the University of Michigan Department of Atmospheric and Oceanic Science.

data are taken from utility bill stubs retained by the household. The end dates are the dates of consecutive meter readings, actual or estimated, provided by Detroit Edison and Michigan Consolidated Gas. Here again, the figures only approximate the actual calendar month. The electricity figures for August, 1978, for example, cover the period from August 8 to September 11. They are expressed as August figures since the majority of days in this period (twenty-three of thirty-four) falls within the month of August. Each utility company tends to read or estimate a particular household's meter on approximately the same day each month. It is a coincidence that both companies adopted billing periods from approximately the ninth of one month to the ninth of the next for this particular household.

Degree-day data for each billing period are computed from daily temperature observations taken at the North Campus and supplied by the University of Michigan Department of Atmospheric and Oceanic Science. Degree-days measure heating load for a given period. They are the average of the daily maximum and minimum temperatures in degrees Fahrenheit, subtracted from 65° F, and then summed over the days in the period. As can be seen in table 1, degree-days are closely related to natural gas consumption by month, but only weakly related to electricity consumption. In the latter case, the relationship may be spurious. For a sample in which air conditioners predominate, cooling degree days might be substituted for heating degree days to measure air conditioning loads.

Using the same conventions and similar data from other households, a composite summary of consumption for each form of energy can be constructed for a sample of households. Table 2 illustrates the results for gasoline. The data refer to gasoline consumption in five automobiles operated by four Ann Arbor households. (Gasoline consumption by the household represented in table 1 is listed as automobile D in table 2.)

Median and upper and lower quartiles are the statistics used to summarize the sample data for each month. By definition half the sample of automobiles used more than the median number of gallons per month, and half used less. A quarter of the sample used *less* than the *lower* quartile number of gallons, and a quarter used *more* than the *upper* quartile number. The difference between the upper and lower quartiles is called the interquartile range. If the automobiles in the

TABLE 2.   Composite Summary of Gasoline Consumption, in Gallons, 1978–80

Month	Automobile					Median and Quartiles		
	A	B	C	D	E	Lower	Median	Upper
July 1978	11.5	85.6	68.9	15.7	39.9	15.7	39.9	68.9
August	29.1	107.4	41.9	5.8	20.8	20.8	29.1	41.9
September	38.5	89.5	65.6	14.7	10.3	14.7	38.5	65.6
October	35.3	86.2	55.9	11.7	20.6	20.6	35.3	55.9
November	25.9	65.2	74.2	14.1	29.6	25.9	29.6	65.2
December	41.2	70.8	83.7	8.4	21.5	21.5	41.2	70.8
January 1979	27.5	87.6	68.2	8.8	20.9	20.9	27.5	68.2
February	23.8	106.8	64.8	2.8	21.6	21.6	23.8	64.8
March	28.3	112.4	63.1	6.6	31.6	28.3	31.6	63.1
April	42.9	40.2	66.4	8.0	20.9	20.9	40.2	42.2
May	29.4	69.6	67.1	7.9	19.9	19.9	29.4	67.1
June	32.2	41.5	67.1	8.8	26.2	26.2	32.2	41.5
July 1979	20.0	77.6	66.3	7.7	98.8	20.0	66.3	77.6
August	31.9	107.5	48.1	11.8	19.5	19.5	31.9	48.1
September	18.8	68.5	69.1	3.8	17.9	17.9	18.8	68.5
October	20.4	34.9	82.5	10.8	20.7	20.4	20.7	34.9
November	18.2	42.6	64.3	12.3	21.4	18.2	21.4	42.6
December	29.1	32.9	93.9	10.0	20.4	20.4	29.1	32.9

Source: Data supplied by four Ann Arbor households.
Note: Underscored figures represent the median value for each month.

sample are ranked by gallons used, the middle half used an amount that falls within this range.[16]

Measures such as these, based on positions rather than averages, are less affected by extreme cases and therefore more stable. For example, in table 2, the extreme high value of 107.4 gallons used in automobile B in August, 1978, could have been as low as 42 gallons without affecting the upper quartile value for the sample; and the extreme low of 5.8 gallons used in automobile D in the same month could have been as high as 20 gallons without affecting the lower quartile. Moreover, atypical values are ameliorated by changes in relative position. As indicated by the underscored medians in table 2, automobile A is typically the median case. But in those months in which significantly more or less than the typical amount of about 30 gallons was used in automobile A, it is displaced as the median case by another automobile in the sample.

Such positional measures from a larger sample would make it easy for an Ann Arbor motorist with a gasoline log to discover where his or her gasoline consumption stands with respect to others. The possibilities go beyond the simple insight that the motorist used more or less gasoline than half the sample, since the interquartile range permits judgments about *how much* more or less *relative* to the rest of the sample. For instance, a motorist who commutes a long distance each workday might be satisfied to keep consumption between the median and the upper quartile. Another motorist who can usually walk or bike to work might be upset if consumption rises above the lower quartile. Such differences in circumstances matter and can be accommodated in a supplementary article, even if they are not represented directly in basic sample statistics. Nevertheless, these positional measures provide for some interesting initial answers to the question, "how much is too much?"

Graphic Presentation

The summary measures in table 2 are not in the most effective form for communicating with a large audience. The basic objectives in designing a more suitable form of presentation are to (1) highlight the most important information, (2) provide additional information for purposes of interpretation, and (3) to do so in an attractive and readable way. (The next section takes up a fourth objective, minimizing the costs of preparing the report.) The task is to use such technical devices as graphs, boxes, arrows, shading, and the like, to realize these objectives. Some compromises are necessarily involved because the objectives are not entirely compatible and because the available technical devices are limited.

Figure 1 presents an illustrative initial design for a community energy report on gasoline, based on the data in table 2. Figure 1 is visually complicated for two reasons. First, it incorporates close to the maximum amount of information one would attempt to put into a single graph. It is easier to improve an initial design by deleting information than by adding new information, as we shall see below. Second, the figure is based on only five cases. With a larger sample, the systematic components of the data would be enhanced relative to the random components, thus improving visual attractiveness and readability.

Figure 1 indicates median consumption of gasoline for July,

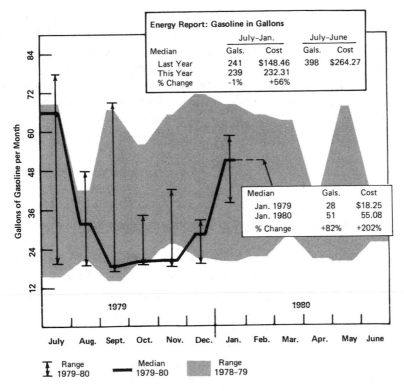

Energy Report: Gasoline in Gallons

	July–Jan.		July–June	
Median	Gals.	Cost	Gals.	Cost
Last Year	241	$148.46	398	$264.27
This Year	239	232.31		
% Change	-1%	+56%		

Median	Gals.	Cost
Jan. 1979	28	$18.25
Jan. 1980	51	55.08
% Change	+82%	+202%

Range 1979–80	Median 1979–80	Range 1978–79

FIG. 1. An initial design for an illustrative community energy report for gasoline. Shaded area indicates the interquartile range for the previous year. Arrows indicate the interquartile range for the current year. (Data from table 2.)

1979, through January, 1980. January's total consumption figures, fifty-one gallons, are given at the right of the median line, along with additional information for interpreting this figure. There has been an 82 percent increase over the twenty-eight gallons used by the median car in January of the previous year. At the current average price paid by the sample as a whole, it cost $55.08, an increase of 202 percent over the cost in the corresponding month in the previous year. In addition, the arrows extending up and down from the median line indicate the interquartile range. In January, 1979, the middle half of the sample used between thirty-eight and fifty-nine gallons of gasoline in January, 1980.

Information on the previous months of the current year beginning July, 1979, can be used for further interpretation of median monthly gasoline consumption. The line shows that median consumption for January was up sharply from the previous five months but still lower than July. The arrows show that the interquartile range was unusually large in July and September. Information on the median car for the year to date is also given. The sum of median consumption from July, 1979, through January, 1980, rounded off to the nearest gallon, was 239 gallons. At the average sample price over this period, the cost was $232.31. Compared to the corresponding seven-month period of the previous year, consumption decreased 1 percent and cost increased 56 percent. Thus the increase in consumption for the month of January brings year-to-date consumption nearly equal to the consumption in the previous year.

Information on the previous year's experience as a whole can be used to clarify expectations about the remainder of the current year and to set goals. The upper box shows that the median car used 398 gallons for all of the previous year at a cost of $264.27. These are the amounts projected for the current year under the assumption that consumption and average prices remain the same. Either of these two amounts can also be used by a reader to set goals for the remainder of the current year. The simplest goal would be a commitment to avoid any increase in gasoline use or cost. Avoiding a cost increase would be the more demanding goal because gasoline prices continue to rise. In addition, the unshaded band across the middle of figure 1 represents the interquartile range for each month of the previous year. It suggests the median and interquartile range over the remainder of the current year if consumption patterns remain approximately the same as last year. It also shows that compared to last year, the range of consumption for October, November, December, and January of the current year has narrowed substantially. The shaded area provides a stable frame of reference within which the current year's experience can be updated as it unfolds.

In summary, figure 1 highlights median consumption in the most recent month for which we have data. This is an appropriate emphasis in view of the need to report current energy consumption levels. Figure 1 also provides sufficient information to interpret this monthly figure in light of the current cost and interquartile range, and to compare it with the corresponding month of the previous year. More broadly, it provides information for further interpretation of the year to date, this year and last year, and last year as a whole. No single reader is likely to be interested in all of this information. But interests differ, and each kind of information is likely to be of interest to some readers in a large, diverse audience. The report, in effect, invites all readers to develop a fuller understanding of local energy consumption and provides the means to do so. The need is not only to report energy consumption levels, but also to encourage clarification and compliance through provision of enough information to stimulate and sustain informal discussion.

The cost of providing a wealth of information is some reduction in visual attractiveness and readability, which reduces the size of the effective audience by an unknown degree. The visual attractiveness of figure 1 would be enhanced by a larger sample size, as previously noted. On statistical grounds, it is reasonable to expect that the interquartile ranges would be more nearly symmetrical about the monthly medians, and that the unshaded area would more nearly approximate a smooth band showing seasonal peaks and troughs that recur from year to year. To enhance readability, various elements of figure 1 might be deleted at the cost of reducing the amount of information provided. The initial design proposed here does not necessarily approximate the optimal trade-off, whatever that may be. Figure 2, which is self-explanatory, illustrates one way of simplifying the initial design. If changes are to be made in the initial design, however, they are best made prior to the onset of publication. It would be unnecessarily confusing to the public to attempt to explain the index while redesigning it.

The extension of the initial design in figure 1 from gasoline to natural gas and electricity is straightforward. The basic frame of reference would be the number of hundred cubic feet or kilowatt hours per month (vertical scale) for each month in the twelve-month year beginning in July (horizontal scale). A minor complication is that the data would be based on a sample of households rather than automobiles. There is a difference. For example, automobiles B and C in table 2 are owned and operated by a single household; and the same household buys electricity under separate accounts for residential service and water-heating service. Sampling gasoline consumption by automobiles

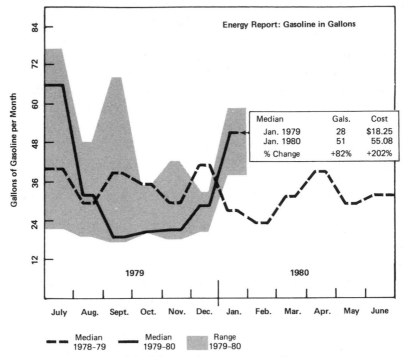

FIG. 2.   A simplified design for an ongoing illustrative community energy report for gasoline. (Format based on fig. 1, data from
table 2.)

is a simple task and provides useful information for single- and mul-
tiple-automobile households alike. Sampling consumption of the other
forms of energy by appliance or end use would be both difficult and
unnecessary because multiple accounts for a single household are not
as common.

Supplementary Articles
A graphed report of fixed design would provide continuity in the focus
of attention from month to month over the course of a year. Only
median consumption represented by the median line and the interquartile range would be extended each month, and the statistical comparisons updated accordingly. Interesting and informative material
that does not fit into the graph itself could be supplied as particular

needs and opportunities arise, through supplementary articles. Supplementary articles would add flexibility and a flow of fresh material to the overall report. They could be based largely on specific examples represented in the data used to prepare the graphed report, but any aspect of the community energy situation is worth consideration. It would be worthwhile to design a logo to identify the energy report, including both its fixed and flexible components.

One purpose would be to help readers answer the question, "how much is too much?" for themselves. An introduction to the graphed report, stories on particular households in the sample, and examples and directions for use of the graphed report would be appropriate. The following headlines suggest some possibilities, with the emphasis on gasoline:

The Ann Arbor Energy Report
   (An introduction to what it is and how to use it)
How One Family Gets By on 10 Gallons a Month
   (An interview with a motorist who consumes at the low end of the sample)
Why 60 Gallons per Month Are Sometimes Necessary
   (An interview with a motorist who consumes at the high end of the sample)
What One Family Learned from the Energy Report
   (An interview with a reader of the energy report)
How to Use Your Household Energy Records
   (Suggestions on using the records in addition to the energy records)

The second and third possibilities would interpret sample statistics in vivid, human terms. For example, in table 2, automobile B is a small, fuel-efficient car used by the head of the household to commute 120 miles each work day. Automobile D is also small but seldom used because the working member of the household was brought up to be energy conscious and prefers to bicycle the short distance to work. Details could be provided in supplementary articles complete with photographs; an asterisk could be inserted in the graphed report to locate consumption in the featured automobile with respect to the rest of the sample. More generally, consumption in each automobile in the sample represents a different mix of miles-per-gallon fuel efficiency and miles driven as well as household preferences and constraints. Such differences in circumstances can be used by readers to assess the applicability of norms implied by sample statistics, and to adjust accordingly.

Of course any public disclosure of household-specific information would require prior approval from the household in question. Furthermore, no useful purpose would be served by publishing value judgments about levels of energy consumption. On the contrary, the point is to encourage readers to make their own assessments of the consumption levels that are reasonable and appropriate for themselves. The examples underscore the proposition that differences in household circumstances warrant different consumption levels, and that each household makes its own energy decisions.

Another purpose would be to help readers understand the causes of changes in energy consumption and energy costs. Among the relevant factors are those the household can influence from day to day (such as use of automobiles, electrical appliances, and gas furnaces) and intermittently (such as replacement of less efficient automobiles and appliances, or the addition of home insulation); and factors that are beyond the household's control (such as the weather and energy prices). Here are some illustrative possibilities, with the emphasis on electricity and natural gas:

> How the Dehumidifier Broke the Electricity Budget
>   (A short item on the unexpected cost of a new appliance)
> Cold Weather: How Much Difference Does It Make?
>   (The relationship between heating degree-days and natural gas consumption for one or more households[17])
> Infiltration and Heating Costs
>   (What happened when a few hours were taken to plug air leaks within a house and to weatherstrip)
> One Family's Energy Plan, and How It Worked
>   (The householder's description and assessment, supplemented by the experts'[18])
> Energy Costs: The Impact of Price Increases
>   (Local trends in energy prices and their impact on the energy consumer)

The first item in this list illustrates how the data on specific households can be used to spot developments worth explaining, and how to do it. The data in table 2 show that unusually large amounts of electricity were used in July and August of 1979. (The low level for June, the intervening month, is an inaccurate estimate.) It took a while for the household to identify the problem: operation of a new dehumidifier in the basement. In this case the household decided a drier basement was not worth the extra cost, and cut back use of the dehumidifier.

Another purpose would be to direct readers to sources of additional information and other services, as a means of helping them solve their own energy problems. A number of suggestions, implicit or explicit, would naturally arise in reporting examples of energy conservation like those above. Other possibilities include the following:

> The Ecology Center's Energy Workshops
> > (A description of an existing program, and what participants gained from it)
>
> The Energy Conservation Information Clearinghouse
> > (An introduction to a new local information service under consideration)
>
> Financing Insulation Through the Gas Company
> > (A new program is being set up under federal and state mandate)
>
> The Energy Consumer's Corner
> > (Letters to the energy editor, including questions, comments, and suggestions)
>
> For More Information . . .
> > (A list of particularly useful or new "how-to" publications for the energy consumer at the public library)

An "Energy Consumer's Corner" would provide an opportunity for members of the community to discuss household energy consumption among themselves, as well as for obtaining feedback for the planning of new supplementary articles.

The suggestions above emphasize specific examples based on the experience of Ann Arbor households as it unfolds. This emphasis stems from the commonplace assumption that specific examples are an effective means of stimulating the interest, comprehension, and involvement of large audiences. They can also provide models that members of the audience can emulate or avoid. Involvement can be further enhanced by making the graphed report and supplementary material available through presentations to neighborhood associations, service organizations, and other civic groups. An Ann Arbor energy report might also provide education material suitable for use in the classroom.

A Pilot Project: Implementation

Since a community energy report of the kind proposed here is essentially untried, it would be prudent to implement it on a pilot basis. A pilot project minimizes initial resource commitments and provides the experience necessary to make an informed decision about whether or not to proceed with a full-scale project. Overall responsibility for a pilot project could be located in the Community Development Office, which administers the Local Energy Conservation Public Awareness Campaign and which has taken the lead on energy policy within the city government.

This section considers three main aspects of implementation: sampling; the mechanics of data collection, processing, and presentation; and the assessment of costs and effectiveness.

Sampling

A large, random sample of Ann Arbor households would provide an ideal basis for a community energy report. The sample statistics—median and interquartile range in particular—become statistically more reliable and representative of the community as a whole as the size of the sample increases and care is taken in the selection of households. Moreover, a large, random sample would be suitable for research purposes as well as for purposes of a community energy report.

However, a large, random sample raises questions of feasibility and necessity. Careful sampling tends to be costly and time-consuming. And each additional household or automobile included in the sample requires the collection and processing of additional data during the start-up period and each month thereafter. Moreover, to stimulate and inform the norm formation process, the primary consideration is that the sample be of interest to members of the audience and perceived to be relevant to their patterns of energy consumption. A large, random sample is one means of providing such "psychological representativeness," but not the only means. A small sample with which the audience can identify could meet this requirement and at the same time hold down costs, if necessary. A small sample could also provide a substantial improvement in reliability over the handful of friends and relatives the interested citizen would otherwise have access to. More generally, the effectiveness of an energy report with respect to its purposes depends more on the skill with which it is designed and presented than on the size of the sample on which it is based.

The implication is that sampling methods and sample size can be adjusted to time and financial constraints, without unduly compromising the effectiveness of a community energy report. This affords a certain amount of flexibility until time and financial constraints can be clarified.

At least two means exist for selecting a probability sample of suitable size with which Ann Arborites might identify. In December, 1979, the Energy Administration of the Michigan Department of Commerce conducted the first phase of the Public Awareness Campaign Evaluation Survey (PACES), a telephone survey of a probability sample of 343 Ann Arbor residents. The next two phases will involve replications with additional samples of approximately 200 each. Several items added to the survey instrument would provide the information necessary to identify participants for a pilot community energy index. The items could be worded to answer the following questions:

> Would the respondent be willing to volunteer monthly data on household energy consumption for the index?
> If so,
>> Does the household keep a gasoline log for its automobile(s)?
>> Does the household use natural gas for space heating?
>> Would the household authorize the office responsible for the index to retrieve its energy records from the gas and electric company?

The last question is important because the utilities are the most convenient source of time series data for the previous year. The question might also be used to filter out those apartment dwellers who do not pay their own utility bills.[19] The next to last question filters out those who use fuel oil rather than natural gas. A "yes" answer to all four questions would identify a respondent eligible to participate in the index. Those eligible would be approximately representative of only part of the community.

An alternative means is provided by the computerized Urban Information System, which is maintained and used by the city planning office. It was recently used to draw a two-stage probability sample of about 3,100 dwellings in Ann Arbor. Each received a letter from the mayor asking the respondent to fill out and return a short, enclosed questionnaire, which includes several items related to energy. Over 81 percent of the sample complied.[20] A similar approach including some items based on the questions above could be used to identify enough households for the sample.

Both of these approaches to a probability sample are costly and time-consuming relative to a third alternative. The Ann Arbor Energy Steering Committee is comprised of twenty-three residents with some interest and background in energy matters. The staff includes four employees of the Community Development Office and two consultants. This nonrandom group of twenty-nine, together with others who participate in task forces and the Community Energy Forum, might be willing to participate in the pilot project as volunteers, although some probably lack gasoline records for the previous year. The question is whether Ann Arborites generally would be interested in the energy consumption patterns of such a sample, and find these patterns relevant to an assessment of their own. The answers may be in the affirmative precisely because the committee and staff are unrepresentative and have assumed responsibility for community leadership in this area.[21] In any case, the visibility if not the influence of the committee and staff would be enhanced.

Data Collection, Processing, and Presentation
Data collection procedures would be significantly simplified and expedited if the committee and staff were selected as the sample. Consequently, let us consider the more difficult case of a more representative sample.

Initially, each household could be visited by a representative from the Community Development Office or its contractor. Aside from answering the volunteer's questions about the project, the representa-

tive would begin the process of data collection. The volunteer participant would be asked to sign a form authorizing access to the household's records at the utility offices and specifying restrictions on project
use of the data. With a signed form, the utilities can provide the appropriate household electricity and natural gas data for the previous thirteen months or more. The project representative could copy (or make
arrangements to photocopy) the automobile gasoline log over the same
period. Finally, the representative could provide a package of oversized,
stamped, and preaddressed post cards, together with instructions for
filling them out and mailing them in each month.

A prototype is shown in figure 3. Each car would be precoded by

Energy Data

Household_____   Month_____

Electricity

Service Period			
From	To	Kilowatt Hours Used	Current Bill

Natural Gas

Billing Period		Units used in	
From	To	100 Cubic Ft.	Amount

Gasoline

Purchase Date	Odometer Reading	Gallons of Gasoline	Amount Paid

FIG. 3.   A prototype postcard for reporting monthly household
energy consumption

household and identified by month. The headings used for natural gas and electricity are taken directly from the utilities' bills to make it easier for the householder to find the necessary information. The headings used for gasoline could also be used in the household's automobile log(s); alternatively, the card itself could serve as the automobile log, with a duplicate provided for each additional car in the household. The card assumes that the project rather than the volunteer participant does the necessary calculations, such as miles driven per month.

The timely return of post cards, accurately and completely filled out, would be stressed. Post cards not filled out and returned by a specified deadline could be traced by telephone, and perhaps the necessary information could be taken over the phone. For electricity and natural gas, the utilities provide a backup source of information, although one to be used as infrequently as possible. Even so, months may arise when a few households are temporarily left out of the report for lack of data. The accuracy and completeness of the information provided by volunteer participants can be assessed within plausible bounds as it comes in. For example, a large and temporary increase in miles driven per gallon for a particular car may signal a gasoline purchase not recorded but nevertheless reflected in odometer readings. Accuracy and completeness can also be assessed at the end of the year by requesting a second time-series printout from the utilities and by taking a second look at the gasoline log.

The processing of the data is a straightforward technical task for which a number of workable procedures could be devised. One is to set up a master data file for each of the three principal energy sources. For example, the raw gasoline data for the previous year taken from one automobile log could be transferred into the format of the gasoline data in table 1 using a hand calculator. The raw data from each additional automobile log could be handled in the same way, with the results inserted in the next twelve lines of the master data file. From the complete master data file, the cases could be ranked by consumption to find the median and interquartile ranges each month; and the time series could be cumulated by month to provide the statistics for year-to-date comparisons of consumption and cost.

Once the master data file is set up for the previous year, it could be updated for each month of the current year by inserting transformed gasoline data from post cards at the appropriate lines. Medians, interquartile ranges, and cumulations for the year to date could be computed as before. Only a few simple calculations would then be required to produce all of the information in figure 1. In addition, the master file could be used to perform more detailed analyses on particular cases or the sample as a whole for purposes of the supplementary articles.

While monthly updates would be manageable with a hand calculator, the processing of the previous year's data at one time would be extremely tedious. In any case, general computer programs already exist (at the University of Michigan, for example) for the most tedious tasks of ranking and cumulating, and for special analyses. Alternatively, a special purpose program to perform all the necessary calculations could easily be written.

The *Ann Arbor News* is a feasible and promising medium for presenting the results each month. The *News* has already demonstrated an interest in local energy matters by publishing a six-day, multiple-part series in September, 1979, with news coverage since.[22] In addition, it is the most widely circulated daily in the area, and apparently a prominent source of local energy information according to the PACES survey. Accompanying articles could be prepared by *News* reporters, the pilot project itself, members of the Energy Steering Committee, and others both able and willing to do so. A number of local organizations such as the Chamber of Commerce and the League of Women Voters have already demonstrated an interest in energy programs, and might be interested in arranging scheduled presentations for members.

Costs and Effectiveness
The need to minimize costs is already reflected in certain aspects of the initial design. First, the initial design is based on observations that would be made whether or not the design is implemented on a pilot basis. This applies not only to electricity and natural gas consumption data, which the utilities collect for billing purposes, but also to gasoline. One criterion for inclusion in the sample is an automobile log covering gasoline consumption in the previous year. Second, the sample size can be scaled down to a level commensurate with the purposes of the report and with the uncertainties inherent in an untried alternative. This minimizes per respondent dollar costs at some

sacrifice in statistical reliability of the sample. Third, the distribution of the work load through time can be rather flat. In particular, the time freed up for project personnel after preparation of data for the previous year can be diverted to special analyses for accompanying articles, since the monthly updates of the index require relatively small amounts of time. This minimizes the expansion and contraction of project person-hours, if not costs.

Other accommodations can be made to reduce direct costs. Sampling can be done more cheaply by adding several items to an already planned survey than by setting up a new survey for purposes of the report. Sampling costs can be reduced still further by selection of the Energy Steering Committee and staff as the sample. The data collection and processing as well as at least some of the special analysis tasks are within the capabilities of university students, who might be interested in joining a pilot project on a work-study or course credit basis. Programming costs can be avoided by using existing general purpose programs supplemented by a few hand calculations. Volunteers from the Energy Steering Committee might be found to make presentations to community organizations. In addition, some costs might be shared with the university (e.g., computer time) and with the *Ann Arbor News* (e.g., artwork, reporting, and newspaper space). The dollar costs of implementing a community energy report on a pilot basis are flexible pending clarification of possibilities such as these.

For the time being, it is worth noting that a decision on a pilot project depends on projected costs (and effectiveness) *relative* to some alternative. As noted earlier, the city has a grant and an obligation under the grant to design and implement an energy awareness program of potential use to other Michigan communities. If care is taken in cost accounting in the execution of a pilot project, it could produce detailed, reliable estimates of the costs of a larger, continuing project to provide a full-scale community energy index.

Assessing the effectiveness of a pilot project is somewhat more difficult than accounting for costs incurred. If the basic purpose is to stimulate, inform, and sustain the development of community energy consumption norms, the most direct indication of success would be an increase in informal conversations comparing and interpreting household energy consumption. Given the spontaneity of such conversations and the need to respect the privacy of those involved, direct systematic measurements would be complicated and obtrusive to say the least. Another complication is the difficulty of disentangling the effects of the pilot report from other factors, such as publicity arising from other local energy projects, possible local energy controversies, or national energy shortages.

A number of assessment possibilities do exist, however.[23] Among them is a detailed study of the sample itself after one year. Interviews with volunteer participants could provide testimony on the extent to which the report stimulated energy conversations with friends and relatives, awareness of household energy consumption levels and reductions in consumption, if any. The data would already be in hand to compare actual energy consumption for the year just ended with the previous year. As participants in the report, the households in the sample would be more likely than the rest of the community to pay attention to the report and respond accordingly. Consequently, if there is any effect, it should be most readily detected in the sample itself.

For an assessment beyond the sample, it would be a mistake to ignore the nonquantitative impressions of reliable observers in various parts of the community regarding any change in the frequency and content of informal conversations about energy consumption. Inexpensive data on one indirect effect—requests for household energy conservation information—could be obtained by asking the suppliers of such information to log the number of such requests during the year of the pilot project, and to ascertain insofar as possible the reasons why each request was made. (This would be simplified if an information clearinghouse were established concurrently with the onset of a pilot project.) The volume of letters to the energy editor is another unobtrusive indicator. More expensive and reliable information could be obtained by drawing a new sample of the community at the end of a one-year pilot project, with interviews and household energy records used to assess the effects. To answer qualitative questions such as "how does it work?" and "under what circumstances?" would require only a small sample. To answer the quantitative question of "how much community impact?" would require a much larger sample.

If a pilot project turned out to be successful, a full-scale community energy index could become an important tool for local energy policy planning and evaluation as well as an instrument to promote energy awareness. For example, time-series data on household energy consumption are necessary to understand at more than a superficial level the energy performance of typical dwellings in Ann Arbor; to improve the diagnosis of energy consumption problems and the prescription of cost-effective retrofits; and to assess the results of retrofits. These are key elements of the "house doctor" proposal, which has attracted some attention in Ann Arbor.[24] Moreover, in the absence of monthly household energy consumption data from a large and statistically reliable sample, Ann Arbor lacks the information necessary to evaluate its developing initiatives in energy policy. The utilities that serve Ann Arbor currently provide only annual electricity and natural gas consumption figures for customers within the city, and the figures are broken down only by rate classifications which are difficult to interpret. The Michigan Energy Administration is the only current source of gasoline consumption data, but the figures are aggregated to the county level and necessarily entail a number of questionable assumptions. A revised and expanded community energy index could generate the data to fill these and other research gaps. Operating responsibility might be turned over to the city planning office, which has the relevant expertise. The data could be made available for research purposes to other parts of the city government, the university, and the community at large.

Conclusions and Recommendations

A community energy index is an essentially untried local energy policy option, but one that merits serious consideration as part of the city's energy awareness program. As an alternative to exhortations and mandatory standards, a well-designed index might stimulate, inform, and sustain the formation of lower household energy consumption norms in Ann Arbor.

We recommend that serious consideration of a pilot project to explore the option begin with the initial design proposed in this chapter. The balance between informativeness on the one hand and visual attractiveness and readability on the other is not necessarily optimal in the graph suggested here. It can be improved through the input of potential users and professional designers alike.

In addition, the operational details of providing the index and accompanying articles can be adjusted to minimize costs and enhance effectiveness. These details include the size and composition of the sample from which data would be collected, and procedures for data collection, processing, and presentation. A number of suggestions have been provided.

A community energy report implemented on a pilot basis for one year could clarify whether or not to proceed with a continuing, full-scale index. Such an index could serve the purpose of local energy policy planning and evaluation as well as community energy awareness.

NOTES

This paper was written in June and revised in July, 1980. The authors wish to thank Lawrence B. Mohr of the Institute of Public Policy Studies, Thomas G. Reike, media consultant to the Ann Arbor Community Development Office, and Raymond J. Sleep of the *Ann Arbor News* for comments on the manuscript. The responsibility is of course the authors' alone.

1. See the testimony of Bill Streng of Davis, California, in U.S., Congress, House, Committee on Interstate and Foreign Commerce, Subcommittee on Energy and Power, *Hearings on Local Energy Policies,* 95th Cong., 2d sess., May 22, June 5 and 9, 1978, Serial No. 95-135, p. 132 (hereafter cited as *Hearings on Local Energy Policies*). The same point is made and additional sources cited by Richard A. Winett and Michael S. Neale, "Psychological Framework for Energy Conservation in Buildings," *Energy and Buildings* 2 (1979):101–16.

2. Winett and Neale report in "Psychological Framework," p. 109, that "of several hundred persons in studies that the senior author has conducted, virtually no one knew how many kwh they used per month or day; most people did not know where their electricity meter was located. (Other investigators in this area have apparently had similar experiences.)"

3. According to a recent survey, only 11 percent of Ann Arborites report their main source of heating fuel is heating oil, while 73 percent report their main source is natural gas. Moreover, heating oil is difficult to incorporate in a monthly energy report because deliveries are relatively infrequent and irregular. For percentages, see Michigan Department of Commerce, Energy Administration, "PACES: Public Awareness Campaign Evaluation Survey; Report on Survey of Ann Arbor Residents," mimeographed (December, 1979), p. 33 (hereafter cited as "PACES").

4. Ann Arbor is also served by the free-circulation monthly, the *Ann Arbor Observer;* by the *University of Michigan Daily;* and by local radio stations. In addition, civic groups serve as media for particular audiences.

5. Robin W. Williams, Jr., "The Concept of Norms," in *International*

Encyclopedia of the Social Sciences, ed. David L. Sills, vol. 11 (New York: Macmillan Co. and Free Press, 1968), p. 204.

6. One of the most insightful studies is Bee Angell and Associates, Inc., *A Qualitative Study of Consumer Attitudes Toward Energy Conservation* (Washington, D.C.: Federal Energy Administration, Office of Energy Conservation and Environment, 1975). On the basis of environmental rather than energy studies, Winett and Neale report in "Psychological Framework," p. 112, that "prompts are inexpensive, relatively simple to deliver, but transient in effect, and only effective with a limited (15 percent) segment of persons."

7. *Hearings on Local Energy Policies,* p. 132.

8. In general, the norm formation process within groups is stimulated by growing recognition of the costs of conventional practices and the perception of unrealized opportunities. Amid initial uncertainty and confusion, the gradual crystallization of norms is facilitated by relative ease of comparison of behavior among group members and by prominent points of reference across the range of behavior. These make it easier for group members to determine when behavior falls within an acceptable range and when it does not. Norms are more readily accepted and internalized by group members to the extent the norms are consistent with the other affiliations of group members. Once established, norms tend to be observed as internalized changes in behavior or enforced through social pressure with government intervention. See Muzafer Sherif, *Social Interaction: Process and Products* (Chicago: Aldine, 1967), chaps. 9, 10, and 11. See also Donald I. Warren, *A Pilot Study Relating Actual Household Natural Gas Usage to Social Organization Patterns of Neighborhoods* (Ann Arbor: Institute of Labor and Industrial Relations, 1976); and Paul C. Stern and Eileen M. Kirkpatrick, "Energy Behavior," *Environment,* December, 1977, pp. 10–15.

9. Bee Angell, *A Qualitative Study of Consumer Attitudes,* illuminates the broad range of motivations involved in household energy consumption.

10. These considerations are broadly consistent with the lessons distilled by Winett and Neale from an attempt to change community energy consumption norms in Washington, D.C. in 1977. See Winett and Neale, "Psychological Framework," p. 115.

11. U.S., Department of Energy, Assistant Secretary for Policy and Evaluation, Division of Environmental and Institutional Impacts Evaluation, *Local Government Energy Activities,* vol. 2, *Detailed Analysis of Twelve Cities and Counties,* DOE/PE-0015/2 (Washington, D.C.: Government Printing Office, 1979), p. 36.

12. Allegheny (Pa.) County, Energy Alert Assessment Committee, "Energy Alert System Manual," mimeographed (Pittsburgh: Allegheny County Department of Planning and Development, 1978), p. 14.

13. "PACES," p. 23.

14. Data suitable for a community energy report may be collected in any case. The City of Ann Arbor, Office of Community Development, "Proposal for

Energy Conservation Public Awareness Campaign," mimeographed (May, 1979), p. 20, notes: "Samples would be taken of overall changes in the average family or renter energy bills over a calendar period. Figures will be obtained for the residential sector elements (homeowners and renters) from the local utilities, Detroit Edison and Michigan Consolidated Gas Company and fuel oil suppliers."

15. This is suggested by the experience of Los Angeles which, during the oil crisis of 1973–74, ran short of oil for generating electricity. The recommendations of a broadly based committee helped assure realistic targets for reduced energy consumption and widespread compliance. See Jan Acton and Ragnhild Sohlberg Mowill, *Conserving Electricity by Ordinance: A Statistical Analysis,* R-1650-FEA (Santa Monica: Rand Corporation, 1975).

16. These simple interpretations recommend the median and interquartile range over means and standard deviations. More technical interpretations and computing conventions can be found in G. Udny Yule and M. G. Kendall, *An Introduction to the Theory of Statistics,* 14th ed. (London: Charles Griffin and Co., 1950), pp. 111–13, 140–42.

17. See Lawrence S. Mayer and Yoav Benjamini, "Modeling Residential Demand for Natural Gas as a Function of the Coldness of the Month," *Energy and Buildings* 1 (1977/78):301–12.

18. See for example Phil McCombs, "Energy-Saving Ideas Work," *Washington Post,* April 14, 1980.

19. Apartment dwellers who do pay their own utility bills would be included. According to "PACES," p. 33, 70 percent of Ann Arbor residents report they pay for both heat and electricity, 21 percent pay for electricity only, 1 percent pay for heat only, and 8 percent do not pay for their own utilities.

20. According to a spokesman for the Ann Arbor planning office, in a telephone conversation, June 25, 1980, the data have been analyzed but the report has not yet been written.

21. This might be a form of modeling, which "is one of the simplest, but most effective, behavior change techniques" according to Winett and Neale, "Psychological Framework," p. 112.

22. Roger Le Lievre and Pamela Klein, "Saving Energy: A Local Perspective," *Ann Arbor News,* September 23–28, 1979.

23. For further insights into evaluation possibilities see Donald T. Campbell, "Reforms as Experiments," *American Psychologist* 24 (1969):409–29; and Donald T. Campbell, "Focal Local Indicators for Social Program Evaluation," in *Evaluation Studies Review Annual,* vol. 2, ed. Marcia Guttentag (Beverly Hills: Sage Publications, 1977), pp. 125–45.

24. Marc Ross and Robert H. Williams, "Drilling for Oil and Gas in Our Buildings," mimeographed report PU/CEES 87 (Princeton: Center for Energy and Environmental Studies, 1979); and Marc Ross, "America Needs House Doctors," mimeographed (September, 1979). Marc Ross is professor of physics at the University of Michigan and a resident of Ann Arbor.

8 An Energy Monitoring System for Municipal Buildings

Mary Ann Preskul, Robin Sandenburgh,

and Susan Scott

The rise in real energy prices, on top of inflationary increases in the prices of other essential goods and services, has become a significant factor in the fiscal planning and management of government operations at all levels. To the extent that the price increases are not controllable, a logical response is to minimize their impact by curtailing consumption. As a result, governmental units, like many householders and businesses, have been forced to seek out ways to identify and discontinue "nonessential" energy use.

Reducing energy consumption by an institution as large, diverse, and decentralized as even an average-sized municipal government presents certain unique difficulties. For one, actual consumption activities are spread over a large number of people and more than one facility. Exhortations to switch lights off and turn thermostats down are far less effective in an office building of 40 or 400 than a household of 4 or 5. Compounding the difficulty is the fact that official policy statements are likely to be ineffective, in and of themselves. Long-term changes in consumption behavior will not occur unless and until direct and measurable actions are taken by managers and department heads in each government-owned or leased building. Finally, systematic feedback on government-wide energy use is far more difficult to obtain than comparable information for a single residential or commercial building.

For all these reasons, an energy monitoring system of some type is essential if a municipal conservation program is to achieve the desired results. Programmatic attempts to make municipal operations more energy-efficient necessarily generate a demand for fairly detailed accounting of progress toward this goal. Obtaining and disseminating the necessary information as efficiently and accurately as possible is the key to an effective monitoring system.[1]

Several municipalities throughout the country have adopted—or are in the process of designing and implementing—systems to monitor and evaluate energy consumption. Interest in an energy monitoring system for Ann Arbor has emerged within various segments of the city government over the last few years, but it was not until the fall of 1979 that an active effort was begun to examine the idea carefully. The next section describes the background situation and considerations that led to this effort. The remaining sections detail the design of a proposed energy monitoring system.

Background of the Energy Monitoring System

In designing an energy monitoring system for Ann Arbor's municipally owned and leased buildings, it was useful to consider the various purposes—internal and external to the city government—such a system would have to fulfill.

Among the internal purposes, the most important was to improve the city's energy management capability. For the city as a whole, the assistant city administrator and the Energy Management Task Force (which he heads) needed better information on where to focus energy conservation efforts to achieve the greatest savings. It was not clear which of more than 150 city buildings were built and managed to be energy-efficient, and which were not. For individual departments or other units, middle-level managers needed better information on the buildings within their areas of responsibility for the same purpose. In addition, some expressed an interest in better information to justify budget requests for energy-related capital improvements. Finally, the Engineering Department could use the results of a comprehensive energy monitoring system to support ongoing activities. One was to help diagnose energy efficiency problems in particular buildings. The other was to expedite reports on the progress of work under state and federal energy conservation technical assistance grants.

The primary external purpose was to demonstrate the city government's commitment to energy conservation in a way that was both measurable and credible. Conservation of nonrenewable energy resources was one of several goals that the mayor began to espouse in earnest in mid-1979. In particular, energy conservation in municipal operations was one of the major policy areas later incorporated into the

1980 Energy Plan. By "cleaning up their own house" with respect to energy conservation, city officials hoped to provide a model of leadership and initiative for households and businesses to follow. Demonstrable cutbacks in energy usage, it was believed, would enhance the credibility of the city's commitment to reducing energy use and expenditures within the city government and the community at large. The Energy Steering Committee as well as the mayor and city council could use better information for this purpose.

To achieve these purposes required a system that could monitor energy use and expenditures in every building on a regular basis. Historically, no such records had been kept, although recently the Engineering Department had begun to track energy consumption in twenty city buildings to fulfill a requirement of the Department of Energy's technical assistance grant program. As a result, the Engineering Department as well as the assistant city administrator, middle-level managers, and elected officials had expressed interest in having the necessary information collected, processed, and reported for all municipal buildings.[2]

It was apparent, therefore, that a number of groups within the city government had been interested in developing an energy monitoring system of some sort for several months. Similar initiatives were in various stages of progress in several other U.S. cities, including Portland, Seattle, Philadelphia, Boston, and Manchester, New Hampshire.[3] The development of a system for Ann Arbor drew on the experiences of these communities as well as the specific needs expressed by city officials.

Basic Design Considerations

It was determined early in the design process that the most cost-effective system would be one that tapped into the city's existing bill payment procedures. On the one hand, the city already paid for gas and electric meters and periodic meter readings through the utilities' monthly service charges. Moreover, city personnel and facilities to process the bills were already in place for the purpose of rendering payment. Finally, the bills contained the most fundamental information— energy use and cost—for *all* buildings owned or leased by the city.

On the other hand, the cost of processing this information to generate a useful set of reports had to be considered. High costs, considerable personnel requirements, and significant disruption of ongoing departmental operations would have seriously hindered the system's chances of receiving high-level approval and internal cooperation. Any of these factors would have rendered the long-term prospects for the system doubtful at best. For these reasons, it was necessary to examine the city's bill payment procedures in detail to identify the least costly, least disruptive way of utilizing bill information.

The Bill Payment Procedure

An overview of the bill payment procedure is presented in figure 1. Bills based on actual or estimated meter readings are sent monthly by Detroit Edison and Michigan Consolidated Gas directly to the building in which the meter is located or to the department or other unit that operates the building. In most cases, they are sent from the department or other unit to the controller's office, from which they are eventually paid.[4] At the time the study began, only a handful of units recorded any information from their utility bills, and these recorded cost but not consumption information. In a few cases, semiautonomous units such as the housing commission and the Ann Arbor Trans-

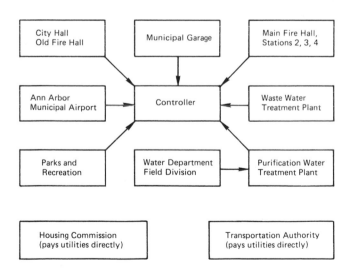

FIG. 1. Schematic overview of bill payment procedure. Not all departments or other units are represented in this overview.

portation Authority paid their bills directly, without going through the controller's office. These semiautonomous units were set aside to focus on the controller's office, where the basic information for nearly all buildings already was brought together each month.

Figure 2 depicts in more detail the flow of bill information. In step 1, the monthly bills received directly from the utility or indirectly from buildings are brought together at the department or other unit, where a clerk codes them with the appropriate account number and forwards them to the controller's office. There, in step 2, another clerk checks the bills for any obvious mathematical or other error, batches the bills together with bills to other units from the same vendor (e.g.,

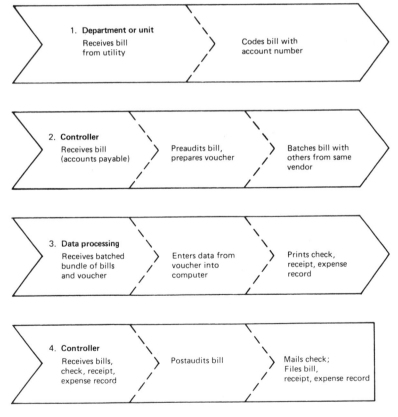

FIG. 2.   Flow of bill information through payment procedure

Detroit Edison or Michigan Consolidated Gas), and sends it in the batch to the Data Processing Department. In Data Processing, step 3, the amount and object of expenditure (e.g., electricity or natural gas) of each bill in the batch are keypunched with the appropriate account number and entered into the computer. The computer calculates the total amount due to the vendor, prints a check for payment, and prints an expense record. (Departmental expenses are also computed and printed out on a monthly, quarterly, and annual basis.) The check, the bills, and the expense record are then returned to the controller's office. There, in step 4, each bill in the batch is post-audited, the check is mailed to the vendor, and the remaining records are filed. Except for the bills received by the semiautonomous units, the sequence is the same for every bill regardless of department or other unit or vendor.

Step 3 was of particular interest because there bills from each of the two utilities are drawn together in the process of batching by vendor. Batched bills sent from the controller's office to Data Processing are accompanied by a "Miscellaneous Payment Voucher" (Form AP-1), reproduced here as figure 3. The voucher is prepared by a clerk in the controller's office, and formats the information to be entered into the computer from each bill in the batch. The numbers under each heading refer to data fields. For example, the budget fund from which payment is to be made is identified by a two-digit number placed in columns 1 and 2. The first four headings—*Fund, Dept., Activity,* and *Element*—refer to various components of the city's accounting system. The next two headings designate the type of expenditure, *equipment* or *object*. The two are mutually exclusive; a purchase is either equipment or object. Payments to utilities are considered object expenditures. *Distribution* refers to the amount of the bill, and *Vendor* refers to the unique four-digit code assigned to each vendor. Thus, for each bill, the information to be retained in computer-readable form is represented as one line of the payment voucher.

A Centralized, Computer-Based Approach
While the existing procedures have been designed for payment and accounting purposes, they can easily be redesigned for purposes of an energy monitoring system. As we have seen, nearly all of the city's gas

Form No. AP-1						Date:_____ 19__	
			Miscellaneous Payment Voucher				
City of Ann Arbor			Payee Name: _____				

Voucher Number	Vendor Number	Invoice Number	Trans Code
22-27	34-37	38-45	79-80
v			08

Account				Code		Distribution Amount
Fund 1-2	Dept. 3-5	Activity 6-8	Element 9-ll	Equip. 12-15	Object 19-21	66-70
					Total	

Prepared by _____

FIG. 3.   Sample miscellaneous payment voucher

and electric bills are brought together in the batching process in the controller's office, and the information to be retained in computer-readable form from each bill is written on the payment voucher. The least costly way to redesign the procedures is to modify the payment voucher to include (from utility bills already at hand) the energy consumption and other information necessary for an energy monitoring system. Implementation would require the training of at least two clerks, one in the controller's office and one in Data Processing, to handle gas and electric bills from the two vendors, and extra time each month to write a few additional numbers on the voucher and to enter them into the computer. With the necessary information stored in the computer, computer programs can be employed to write energy use reports as needed. The required programming is not likely to require more than several days, and a fully computerized system probably could be operational in a month's time.[5]

Consider the alternatives to this centralized, computer-based approach. Bill information could be recorded on a decentralized basis at the departmental level, but this would entail the training of at least one person in each department or other unit, interdepartmental coordination, and the risk of missing or delayed information. In all likelihood, recording energy data would be a lower priority than other departmental tasks; during periods when the work load is especially heavy, recording might be skipped or delayed and the utility of the monitoring system thereby reduced. Bill information could be processed manually to produce energy use reports, but this would be extraordinarily time-consuming and expensive because the city owns and leases more than 150 buildings. Moreover, computer programs are much easier to modify or expand than manual data processing systems. The flexibility of a computer-based system is particularly desirable in the short run, as the appropriate content, form, and frequency of energy use reports are refined through experience.

Having chosen a centralized, computer-based design for an energy monitoring system, attention turned to the detailed specification of the data to be entered into the system and the reports to be written from it—in short, to system *inputs* and *outputs*. The results are reviewed in the next two sections. For purposes of illustration, we shall use raw data from the utility bills of Ann Arbor's four fire stations for the 1978–1979 and 1979–80 fiscal years. The raw data for the Main Fire Hall (located across North Fifth Avenue from City Hall) are reproduced as Table 1. Such raw data, for many different buildings with different meter reading schedules, are of little direct use for comparative, analytical, or promotional purposes; hence the need for an energy monitoring system.

System Inputs

To fulfill its purposes, the system requires energy consumption and cost data on a building-by-building basis and additional information to help interpret and report the results. The additional information includes outdoor temperature and the characteristics of each building as well as utility bill data. This section describes each of the three kinds of system inputs.

TABLE 1.   Illustrative Data from Utility Bills, Ann Arbor Main Fire Station

Natural Gas				Electricity			
Billing Period				Billing Period			
From	To	Use (ccf)	Cost ($)	From	To	Use (kwh)	Cost ($)
1978–79							
6–10	7–10	250	$43.20	6–12	7–12	40,160	$1,484.20
7–10	8–7	399	58.88	7–12	8–11	37,280	1,652.50
8–9	9–10	208	51.68	8–11	9–12	42,080	1,818.33
9–10	10–9	251	61.89	9–12	10–11	23,520	1,171.20
10–9	11–9	797	193.88	10–11	11–9	24,000	1,310.57
11–9	12–7	1,933	464.39	11–9	12–11	27,840	1,459.53
12–7	1–8	3,604	863.37	12–11	1–12	35,040	1,905.67
1–8	2–8	4,657	1,112.76	1–12	2–9	27,040	1,347.99
2–8	3–9	3,535	838.44	2–9	3–13	29,120	1,561.91
3–9	4–9	2,412	582.14	3–13	4–12	28,000	1,504.29
4–9	5–8	910	244.71	4–12	5–11	24,960	1,441.65
5–8	6–8	741	203.84	5–11	6–12	30,080	1,641.24
1979–80							
6–8	7–9	202	36.68	6–12	7–12	29,760	1,599.92
7–9	8–9	157	49.06	7–12	8–13	36,960	2,091.73
8–9	9–9	202	22.82[a]	8–13	9–12	30,240	1,656.46
b	b	b	b	9–12	10–12	24,000	1,362.34
9–9	11–8	1,247	501.81	10–12	11–9	22,240	1,214.79
11–8	12–7	2,000	635.69	11–9	12–11	25,120	1,403.30
12–7	1–7	2,733	862.80	12–11	1–14	26,720	1,400.96
1–7	2–8	4,655	1,480.34	1–14	2–12	27,840	1,512.35
2–8	3–11	3,686	1,185.84	2–12	3–12	24,800	1,440.30
3–11	4–9	2,566	835.92	3–12	4–11	23,840	1,388.86
4–9	5–9	802	290.56	4–11	5–12	25,440	1,546.37
5–9	6–9	373	138.91	5–12	6–11	28,160	1,813.64

Source: City of Ann Arbor, Fire Department
a. This figure includes a credit refund of $40.94.
b. Records show no bill for this month, followed by a bill for two months.

Utility Bill Data

As we have seen, the Miscellaneous Payment Voucher (fig. 3) is the logical place to modify the system in order to incorporate more utility bill data. For gas and electric bills a new form, an Energy Payment Voucher, would be substituted for the existing form. (The existing voucher would continue to be used for all other bills.) Figure 4 proposes a layout for the Energy Payment Voucher, which would be mimeographed on colored rather than white paper in order to distinguish it easily from the existing form. Fire Department data are entered on the form as they would have been if the system had been in effect in March, 1980.

As a comparison of figures 3 and 4 indicates, all of the data specified in the existing form are retained in the same data fields in the new form: *fund* is still identified in columns 1–2, *department* in columns 3–5, and so forth. This minimizes disruption and makes the

Form no.							Date:	<u>March</u>	19 <u>80</u>
Energy Payment Voucher									
City of Ann Arbor							Vendor:		Michigan Gas

Voucher Number 22-27	Vendor Number 34-37	Invoice Number 38-45	Trans Code 79-80
V			08

A C C O U N T   C O D E

Fund	Dept.	Activity	Element	Bldg.	Object	Amount Used	First Day	Last Day	Distribution Amount
1-2	3-5	6-8	9-11	12-14	19-21	28-33	46-49	50-53	66-70
:	:	:		:	:	:	:	:	:
10	032	110	· · ·	AAA	221	3686	0208	0311	1185.84
10	032	110	· · ·	BBB	221	104	0214	0316	39.94
10	032	110	· · ·	CCC	221	1752	0204	0305	501.56
10	032	110	· · ·	DDD	221	898	0218	0320	295.19
:	:	:		:	:	:	:	:	:
								Total	

Form no.							Date:	March	19 <u>80</u>
Energy Payment Voucher									
City of Ann Arbor							Vendor:		Detroit Edison

Voucher Number 22-27	Vendor Number 34-37	Invoice Number 38-45	Trans Code 79-80
V	0094		08

A C C O U N T   C O D E

Fund	Dept.	Activity	Element	Bldg.	Object	Amount Used	First Day	Last Day	Distribution Amount
1-2	3-5	6-8	9-11	12-14	19-21	28-33	46-49	50-53	66-70
:	:	:		:	:	:	:	:	:
10	032	110		AAA	222	24800	0212	0312	1440.30
10	032	110		BBB	222	2079	0205	0305	124.35
10	032	110		CCC	222	2621	0213	0317	158.11
10	032	110		DDD	222	1702	0227	0326	105.96
:	:	:		:	:	:	:	:	:
								Total	

FIG. 4.   Input files. (Data from Fire Department utility bills.)

new system compatible with the old. However, the previously unused data fields are used to incorporate additional data necessary for the monitoring system.

First, a building code has been inserted in columns 12–14, which are unused in the payment of gas and electric bills but not other bills. AAA, BBB, CCC, and DDD refer, respectively, to the Main Fire Hall and Fire Station Nos. 2, 3, and 4. These letters would be replaced by numbers ranging up to 999 before the system becomes operational. A building code is necessary because the existing account codes are neither building- nor department-specific, and because the energy monitoring system must track energy consumption on a building-by-building basis to fulfill its purposes.

Second, *amount used* has been inserted in columns 28–33. For the Main Fire Hall (building code AAA), the amount of natural gas used according to the March, 1980, bill was 3,686 ccf and the amount of electricity used according to the March bill was 24,800 kwh. The system can distinguish between hundreds of cubic feet and kilowatt hours because the object codes for natural gas and electricity are 221 and 222, respectively. Amount used is obviously important because a basic purpose of the system is to keep track of how much energy is used in each building. The dollar amount of the bill, already included in columns 66–70, is not sufficient for this purpose because the dollar amount varies with rate changes as well as consumption.[6]

Third, the billing period has been entered into columns 46–53. For example, the March, 1980, bill for the Main Fire Hall showed that the 3,686 ccf were used during the thirty-two-day period from February 8 to March 11. Consequently, the first day of the billing period for that building is coded as 0208 in columns 46–49, and the last day is coded as 0311 in columns 50–53. Notice that the billing periods are not synchronized; rather, they vary in length from station to station and from gas to electricity for the same station. Billing periods need to be included in the system because they affect interpretations of the amount used. Other things being equal, we expect less energy to be used in a twenty-eight-day period than a thirty-five-day period.

Degree-Days
Outdoor temperature also affects the amount used, and therefore needs to be incorporated into the system as a data input. The most

convenient way to do this is to maintain a file of heating degree-days in the computer system. (Cooling degree-days might also be included depending upon the significance of the summer air conditioning load.) Degree-days data are collected, computed, and distributed by the University of Michigan Department of Atmospheric and Oceanic Science. It would be a fairly simple task for a public employee to obtain these data on a monthly basis. Table 2 presents an example of a degree-days file, with illustrative figures keyed to the billing periods in figure 4. The data input are shown on the left; the data computed from the inputs are shown on the right. For any particular day, the computer could be programmed to "look up" the cumulative degree-days to date for the current year and compare it with the previous year. For any particular billing period, the computer could be programmed to "look up" cumulative degree-days for the first and last dates of the billing period, and compute the difference. The result would be the number of degree-days accumulated during the billing period. This would improve the diagnostic potential of energy use reports, since the weather component in changes or differences in the amount of natural gas used could be signaled in the reports or statistically removed.

TABLE 2. Heating Degree Days

| | Daily Degree Days | | | Cumulative Degree Days | |
Date	1978–79	1978–80	Day No.	1978–79	1979–80
2/8	56.5	44.0	223	4,464.5	4,152.5
2/9	63.5	41.5	224	4,528.0	4,194.0
2/10	60.0	42.5	225	4,588.0	4,236.5
2/11	61.0	46.0	226	4,649.0	4,282.5
2/12	55.0	43.5	227	4,704.0	4,326.0
3/8	26.5	38.0	251	5,676.5	5,380.0
3/9	32.5	37.5	252	5,709.0	5,417.5
3/10	42.0	33.5	253	5,751.0	5,451.0
3/11	50.5	45.5	254	5,801.5	5,496.5
3/12	39.0	47.5	255	5,840.5	5,544.0

Source: University of Michigan Department of Atmospheric and Oceanic Science
Note: Degree days for each day are computed as 65° F minus the average of the daily maximum and minimum temperature in ° F. Cumulative degree days are computed from July 1, the beginning of the city's fiscal year.

Building Characteristics

Finally, it is necessary to maintain in the computer system a permanent file identifying the characteristics of each building. The most important characteristics are *building name, square footage,* and *report code.* Building name is important to facilitate quick and easy interpretation of energy use reports. Results attributed to the Main Fire Hall are better in this connection than results attributed to building AAA or accounting unit 10-032-110. Square footage can be used to improve the diagnostic capability of the system since energy consumption varies with building size. For example, consumption figures for a sample of buildings can be expressed per square foot of building area in order to clarify which are less energy-efficient. Report codes are necessary to instruct the computer to include (or not include) data for each building in each of the various reports. For example, a report to the head of the Fire Department should include data for each of the fire stations, but not necessarily data for other city buildings. This is considered in more detail in the next section. For now it is worth pointing out that the report code mechanism is a convenient and flexible way of specifying who should get what information. Finally, other information could be added to the building characteristics file as needed. Among the possibilities are rate codes under which electricity and natural gas are sold by the utilities, and address of the building. Table 3, which is self-explanatory, illustrates the format and content of a building characteristics file.

In summary, the system inputs consist of additional utility bill data (building code, amount used, and billing period) entered through

TABLE 3.   Building Characteristics

No.[a]	Building Name	Location	Sq.Footage	Report Code[b]	Rate Code[c]
AAA	Main Fire Hall	N. Fifth Ave.	43,900		C
BBB	Fire Station No. 2	Stadium Blvd.	11,400		C
CCC	Fire Station No. 3	Jackson Rd.	5,800		C
DDD	Fire Station No. 4	Huron Pkwy.	5,000		C

a. Numbers are to be assigned after system is adopted.
b. Report codes are to be assigned after system is adopted. See the section on system outputs for more details.
c. Code C designates the commercial rates under which these buildings fall.

a new Energy Payment Voucher, degree-days data, and building characteristics data.

System Outputs: Energy Use Reports

Energy use reports should communicate the essential information in a straightforward manner to the people who need it at appropriate intervals. This is easier said than done, because needs vary from one group to the next in a multipurpose energy monitoring system, and because there are many options in specifying the scope, frequency, format, and content of energy use reports. This section reviews the main design issues and then proposes two reports that are complementary but addressed to different user groups.

Design Issues

Different needs. The heads of functional units having responsibility for a set of buildings are middle-level managers. As discussed in the "Background" section of this chapter, they constitute only one of several groups whose needs might be met by an energy monitoring system. The others are the assistant city administrator and the Energy Management Task Force, the Engineering Department, and the mayor and council as well as the Energy Steering Committee. The various needs are only partially overlapping. For this reason, it seemed prudent as a first approximation to design separate reports that conveyed only the essential information to the appropriate group. To convey relatively complete information based on all system inputs would render the reports less useful.

At least two kinds of reports were considered essential. Mid-level reports, each based on a different subset of buildings but having the same format, would enable mid-level managers to spot trends in efficiency or inefficiency and to make comparisons among the buildings within their respective areas of responsibility. More detailed, diagnostic data and data on other buildings were not considered essential for their purposes. Citywide reports, based on all buildings owned and leased by the city, would enable the Energy Management Task Force to spot the strongest and weakest performances through a selective summary of building-level data and to monitor aggregate progress through totals across all buildings. These reports would also serve the purposes of mayor and council and the Energy Steering Committee. Finally, the task of using the energy monitoring system to diagnose energy efficiency problems on a building-by-building basis, and to facilitate grant reporting on some twenty of them, would be left to the Engineering Department. The proposed system inputs already include such data as square footage for these purposes; what remains to be added are sophisticated analysis programs written by the Engineering Department and tailored to its needs.

The set problem.   Utility bills, as we have seen, provide the foundation for the system. Each bill corresponds to a single meter and in nearly all cases to a single building. A problem arises, however, because there is no one-to-one correspondence between physical units like buildings and functional units like departments. For example, City Hall on North Fifth Avenue houses some twenty departments, while some departments like Fire oversee several buildings scattered throughout the city. Moreover, some functional units are not departments for purposes of an energy monitoring system. An example is a department like Parks and Recreation, where responsibility for building energy efficiency might best be distributed among subdepartmental units.

Ideally, a mid-level report on a set of buildings should go to the head of the functional unit that has responsibility for energy efficiency in those buildings. In practice, the problem is to identify the appropriate functional units, and departments provide only a partial guide. The matter is best left to the Energy Management Task Force, since it involves some potentially important managerial decisions. Given a complete list of buildings on the one hand and a complete list of administrative units (departmental and nondepartmental) on the other, the task is to assign buildings to units. The results can be coded into the building characteristics file (table 3). The *report code* column provides a means of specifying the problem, implementing the solution, and modifying lines of responsibility as unforeseen needs and opportunities arise.

Frequency.   Most representatives of the various user groups contacted for this study indicated they would like to receive energy use reports every month. Monthly reports seemed logical for mid-level managers who have day-to-day responsibility for a set of buildings and could make use of the most timely data. The need for monthly reports was less apparent in the case of officials with citywide responsibilities, most of whom already are inundated with memoranda, reports, issue papers, and the like. Contributing a monthly addition to this "paper flood" could have a perverse rather than a positive effect, to the extent that information overload caused the energy use reports to be reviewed less carefully or not at all. Any information system includes people as well as machines, and should be designed with the interests and capabilities of people in mind.

A related consideration was that monthly reports are less likely to present a reliable picture of energy consumption trends than reports spanning longer periods of time. Unusual events in a particular month can cause reported consumption to rise or fall sharply, and thereby obscure rather than clarify the underlying trend. Such events might result from operations in a building or simply reflect an accounting anomaly. For example, as shown in table 1, the Main Fire Hall did not receive a natural gas bill in October, 1979, but received a two-month bill in November. Mid-level managers deeply involved in operations in a set of buildings are more likely to understand the causes of sharp fluctuations. Higher-level officials with broader responsibilities are more likely to misinterpret them. Their needs would be better served by less frequent reports that are more reliable.

In view of these considerations, the recommendation is to generate mid-level reports for departmental or other units on a monthly basis, and to generate citywide reports for higher-level officials on a quarterly basis. The proposed format and content of these two kinds of reports are outlined in the remainder of this section.

Mid-Level Energy Use Reports
Monthly reports for mid-level managers were designed to provide a succinct and useful summary of energy consumption and costs in the buildings operated by particular departments or other units. An example of the form and content of a mid-level energy use report, based on Fire Department data, is presented in table 4.

The format consists of four blocks of information, the first two for natural gas and the second two for electricity. For each energy source,

TABLE 4. Fire Department Example of Mid-Level Energy Use Reports

To: M_____
Chief, Fire Department
111 N. Fifth Avenue

Energy Use Report: Fire Department, March, 1980

Natural Gas: This Month									
Building	Days	To	Degree Days	% Change	ccf Used	% Change	$ Cost	% Change	
Main Fire Hall	32	03–11	1,344	8	3,686	4	1,186	41	
Fire Station No. 2	31	03–16	1,269	11	104	1	40	33	
Fire Station No. 3	30	03–05	1,284	−3	1,752	6	502	27	
Fire Station No. 4	31	03–20	1,182	10	898	8	295	24	
Total					6,440	3	2,023	35	

Natural Gas: Year to Date									
Building	Days	To	Degree Days	% Change	ccf Used	% Change	$ Cost	% Change	
Main Fire Hall	255	03–11	5,497	−4	14,882	−5	4,815	31	
Fire Station No. 2	260	03–16	5,678	−4	764	−2	291	54	
Fire Station No. 3	249	03–05	5,296	−6	7,423	10	1,962	9	
Fire Station No. 4	264	03–20	5,780	−4	4,070	−15	1,337	13	
Total					27,139	−8	8,679	25	

Electricity: This Month									
Building	Days	To	Degree Days	% Change	kwh Used	% Change	$ Cost	% Change	
Main Fire Hall	29	03–12			24,800	−14	1,440	−8	
Fire Station No. 2	29	03–05			2,079	−20	125	−14	
Fire Station No. 3	33	03–17			2,621	−7	158	16	
Fire Station No. 4	28	03–26			1,702	−13	106	−4	
Total					31,202	−14	1,829	−6	

Electricity: Year to Date									
Building	Days	To	Degree Days	% Change	kwh Used	% Change	$ Cost	% Change	
Main Fire Hall	256	03–12			247,680	−13	13,682	0	
Fire Station No. 2	249	03–05			17,580	−30	974	−18	
Fire Station No. 3	261	03–17			17,195	5	1,001	9	
Fire Station No. 4	270	03–26			14,963	−7	874	2	
Total					297,418	−14	16,531	−2	

Source: Data from the City of Ann Arbor, Fire Department

Note: Percentage changes are based on the corresponding period of the previous year. Cooling degree-days (optional) could be inserted in the "degree days" and "percent change" columns for electrical use. Cooling degree-days are calculated as the excess of the average of the daily maximum and minimum temperatures in ° F over a base of 65° or 75° F.

the first block provides information on the current month while the second block provides information on the fiscal year to date. (On wider computer paper, the current month and year-to-date blocks for each source might be printed side by side.) Within each block, the data are presented in a common format, which draws attention to unit totals and a building-by-building breakdown for the unit.

The standard of comparison for a building's energy consumption and cost is the same building's consumption and cost in the corresponding period of the previous year, expressed as a percentage change. The number of days in the period, and the number of degree-days in the period, are included to assist interpretation of the percentage changes. Current monthly data, as we have seen, can be interpreted and responded to quickly by mid-level managers, even though such data are inherently less reliable. Year-to-date data provide a cumulative score card coincident with the city's fiscal year. A missing bill, a meter estimate, or a short billing period in one month tends to be followed in the succeeding month by a two-month bill, a meter reading, or a longer billing period that reestablishes the nominal schedule. Moreover, unusually high or low consumption periods become an increasingly small proportion of the year-to-date cumulation through the course of the fiscal year, thus emphasizing the underlying trend rather than short-term departures from it. Year-to-date figures provide not only a basis for interpreting the monthly data, but also a means of charting progress (or the lack of it) through the course of the fiscal year.

To illustrate the use of such a report, consider the data in table 4. The chief of the Fire Department could note that natural gas consumption for the department on a year-to-date basis is down by 8%. Although the Main Fire Hall accounts for more than half of the department's natural gas consumption, the best performance has been turned in by Station No. 4 (a 15 percent decrease) and the worst by Station No. 3 (a 10 percent increase). Degree-days data indicate that the first eight months of the current fiscal year have been slightly warmer relative to the previous year; thus the heating load has been less, accounting in part for the overall reduction in consumption.

However, for the monthly billing period ending in March, 1980, the heating load has been generally higher relative to the same monthly billing period in the previous year. Fire Station No. 2, which is farthest behind the pace it set for itself the previous year, turned in the smallest increase in consumption in the current month. Costs are up substantially from the previous year, but the percentage changes in cost bear no simple relationships to the percentage changes in consumption on a building-by-building basis. The implication is that the rate structure is worth looking into, to the extent that cost reductions are a significant objective. (A dollar saved in energy costs might be freed up for other departmental expenses.) A similar analysis can be made in the case of electricity.

The length of the mid-level monthly report will vary from one unit to the next, depending upon the number of buildings for which the unit has assumed responsibility. While a four-building report is required for the Fire Department, a one-building report may be required for a smaller unit and a many-building report for a larger one.

City-Wide Energy Use Reports
Quarterly reports for higher-level city officials were designed to provide a succinct and useful summary of energy consumption and costs across all buildings owned or leased by the city. No illustration is provided here because we lack data equivalent to the Fire Department data for all other units. However, citywide reports are easily visualized as an extension of mid-level reports.

For reasons of reliability already discussed, the citywide reports are based only on year-to-date blocks prepared for all units for the months of September, December, March, and June. At these intervals, the computer would rank each of the more than 150 buildings by percentage change in natural gas consumed and percentage change in electricity consumed, and calculate the total consumption and cost of each energy source across all buildings. There would be little point in printing out the entire rank ordering for each energy source; each rank ordering contains too much information to absorb and use effectively. Rather, the computer would print out data using the format in table 3 for the 5 to 10 buildings with the largest pecentage reductions and the 5 to 10 buildings with the largest percentage increases (or smallest percentage reductions) for each fuel.

Under the five-building option, the gas and electricity reports would each consist of ten lines of data plus a line giving citywide year-to-date consumption and cost totals, and the percentage changes in the totals from the previous year. For example, the quarterly citywide natural gas report for March, 1980, would have included the line for Fire Station No. 4 from the second block of the Fire Department report in table 4, if that station's performance (a 15 percent reduction) had been among the five best in the city. Similarly, the quarterly report would have included the line for Fire Station No. 3, if that station's performance (a 10 percent increase) had been among the five worst in the city.

With such a report, the assistant city administrator and the Energy Management Task Force initially could decide which buildings (and the units responsible for them) deserve commendation, and could define priorities as to which buildings require modifications in operations or structural improvements. The latter would provide an indication of how to allocate the limited technical audit and building retrofit capabilities of the Engineering Department in order to realize the greatest payoff—in energy saved or costs avoided—to the city. The greatest payoff will not necessarily be realized in the building(s) with the highest percentage increases in consumption, but in the building(s) with relatively high percentage increases *and* relatively high levels of energy consumption. Preliminary judgments about the greatest payoffs might be refined by directing the Engineering Department to perform more detailed statistical analyses of the performances of the worst five or ten buildings, taking into account such additional information as square footage. Over a period of time, the Energy Management Task Force could use the citywide report to monitor the effectiveness of previous commendations in holding down energy consumption in the best buildings, and the effectiveness of directives to modify operations or structures in increasing efficiency in the worst buildings. The effects of changes in operations should be apparent more quickly than the effects of building retrofits.

The citywide totals of energy consumption and costs, and their percentage changes, could be used to monitor aggregate progress toward improvement in the energy efficiency of city buildings. These figures would also be of use to the mayor and city council and to others interested in promoting improvements in *community* energy efficiency through documentation of the city government's leadership by example.

These energy use reports, which constitute the outputs of the energy monitoring system, are a first approximation. Refinement of their number, scope, frequency, format, and content can and should be undertaken on the basis of initial operating experience.

Further Considerations

Transforming the energy monitoring system from the proposal stage to a fully implemented, workable system is likely to introduce some operational considerations not addressed in the preceeding description of how such a system *might* work. Some of these have been anticipated and are discussed in this section.

System Costs

The costs of implementing and maintaining this energy monitoring system are not likely to be prohibitive. The major start-up activities will be (1) explaining the use of the Energy Payment Voucher to clerks in the controller's office and Data Processing, (2) setting up input files for degree-days and building characteristics, and (3) programming the computer to generate energy use reports.

The first activity is a minor one in terms of costs. Training clerks can be expected to take, at most, a few hours of time on the part of the person explaining the new Energy Payment Voucher and the clerks themselves. The second activity requires more time and effort, but the amount is difficult to estimate. Degree-days data are readily available in convenient form; building characteristics data might require more time to assemble from various city offices. Including the entry of these data into the computer system, this technical part of the task might require a week's time. The managerial part, involving the assignment of buildings to administrative units for energy conservation purposes, might require considerably more or less than a week's time. The amount depends upon the extent to which the lines of responsibility are already clear and accepted. The third major activity might require a week of a programmer's time to write and "debug" the necessary programs.[7] Data Processing already employs a few programmers who know the system, and the programming task is not a particularly difficult one given precise specification of inputs and outputs.

Once the system is operating, the monthly costs will be modest. Entering data from utility bills will require about nineteen additional keystrokes for each bill each month plus a few additional keystrokes for the daily degree-days accumulated during the month. (The static building characteristics file does not require a monthly update.) An experienced keypuncher can accomplish the task in about two hours each month.[8] The other operating costs will be the computer time and paper necessary to generate the monthly and quarterly energy use reports, and of course the time required to read and understand them. The potential savings in energy costs, we believe, more than justify these modest costs.

Previous Year Data

The energy use reports include references to consumption and costs in the previous year for purposes of comparison. Obviously, these references will present some difficulties in the first year of implementation, since previous year data in the specified format will not be available. One solution is to treat the first year of the project as a start-up phase and to issue mid-level reports without the previous year comparisons. (Citywide reports require percentage change data for ranking purposes.) Such mid-level reports would not be as informative or useful, but could serve to introduce the system and draw attention to the city's commitment to energy efficiency. This solution avoids the large and possibly excessive cost of assembling a massive body of data from the files of the utilities or the city.

Filling Gaps

There are some gaps in the proposed energy monitoring system that merit attention after the system has been implemented. As noted previously, a few semiautonomous units such as the housing commission and the Ann Arbor Transportation Authority pay their utility bills directly, without going through the controller's office. Moreover, the proposed system excludes fuel oil that is used in a relatively small number of buildings instead of natural gas.

How these additional units and fuel oil might be incorporated into the system, and whether the payoffs would justify the expense, remain to be seen. Fuel oil probably presents the more difficult problem, since it is delivered on an irregular basis. The monitoring of consumption would entail the time-consuming task of gauging tanks each month. It is worth noting that the Engineering Department has been developing a computerized system to monitor the consumption of gasoline and diesel fuel through the city's own pumping stations.

Conclusion

The energy monitoring system outlined in this paper has been designed to meet certain needs expressed by various city officials. These include the comparison of progress toward improved energy efficiency among buildings on a unit and citywide basis, statistical diagnosis of energy efficiency problems on a building-by-building basis, and demonstration of the city government's leadership in energy conservation. The system is designed to meet these needs at minimal cost and disruption by tapping into the existing centralized and computerized bill payment procedures.

The principal recommendation is to begin implementation as soon as possible by substituting the new Energy Payment Voucher for the existing Miscellaneous Payment Voucher. This is the key step because a fully implemented system requires a file of data for the previous year to gauge progress. Other essential steps can be undertaken while the previous year data is accumulated in the computer system. These steps include setting up the degree-days and building characteristics files, adoption of a final design for energy use reports, and development of the computer programs to produce such reports. After a one-year start-up phase, Ann Arbor can have a valuable managerial tool that draws attention to problems and progress in improving the energy efficiency of city buildings, and to the city government's leadership in energy conservation.

NOTES

Research for this study was begun in September, 1979. A preliminary draft was completed and circulated for comments in May, 1980. Final revisions and additions to the proposal, based on the preliminary draft, were made between November, 1980, and June, 1981. The authors would like to thank Tom Collins, Dan Hanlon, Tom Murray, and Barry Tilmann for their helpful reviews of the proposed system. Responsibility is the authors' alone.

1. Internal energy management is one of three basic programs outlined in Don Spangler, *Establishing an Energy Office: Seven County Programs*

(Washington, D.C.: National Association of Counties Research Foundation, 1979), p. 43.

2. Gasoline and diesel fuel consumption are included in a complementary energy monitoring system being designed by the Engineering Department.

3. Boston hired a consulting firm to develop its Computerized Energy Management System (CEMS) which monitors consumption in all city buildings. Philadelphia also hired a private consultant to design its Utility Forecasting and Monitoring System (UFMS) and later redesign several aspects of the system. Portland's 1979 Energy Conservation Ordinance included plans to develop an energy monitoring system. In 1980, Manchester, New Hampshire, instituted a noncomputerized but comprehensive Manchester Energy Management Information System (MEMIS).

4. Departments are sometimes but not always the appropriate administrative units for purposes of an energy monitoring system.

5. These estimates are based on conversations with Tom Murray of the Data Processing Department on June 10 and 11, 1980.

6. In modifying the Miscellaneous Payment Voucher, it was noticed that the data field for distribution amount was too narrow to accommodate an amount in excess of $999.99. Because the existing system evidently handles bills in excess of this amount by some method, we have left the data field for distribution amount in its original form.

7. This is more than twice the time estimate given by Tom Murray of Data Processing in order to allow for unanticipated difficulties. Mr. Murray's estimate was based on a verbal description of the proposed energy monitoring system.

8. An average speed for an experienced keypuncher is eighty cards per hour. Each card has eighty columns, although all columns are not necessarily used.

PART 3: EVOLUTION

9 The Search for Solutions

Ronald D. Brunner and Robin Sandenburgh

The six chapters of Part 2 constitute only a modest part of the Ann Arbor energy initiative. Others in the city have analyzed the same program options, and many other program options have been considered and in some cases implemented. Moreover, the analyses above are merely snapshots in a moving picture. Each has been revised in the light of new developments and the comments and criticisms of private citizens and public officials alike.

In this concluding chapter we attempt to bring each of the six options up to date, as of mid-1981, emphasizing the contributions of others. The purpose is not only to place these analyses in proper perspective; more importantly, it is to underscore the limitations of analysis and the importance of open and informed policy processes in the search for solutions. This point is developed in the next section. After a review of each option, the concluding section reexamines developments at the federal level since 1979, when chapter 1 was first written.

The Limitations of Analysis

While policy and program analysis can reduce uncertainties about the next steps that are likely to be feasible and worthwhile, such analysis is inherently limited. This is so because every analysis is both an elaboration of the viewpoint of the analyst and an incomplete attempt to understand things as they are.

No one, at the start of an analysis, can completely set aside the particular perceptions, preferences, and interests that he or she has acquired through the course of a lifetime. Moreover, no one, during the course of an analysis, can completely understand how it will be perceived by others who have different viewpoints. Such biases and limitations of perspective are not isolated from analysis, but expressed through it. They can be mitigated, but not eliminated, by adherence to

254

standards of evidence and inference. The result is that no set of recommendations based on policy or program analysis can incorporate *all* the factors that are (or might turn out to be) significant from every viewpoint. People differ in their interests and outlooks; analysts are no exception.

Everyone has some experience in which things as they are turned out to be different from things as they were perceived to be. Some people may have more foresight than others, but no one has a completely reliable crystal ball. At a fundamental level, the problem is that knowledge of external reality is in principle restricted to the past. Because we have no observations or data on the future, we therefore have no direct knowledge of it. Instead, we make inferences about future possibilities on the basis of present knowledge, and these inferences are routinely undermined in some respects, major or minor, by unfolding experience.[1] We nevertheless must make such inferences if we are to act with our eyes open to realize some of the preferred possibilities, such as improvements in community energy efficiency.[2]

In short, *there are no purely analytical or technical solutions to policy problems.* The implication is not to retreat from the discipline of analysis into willful ignorance or inaction. Rather, the implication is to subject the recommendations arising from policy and program analysis to the marketplace of ideas and to the tests of experience. This procedural approach is as American as apple pie; our culture prizes democracy and pragmatism, as well as science.[3] The alternative to the interplay of many viewpoints through an open and informed policy process is not *the* rational solution, but the imposition of *someone's* solution. Similarly, the alternative to continuous monitoring and evaluation of results is not *the* rational solution, but an inability to learn from experience and a tendency to repeat our mistakes. The rational course of action is not a matter settled a priori and in isolation by the analyst. The search for solutions is open-ended, and is more likely to produce satisfactory if not rational results where it is conducted with respect for differing viewpoints and the complexity of the world around us.[4]

One example of the search for solutions has already been presented in chapter 2, which describes the evolution of Ann Arbor's energy work plan. What remains is to review the evolution up to mid-1981 of the program options considered in the other chapters.

Program Evolution: Ann Arbor

Energy Monitoring System
On November 5, 1980, the city's Energy Management Task Force
approved an energy monitoring system for municipal buildings based
on substitution of an Energy Payment Voucher for the existing
voucher in the city's computerized bill payment procedure. The next
day, on recommendation of the Promotional Task Force, the Energy
Steering Committee unanimously added its endorsement. In both actions, the proposal was not controversial in part because the basic
design had been worked out in collaboration with city officials and in
part because the need for such a system was widely recognized. Implementation has been delayed, however, because of a bottleneck in
the Engineering Department arising from its responsibility for a number of more urgent projects and a resignation. At mid-1981, a consultant to the community development staff has been assigned to put two
weeks into the energy monitoring system in order to expedite entry of
the necessary additional data into the computer system.

Community Energy Report
Over the winter of 1980–81, three members of the Promotion Task
Force completed a pilot project to develop a community energy report.[5]
The pilot project relied on the collection of household energy data from
a sample of volunteers comprised of members of the Energy Steering
Committee, its task forces, and the community development staff. A
proposal is now being prepared to fund a more ambitious project that
incorporates the lessons learned from the pilot project.

The pilot project proposal was presented to the Energy Steering
Committee and approved on September 25, 1980. On that occasion
and at subsequent meetings of all task forces it was emphasized that
members who volunteered were expected to do two things. One was to
return signed forms authorizing Detroit Edison and Michigan Consolidated Gas to release account data over the previous year. The other
was to fill out and mail in at the end of each month a form (similar to
fig. 3 in chap. 7) to report household energy consumption data. Reporting would begin in October and continue through March. About
forty-five volunteers signed up for the pilot project.

Gasoline data were dropped from the project rather early when it was discovered that few households kept (or could be persuaded to keep) a gasoline log, and that the gasoline data reported was of poor quality. Tables 1 and 2 summarize the sample data for electricity and natural gas usage. The background or comparative data covering the period from October, 1979, through September, 1980, were obtained from the utilities after submission of the signed release forms by the project team. Maximum monthly sample size (number of households) dropped from a potential high of forty-five to thirty-six in the case of electricity and thirty in the case of natural gas. Some volunteers did not have natural gas service or accounts. Otherwise, the shrinkage in sample size reflects unsigned or unreturned release forms and relatively short account histories for those volunteers who had moved residence within the period. The volunteers mailed in reports for the first month, October, 1980, at a relatively high rate, but participation quickly dropped off to substantially

TABLE 1.   Sample Data of Electricity Usage from a Community Energy Report Pilot Study, in Kilowatt Hours

	No. of Households	Quartile Range			Mean	Min.	Max.
		Lower	Median	Upper			
Data from Utilities							
October, 1979	32	207	392	569	419	0	1,125
November	33	212	424	809	510	10	1,929
December	34	173	456	705	519	0	1,929
January, 1980	34	226	481	930	666	43	3,795
February	35	208	431	705	524	0	3,273
March	36	224	353	643	542	66	3,530
April	36	201	373	645	484	36	2,719
May	36	182	323	570	410	25	1,404
June	36	85	276	507	342	10	1,179
July	36	167	350	644	430	4	1,284
August	36	199	379	750	522	0	1,828
September	35	167	396	787	509	1	1,504
Data from Volunteers' Reports							
October, 1980	37	199	298	623	412	10	1,065
November	30	224	283	558	419	31	1,379
December	14	210	373	694	422	91	904
January, 1981	13	228	384	774	529	84	1,226
February	12	205	325	520	450	88	1,725

Source: Sue MacKenzie, Jackie Krieger, and Karen Rutledge

TABLE 2.   Sample Data of Natural Gas Usage from a Community Energy Report Pilot Study, in Hundred Cubic Feet

	No. of Households	Quartile Range			Mean	Min.	Max.
		Lower	Median	Upper			
		Data from Utilities					
October, 1979	23	24	57	86	61	3	177
November	27	55	130	153	109	0	206
December	28	78	162	217	150	4	360
January, 1980	27	146	196	248	189	1	415
February	27	172	222	320	239	4	642
March	26	191	261	297	231	4	408
April	27	100	179	250	237	4	1,678
May	29	57	108	139	120	4	606
June	28	32	40	56	49	8	141
July	28	21	35	43	63	2	892
August	29	21	27	50	39	6	160
September	30	11	30	44	30	0	78
		Data from Volunteers' Reports					
October, 1980	27	24	56	79	53	5	129
November	13	76	143	160	126	17	226
December	12	87	181	215	150	6	249
January, 1981	10	109	184	307	203	81	346
February	11	160	193	270	199	68	323

Source: Sue MacKenzie, Jackie Krieger, and Karen Rutledge

lower levels. By November, only thirteen natural gas reports were received; by December, only fourteen electricity reports were received. The assumptions about voluntary participation in the original design of a community energy report turned out to be optimistic.[6]

Assumptions about dissemination of the monthly reports also turned out to be optimistic. After an initial story that presented the background data and attempted to explain the basic rationale, the *Ann Arbor News* published only one other story from the project.[7] A third story with interviews from the median cases (gas and electricity) for the month was prepared by the Promotion Task Force team but delayed and later canceled. The problem resulted in part from delays in receiving data from the volunteers, which reduced the timeliness of the reports and in part from different conceptions of what constituted useful and interesting information for readers.

Because the initial design failed to foresee these problems of data collection and report dissemination, the pilot study did not progress far enough to clarify the basic question of whether a community energy report might stimulate comparisons of energy consumption levels among households and eventually help lower energy consumption levels on a communitywide basis. It is worth noting, however, that the project did stimulate comparisons and competition to reduce consumption among several volunteers in the sample.

The proposal now in preparation attempts to address these problems. On the one hand, current data will be collected on a more personal basis by telephone rather than by mail, and participation will be reinforced by quick reports to each volunteer showing his or her consumption relative to the median and interquartile range each month. On the other hand, editorial differences might be resolved through closer collaboration, and alternative means of dissemination will be explored. For example, copies of monthly community energy reports could be distributed free through banks, libraries, and other public places. The number of copies picked up could serve as a rough indication of the level of community interest.

Solar Applications at City Parks
On April 9, 1981, city council approved a resolution to initiate solar applications at city parks. It directed the Engineering and Parks and Recreation departments to

1. study the feasibility and cost-effectiveness of an active solar system for water and space heating at Fuller Park, and report back to City Council;
2. study the feasibility and cost-effectiveness of pool covers for passive solar heating at either Veterans or Buhr Park, and report back to City Council; and
3. monitor the consumption of natural gas by each boiler at Fuller, Veterans, and Buhr Parks through the installation of elapsed-time clocks and periodic readings.[8]

From a federal Energy Conservation Technical Assistance grant, eighteen hundred dollars has been set aside for the consulting services of Sunstructures, Inc., for solar heating analysis. The balance of costs will be covered by the city through staff support. Elapsed-time clocks were installed during the heating of Fuller Park pool prior to its open-ing for the 1981 swimming season, and additional clocks have been ordered for installation at Buhr and Veterans parks.

After the basic analysis reported in chapter 5 had been com-pleted, research on solar applications at city parks continued in the fall of 1980. Further investigation did not reduce major economic uncer-tainties, but it did confirm the initial impression that a glazed hot water collector might have substantial advantages over a simpler pool heater in terms of financial costs and benefits and demonstration value. The site of the proposed demonstration project was moved from Veterans to Fuller Park for two reasons. One was increasing concern that the roof of the ice arena at Veterans Park could not support the weight of a glazed collector array. The other was the breakdown of an industrial-sized boiler at Fuller Park. It was repaired and put back into service temporarily, but there is now an opportunity to replace it with a smaller and less expensive boiler supplemented by a domestic solar water heating system. The effect would be to reduce the initial cost of a solar demonstration project at Fuller Park and thereby improve the payback period (see fig. 3 in chap. 5).

The Energy Steering Committee cleared the proposal for public review on February 5, 1981, and voted unanimously to recommend it to the city council on March 19. During the intervening period, the Promotion Task Force contacted by telephone more than thirty people from a variety of groups—schools, churches, city government, solar and other businesses, service organizations, neighborhood organiza-tions, and swim clubs—who agreed to review and comment on the solar applications report. Those who did not respond to the written report and its covering letter within two weeks were contacted again by phone. By the March 19 meeting of the steering committee, nearly twenty responses had been received including an editorial endorse-ment from the *Ann Arbor News*.[9] Discussion focused on reservations expressed in a letter from the superintendent of the Parks and Recre-ation Department, most of which had been satisfied in a prior meeting with two committee members. The Republican member of the city council on the steering committee resolved concern about the mar-ginal economics of the project with the observation that the city parks system as a whole could not be expected to turn a profit either. The chair of the committee, a solar expert, confirmed that the project was valuable as a demonstration of the solar domestic water heating potential in Ann Arbor.

Within the city government, the city parks project has been associated with another project. In a memorandum distributed to city council members prior to its action on April 9, a city engineer noted the following:

> Working with the City staff, the Energy Steering Committee has developed a preliminary analysis for a solar demonstration program for Ann Arbor to incorporate two (2) facilities. The first facility is the Fuller pool and recreation center and the second facility is the South Industrial Utilities Maintenance Facility.[10]

The Energy Steering Committee was advised of the South Industrial project but did not participate in the planning of it. However, the project provides another opportunity to generate information on the solar potential in Ann Arbor. Sunstructures, Inc., has done the engineering which involves active and passive solar retrofit of the existing facility. Funding has been secured for the project pending final approval by council.

Feasibility analysis of the Fuller Park solar demonstration project using new data on natural gas consumption is expected to be completed by the fall of 1981. It will be important at that time to reemphasize that the major goal of the project is to generate reliable data on the solar potential in Ann Arbor, not dollar savings. If the decision is made to install an active solar domestic hot water heating system at Fuller Park, the top priority should be to monitor the reductions in natural gas consumption and to compare them with consumption at one of the other parks as a control. Evaluation is key to the success of the project.

Feedback for Energy Consumers
The proposal to improve feedback for energy consumers through revision of utility bills was presented to the Michigan Public Service Commission in December, 1980, and January, 1981, in connection with hearings to implement lifeline electric rates.[11] On May 27, 1981, as part of its order in the proceedings, the commission deferred consideration of the feedback proposal for at least one year pending clarification of customer reaction to the new rates.[12]

In Ann Arbor the previous fall, the feedback proposal had been vigorously and thoroughly debated by members of the Promotion Task Force over several meetings.[13] The central issue to emerge was the inclusion of marginal rate information in the feedback message (see fig. 4 in chap. 6). Opponents led by the manager of the Ann Arbor Division of Detroit Edison contended that the inverted block rate structure was complicated and that the marginal rate information, in particular, would unnecessarily confuse a substantial proportion of utility customers. Proponents advanced the viewpoint that while some confusion was inevitable, this was insufficient reason to keep customers in the dark as to the rates they paid, and that marginal rate information was the simplest and most appropriate price signal.

A staff member of the Washtenaw County Consumer Protection Agency helped resolve the issue. Several of his suggestions to reword the feedback message for purposes of clarity had already been accepted by feedback proponents before he attended the task force meeting on October 27, 1980. At the meeting he testified that, although some people do not benefit from consumer information even if it is easy to read, he nevertheless felt that such information should be made available. With eight in favor, two opposed, and one abstaining, the task force voted to recommend the feedback proposal to the Energy Steering Committee.

The proposal was taken up by the committee at the meeting of November 6, 1980. It took the form of six pages of documentation and a resolution that would be recommended to city council if approved by the committee. Detroit Edison chose not to oppose the feedback proposal directly; instead, it submitted a statement that was read at the meeting. It said in part:

> While we know that this proposal would result in additional costs and computer processing time, we cannot quantify precisely the expense that would be incurred since a number of other changes must be made that will impact the bill format. We are also concerned about the potential effect of this proposal on our customer's understanding of the bill, but cannot assess this until we know what form the other changes will take.[14]

The "other changes" would be necessary because of 1980 Public Act 139 of the State of Michigan, which directed the Michigan Public

Service Commission to implement lifeline electric rates. Michigan Consolidated Gas sent three representatives who expressed similar reservations and noted that it would be difficult to incorporate the feedback proposal into a new bill format scheduled for implementation early in 1981. After much discussion, the steering committee approved the proposal with thirteen ayes, one nay, and two abstentions.

On November 17, city council adopted the resolution unanimously after it was endorsed by two of its members, a Democrat and a Republican, who were also members of the steering committee. The resolution summarized the proposal and the case for it, and concluded

> NOW, BE IT THEREFORE RESOLVED, that the City Council of Ann Arbor endorses such improved feedback through monthly natural gas and electric bills and authorizes a representative of the Ann Arbor Energy Steering Committee to present a proposal for such improved feedback before the Michigan Public Service Commission.[15]

It was noted in the discussion that the resolution made no claim on the time of the city attorney, and that the Public Service Commission had more expertise to deal with the issue raised.

In the proceedings in Lansing, the commission's attention was focused on implementing 1980 Public Act 139. Revision of bill information was a subsidiary matter. Under the act, the commission was directed to increase the rate differentials between blocks of residential electricity consumption. The rate for the first several hundred kilowatt hours consumed per month (the lifeline block for essentials) was to be reduced; the rates for the higher blocks of consumption were to be increased, in some cases substantially. The central issue in the proceedings was the determination of blocks and rates within the framework of the act. The issue was complicated by uncertainties about the aggregate response of residential electricity demand to this major change in the rate structure. The act mandated a review of the new rate structure by the commission one year after implementation.

As pointed out in cross-examination, the combination of reduced rates for the lifeline block and the proposed feedback message could give rise to an anomaly. During the first year of lifeline rates, the lower portion of the feedback message could show *savings in costs* for those customers who *increased consumption* but stayed within the reduced-rate lifeline block. (This would occur when the reduction in rate more than compensated for the increase in consumption.) To correct this problem, it was proposed to program the computer to detect this combination of circumstances and to print a different message in the lower portion of the bill, or to implement the feedback message one year after implementation of the lifeline rates. Under the latter alternative, the original message would serve because rates in all blocks almost surely would stay the same or increase after the first year. Near the end of its May 27 order, the commission did not direct the utilities to implement either of these feedback alternatives, but noted that

> a substantial record has been developed on this issue and there may not be a need to present further testimony next year. However, the Commission and the other parties may learn a lot about customer reaction to lifeline rates during the next year, and that reaction may be helpful in assessing whether or not marginal pricing information should be ordered. The companies are of course free to offer this information voluntarily at this time if they so desire.[16]

We have as yet no indication that Detroit Edison intends to do so.

Should the Energy Steering Committee or its successor choose to, the feedback proposal can be reintroduced at the lifeline rates proceeding next year. Natural gas rate cases provide another opportunity, as yet untried, to raise the feedback issue. In any case, the proposal has attracted some interest from public interest groups who intervene in cases before the commission and lobby the state legislature.

Resource Recovery

On May 25, 1981, city council amended the city administrator's proposed 1981–82 budget to include fifty thousand dollars for recycling. The general plan is to use this money to expand the recycling operations of two private, nonprofit groups, the Ann Arbor Ecology Center and Recycle Ann Arbor. About half of the money will be used to buy a vehicle to facilitate collections and about half to buy materials to construct on city-owned land a shed to store recyclables and to house Recycle Ann Arbor's paper baler. (Baled newsprint can be sold for almost twice as much as unbaled.) A specific agreement between the city and the two private groups has yet to be worked out.[17]

The Ecology Center and Recycle Ann Arbor have provided much of the impetus for this major step toward a citywide, multimaterial recycling program. As noted in chapter 4, the Ecology Center has maintained a recycling station on land leased from the city for a dollar per year since 1970. Recycle Ann Arbor was founded in 1978. It is providing curbside pickup of paper, glass, and metal once a month in an area comprising about 20 percent of Ann Arbor's households. The two groups have coordinated their programs under an operating agreement.

Recycling options received early and detailed attention from the Renewable Resources Task Force. On February 5, 1981, the task force brought a resolution to the Energy Steering Committee in anticipation of city council action on the 1981–82 budget the next week. A sum of money for "recycling centers" had already been included in the 1983–84 capital improvements budget; the resolution called for council to make fifty thousand dollars available in the coming fiscal year for a shed and a vehicle. The two members of council who also sat on the Energy Steering Committee supported the resolution, which was approved unanimously. Final action on the 1981–82 budget, including the recycling project, was deferred until late May, after Michigan voters had turned down a ballot proposal that would have drastically affected city revenues.

Meanwhile, the Renewable Resources Task Force brought a more complete proposal to the Energy Steering Committee on March 5. The proposal was cleared unanimously for review through the public outreach plan, but initiation of the review has been deferred pending completion of documentation. The proposal does, however, appear as a major section of the task force report.[18] In addition to the fifty thousand dollar budget request, it included several other recommendations. One was enactment of an antiscavenging ordinance to deter unauthorized pickups that might otherwise undermine the program. Another was to provide a subsidy of ten dollars per ton to participating nonprofit groups that recycle multiple materials on a year-round basis. This subsidy was intended to reflect the approximate average costs avoided by the city's solid waste department, and to provide compensation for employees of the nonprofit groups. Finally, it was recommended that a mandatory recycling ordinance be submitted to voters as a ballot proposal approximately two years after the start of a citywide, multimaterial recycling program. Passage of such a proposal would increase the rate of participation in the program by Ann Arbor households and enhance the program's financial feasibility.[19]

In the months ahead, the top priority will be to complete arrangements for constructing a shed and buying a vehicle. This effort will include a lease for these facilities from the city to one or both of the nonprofit groups, and a decision about the location of the shed. The two alternatives are the current location of the recycling center near the middle of the city and the city's landfill located at the outskirts. The landfill site would increase hauling distances but facilitate alternative uses of the shed, if necessary. No action on the other recommendations has been initiated, so far as we know.

Still under consideration are facilities to produce energy directly from solid waste. The city has completed a $34,394 project (of which $23,860 was funded by the state Energy Administration) to analyze the quality and quantity of the Ann Arbor solid waste stream as a source of energy.[20] The results will be used to refine estimates of the financial feasibility of waterwall or modular combustion incinerators (now referred to as mass burning facilities) and a refuse-derived fuel facility. Interest in mass burning among city officials and others appears to have increased, in large part because the technology is relatively reliable. Interest in refuse-derived fuel has been sustained by a $260,765 feasibility study supported in part by a $195,038 grant from the Department of Energy.[21] The project under consideration in this study would produce refuse-derived fuel at the city's landfill and burn it to produce steam for electricity generation and space heating at a proposed power plant on the University of Michigan's North Campus. The study is a joint undertaking of the city and the university.

The Hydro Option

The possibility of reactivating one or all of the four former hydroelectric sites now owned by the city has been under study for more than two years since the basic analysis in chapter 3 was completed in June, 1979. The city engaged Ayres, Lewis, Norris, and May, Inc., to do a preliminary feasibility study of the four sites at a cost to the city of $5,311. The results, summarized in a Phase I report issued in May, 1980, were sufficiently promising to justify a Phase II assessment funded by a $38,412 loan from the federal government and $1,595 in city funds.[22] The Phase II report was issued in April, 1981, and has been reviewed by city engineers, the Renewable Resources Task Force, and others. On May 4, 1980, city council approved a resolution authorizing continuation of city activities toward reactivation of hydro-electric potential at the Huron River dams. As we shall see, the resolution moves the hydro option forward but falls short of a full commitment pending clarification of certain issues.

The summary economic analyses of the Barton Dam site from the Phase I and Phase II reports are compared in table 3. In the best case analysis, the Phase I report concluded that reactivation of the Barton site would produce a first-year profit of $50,718 and a life-cycle ben-

TABLE 3.　A Comparison of Phase I and II Results Regarding Reactivation of the Barton Dam Hydroelectric Site

	Phase I		
	Best Case	Worst Case	Phase II
Results			
Estimated or proposed installed capacity (in kw)	800	800	900
Projected average annual production (in kwh)	4,200,000	4,200,000	3,600,000
Projected first year revenue	$126,000	$126,000	$110,520
Projected or estimated development cost	$644,000	$1,472,000	$1,466,000
Net first year revenue	$50,718	$(20,358)	$(75,803)
Life cycle benefit/cost ratio	2.86	1.58	1.39
Assumptions			
Plant life (in years)	25	25	35
Annual escalation of energy prices	8%	8%	8%
Annual escalation of O & M costs	6%	6%	6%
Discount rate	8%	8%	10.5%
Avoided cost value of electricity (per/kwh)	3.00¢	3.00¢	3.07¢

Source: Ayres, Lewis, Norris, and May, Inc., *Preliminary Assessment of the Feasibility of Hydroelectric Development of Four City-Owned Dams for the City of Ann Arbor, Michigan* (Ann Arbor: Ayres, Lewis, Norris, and May, Inc., May, 1980), p. I-5; and *Assessment of the Feasibility of Hydroelectric Development of Four City-Owned Dams, City of Ann Arbor, Michigan, Phase II* (Ann Arbor: April, 1981), p. 4.

efit/cost ratio of 2.86. Although the assumptions differ from those used in chapter 3, the conclusions are approximately the same. Chapter 3 projected a first-year profit of $59,300 and a benefit/cost ratio of 3.4 for 830 kw of installed generating capacity. The economic projections are less favorable in the Phase I report's worst case, and still less favorable in the Phase II report. The latter projects that the best alternative at the Barton site would generate expenses in excess of revenues for eight years (including a loss of $75,803 in the first year) and a benefit/cost ratio of only 1.39. The Barton site is the most attractive of the four; the report shows that the Superior Dam site is the only other with a benefit/cost ratio greater than 1.0.[23]

The Phase II report attributes the differences in results from Phase I to several factors. First, while the earlier report based estimated development costs on summaries of forty-nine feasibility studies and fifteen demonstration projects the later report based estimated development costs and energy production on site-specific designs and engineering analyses, which are considered more reliable. Costs ranged from $644,000 to $1,472,000 in the Phase I report, and turned out to be at the high end of the range in the Phase II report.[24] Second, while the first report used a twenty-five-year project life and an 8 percent discount rate, the second used a thirty-five-year project life and a 10.5 percent discount rate.[25]

The Phase II results are based on installation in the Barton power house of two vertical turbines, of the same general type as the original turbines, rated at 600 kw and 300 kw. The electricity generated would be sold directly to Detroit Edison at a rate to be determined by the Michigan Public Service Commission but equal, under federal law, to the utility's avoided cost—that is, to the price the utility would pay to generate the power itself or add to its system. Ayres, Lewis, Norris, and May estimated this rate at 3.07¢ per kwh. It recommended financing of the project through general obligation bonds and contributions from other sources, private investors, or delaying the project until interest rates on municipal bonds decline. Nationally, there has been a surge in private investor interest in small hydro developments as a result of the avoided cost provision (Section 210) of the Public Utility Regulatory Policies Act of 1978 and a 21 percent investment tax credit for small hydro projects.[26] The latter is 11 percentage points higher than the standard investment tax credit, and is worth almost $304,000 on a project that costs as much as the Barton project estimate, $1,466,000.

The Phase II report concludes that

> The decision regarding whether or not to develop the sites is judgmental and can be made only by the City. However, judgment based strictly on engineering analyses and an economic evaluation which considers only tangible benefits directly associated with the hydro projects indicates only Barton and possibly Superior are viable hydro development projects at this time.[27]

The Renewable Resources Task Force found itself "in general agreement with the major conclusions of the [Phase II] Report . . . and supports the City's reactivation of two or more of its Huron River Dams for hydroelectric power generation."[28] In the task force's view, the life-cycle benefit/cost ratios in the Phase II report "represent a worst case scenario based on conservative projections."[29] The task force also responded to issues of marketing, financing, and timing. First, it recommended further review of the two principal alternatives for marketing the power produced, selling it to Detroit Edison or using it at city-owned facilities.[30] Second, it contended that private financing through a long-term lease with a private developer or investment group was not in the best interest of the city. (The mayor had been approached by a local investors' group as early as the summer of 1979; one of the principals of this group is mentioned without endorsement in connection with financing options in the Phase II report.) In addition, the task force urged the city to take certain steps at the state and federal levels as soon as possible in order to minimize regulatory delays.

The city council's May 4 resolution authorized further action with respect to all four sites, not just Barton and Superior.[31] Two actions were addressed specifically to the negative cash flows projected in the Phase II report. With regard to marketing, the city staff was directed

> to begin negotiations with Detroit Edison and other potential power purchasers to establish the most viable markets for the purchase of the power produced at the developed sites, and to develop a positive cash flow for each year of the life of the project.[32]

No direct reference was made to the alternative of using the power at city-owned facilities as opposed to selling the power to someone else. With regard to financing, the city staff was directed

> to develop other financing alternatives that will also produce positive cash flows throughout the life of the project, including but not limited to leasing for operation to private developers. A report will be developed by the Engineering Department for review by City Council discussing the financing alternatives examined.[33]

The reference to "leasing for operation" is unclear because operating expenses (exclusive of debt retirement) are only a minor part of the cash flow problem. In addition, city staff was directed "to continue licensing efforts to secure appropriate governmental approvals."[34] City council also directed the city administrator to report on progress of the hydro project every three months.

The council resolution acknowledged the inputs and the endorsements of Barton Hills Village, the Washtenaw Historical Society, and the Energy Steering Committee, all of which can be expected to participate in the resolution of the remaining issues. These include marketing, financing, timing, and the question of how many (if any) of the sites to reactivate.

Program Evolution: The Federal Level

Federal programs that stimulate and support local energy policy processes as an instrument of national energy policy are currently in a state of flux.[35] Under the Reagan administration, the general direction is toward cutbacks and consolidation, and energy is no exception. The expectation is that when action has been completed on the federal budget for the fiscal year beginning October 1, 1981, a variety of categorical programs to provide assistance for energy conservation and renewable resources development will have been consolidated into block grants at a reduced level of funding. One early result is the termination of the President's Clearinghouse for Community Energy Efficiency as of June 30, 1981, although plans for an energy management center to replace it are being discussed.

Under the previous administration, the Department of Energy

completed a study on the local role in energy policy and initiated such programs as the Comprehensive Community Energy Management Program (CCEMP) and the Decentralized Solar Energy Technology Assessment Program (TAP), both of which were described at the end of chapter 2.[36] In addition, the Solar Energy Research Institute (SERI), which is operated by the Midwest Research Institute for the Department of Energy, sponsored conferences on community renewable energy systems that were well attended by local energy officials.[37] The administration's major legislative initiative in this area was the Energy Management and Partnership Act of 1979 (S. 1280). Although addressed primarily to the states, it provided for grants through the states to local governments to develop and implement special energy projects.

> This feature of the bill would provide the flexibility necessary to support innovative projects which may not qualify under existing categorical programs but which are nevertheless worthy of federal support. Projects having national applicability are given preference under this program.[38]

The bill was passed by the Senate on July 25, 1980 and reported out of the House Interstate and Foreign Commerce Committee on September 5. However, the House did not take up the bill before the end of the Ninety-sixth Congress.

Another bill and an amendment more directly focused on the local role were developed and introduced by members of the Ninety-sixth Congress, but neither became law. On July 18, 1979, Senator Charles Percy of Illinois reintroduced the Local Energy Management Act of 1979 (S. 1537).[39] It would establish three modestly funded, interlocking programs. The first, a demonstration grants program, was designed to stimulate energy innovation within individual localities. The second was

> the documentation and distribution grants program [that] would provide funding to a limited number of localities which have already developed innovative energy programs. Localities receiving these grants would prepare and publish practical brochures on energy measures they have undertaken, and would make this information available, free of charge, to other localities.[40]

The third component of the bill was a local energy reference center to

> serve as a data bank and information clearinghouse on local energy initiatives . . . [drawing] upon the information gathered through the documentation and distribution grants program as well as other sources.[41]

The function was similar to that of the President's Clearinghouse for Community Energy Efficiency. The bill proposed an authorization of $15 million for the first year.

On October 12, 1979, Congressman Phil Sharp of Indiana introduced an amendment to the Department of Energy authorization bill (H.R. 3000) on information assistance for local conservation activities. The amendment proposed to set aside $2.3 million of funds authorized for the Energy Information Administration to facilitate the sharing of information on practical experience with energy programs at the local level. The funds would support a local energy reference center and provide for the reimbursement of local governments that supplied information on their programs. The House agreed to the amendment but failed to complete action on H.R. 3000.[42]

Whether these threads are picked up by the Ninety-seventh Congress or the new administration remains to be seen. However, a substantial federal role in local energy initiatives was not essential in Davis, Seattle, or Springfield, nor in other communities including Ann Arbor. There is every indication that a federal role can be helpful but will not be essential for further progress. Energy price increases and threats of energy supply curtailments arising, ultimately, from the global energy transition, continue to have an impact on local communities. And local policy processes continue to supplement market and federal policy processes in the search for solutions.

NOTES

This chapter was completed on July 1, 1981. The authors acknowledge with thanks in the notes that follow the people who have supplied information on particular projects, and Cynthia Conklin, Lawrence B. Mohr, Tom Rieke, and Barry Tilmann, who reviewed all or part of the draft. Responsibility rests with the authors, not their colleagues.

1. Assessments of forecast accuracy in a number of fields, including energy, can be found in William Ascher, *Forecasting: An Appraisal for Policy-Makers and Planners* (Baltimore: Johns Hopkins University Press, 1978).

2. Compare Bertrand de Jouvenel, *The Art of Conjecture* (New York: Basic Books, 1967), p. 5: "The expression 'knowledge of the future' is a contradiction in terms. Strictly speaking, only *facta* can be known; we can have positive knowledge only of the past. On the other hand, the only 'useful knowledge' we have relates to the future."

3. See Abraham Kaplan, *American Ethics and Public Policy* (New York: Oxford University Press, 1963), especially the section entitled "Methodology of Morals."

4. On the interested as opposed to disinterested role of analysts see James R. Schlesinger, "Systems Analysis and the Policy Process," *Journal of Law and Economics* 11 (October, 1968):281–98. On rationality see Herbert Simon, "Rationality as Process and as Product of Thought," *American Economic Review* 68 (May, 1978):1–16. On the need for humility in social science see Joseph J. Spengler, "Social Science and the Collectivization of Hubris," in *Propaganda and Communication in World History,* ed. Harold D. Lasswell, Daniel Lerner, and Hans Speier, vol. 3, *A Pluralizing World in Formation* (Honolulu: University of Hawaii Press, 1980).

5. The three were Susan Mackenzie, Jackie Krieger, and Karen Rutledge, who provided material for this update.

6. Table 1 also illustrates some important properties of the data. Notice particularly the minimum and maximum consumption levels in the monthly samples. Zero minimums indicate missing data in at least one account; unusually high maximums indicate multiple-month account data, or, in the case of electricity, electric space or water heating. Examples of unusually high maximums can be found in the natural gas data for April and July, 1980, which show maximum consumption increasing by more than a factor of four from colder to warmer months. A few extreme values distort the sample mean, but leave the median and interquartile range unaffected.

7. See Chong W. Pyen, "How Normal Are Your Gas, Electric Bills?" *Ann Arbor News,* December 29, 1980; and Chong W. Pyen, "We're Saving Energy—But Not Money—Because of Rate Hikes," *Ann Arbor News,* February 27, 1981.

8. "Resolution to Initiate Solar Applications at City Parks," Ann Arbor City Council, filed April 9, 1981. Cindy Conklin, Susan Greenberg, and Gary Woodard provided material for this update.

9. "Fuller Pool Solar Idea Sounds Good," *Ann Arbor News,* March 3, 1981.

10. Memorandum from Leigh A. Chizek to Godfrey W. Collins, Assistant Administrator, March 27, 1981, on Energy Conservation/Technical Assistance (ECTA) Program Proposal Evaluations.

11. Ronald D. Brunner, "Direct Testimony Before the Michigan Public

Service Commission, Case No. U-6590," mimeographed (December 19, 1980). Cross-examination occurred on January 26, 1981.

12. Michigan Public Service Commission, "Order Implementing Lifeline Rate Structure, Case No. U-6590," mimeographed (May 27, 1981).

13. The "Summary of Meetings" of the Promotion Task Force shows references to and discussion of the proposal at the meetings of September 15, 22, and 29, and October 6, 13, and 27.

14. Detroit Edison, "Statement Concerning Professor Brunner's Recommendation," mimeographed (November 6, 1980). See also Chong W. Pyen, "Energy-Saving Proposal May Stir Energetic Debate," *Ann Arbor News,* November 6, 1980.

15. "Resolution Promoting Improved Communications for Ann Arbor Energy Consumers," Ann Arbor City Council, filed November 17, 1980.

16. Michigan Public Service Commission, "Order Implementing Lifeline Rate Structure, Case No. U-6590," p. 32.

17. Material for this update has been provided by Sydney Solberg and Wendy Wilson.

18. Renewable Resources Task Force, *Ann Arbor Energy Plan: Renewable Resources Task Force Report* (Ann Arbor: Energy Steering Committee, 1981), pp. 33–45.

19. Another recommendation was either to enforce an existing provision of the city code limiting residential refuse pickup to no more than three twenty-five gallon containers per household per week or to charge extra for any more than three such containers. By council resolution the number of containers permitted had been increased to ten to accommodate grass clippings and leaves. The purpose of the recommendation was to underscore the cost of collecting and burying material that could easily be composted, and to avoid that cost.

20. Budget figures are from Community Development Office, "Summary of City Energy Programs," photocopied (September 30, 1980), p. 13. The report from the study was made available to the public late in July, 1981.

21. The Community Development Office "Summary of City Energy Programs," also shows, p. 13, that the state share was $23,860, the city share was $19,068, and the university share was $22,800. This report also was made available to the public late in July, 1981.

22. Community Development Office, "Summary of City Energy Programs," p. 14. For results see Ayres, Lewis, Norris, and May, Inc., *Preliminary Assessment of the Feasibility of Hydroelectric Development of Four City-Owned Dams for the City of Ann Arbor, Michigan* (Ann Arbor: Ayres, Lewis, Norris, and May, 1980); and Ayres, Lewis, Norris, and May, Inc., *Assessment of the Feasibility of Hydroelectric Development of Four City-Owned Dams, City of Ann Arbor, Michigan, Phase II* (Ann Arbor: Ayres, Lewis, Norris, and May, 1981). Material for this update was supplied by Owen Jansson and Barry Murray.

23. The Phase II report, p. 4, gives benefit/cost ratios of 1.11, 0.68, and 0.76 for Superior, Argo, and Geddes dams, respectively.

24. Development cost estimates are thus the major analytical weakness of both chapter 3 and the Phase I report.

25. In the Phase II study, the discount rate is set equal to the interest rate for municipal bonds. However, the analysis includes an 8 percent annual increase in energy prices. The net effect (ignoring operation and maintenance cost increases) is equivalent to the 2.5 percent discount rate used in chapter 3. The Phase I analysis was done in current dollars; the chapter 3 analysis was done in constant dollars.

26. Richard Corrigan, "With an Off-Handed Push from Congress, Speculators Plunge into Small Hydro," *National Journal,* May 30, 1981, pp. 974–77.

27. From pp. 3, 5 of the Phase II report.

28. Renewable Resources Task Force, *Ann Arbor Energy Plan: Renewable Resources Task Force Report,* p. 27.

29. Ibid., p. 30.

30. Ibid.

31. In an April 4 memorandum to mayor and council, Leigh A. Chizek, City Engineer, recommended "maintaining all four (4) dams within the scope of the project in order to most effectively study all possible alternatives."

32. "Resolution Authorizing Continuation of City Activities Toward Reactivation of Hydroelectric Potential at the Huron River Dams," Ann Arbor City Council, filed May 4, 1981.

33. Ibid.

34. According to Barry Murray of the Renewable Resources Task Force, Ann Arbor applied in March, 1980, to the Federal Energy Regulatory Commission for preliminary permits to secure priority of application for licenses required to operate dams as generating facilities. The preliminary permits were received in October, 1980.

35. For a recent account see Beverly A. Cigler, "Organizing for Local Energy Management: Early Lessons," *Public Administration Review* 41 (July/August, 1981):470–79.

36. U.S., Department of Energy, Assistant Secretary for Policy and Evaluation, *Local Government Energy Activities,* 3 vols. (Washington, D.C.: Government Printing Office, 1979).

37. The proceedings of the first conference can be found in Robert Odland, ed., *Community Energy Self-Reliance* (Washington, D.C.: Government Printing Office, 1980).

38. From a letter by Jimmy Carter transmitting the Energy Management Partnership Act of 1979 to the Senate, *Congressional Record,* June 5, 1979, p. S6969.

39. The first version of the bill, S. 931, can be found in the *Congressional Record,* April 9, 1979, pp. S4199–4202. See also Ronald D. Brunner,

"Suggestions for Revision of S. 931," photocopied (Ann Arbor: Institute of Public Policy Studies, May 9, 1979).

40. From the remarks by Senator Percy introducing S. 1537, the Local Energy Management Act of 1979, *Congressional Record,* July 18, 1979, p. S9785.

41. Ibid.

42. *Congressional Record,* October 12, 1979, pp. H9059–60.

Bibliography

This bibliography is divided into three sections. The first consists of references on the Ann Arbor energy initiative, the second consists of other energy references, and the third collects references to the general public policy literature.

The Ann Arbor Energy Initiative

Ann Arbor, Ad Hoc Committee on Solid Waste Disposal. "Final Report to Ann Arbor City Council." Mimeographed. Ann Arbor: Ad Hoc Committee on Solid Waste Disposal, May 17, 1977.

Ann Arbor, Community Development Office. "Proposal for Energy Conservation Public Awareness Campaign." Photocopied. Ann Arbor: Community Development Office, 1979.

———. *1980 Energy Plan*. Ann Arbor: Community Development Office, January, 1980.

———. "Summary of City Energy Programs." Photocopied. Ann Arbor: Community Development Office, September 30, 1980.

Ann Arbor, Department of Solid Waste. "Solid Waste Disposal in Ann Arbor: An Evaluation and Recommendation." Mimeographed. Ann Arbor: Department of Solid Waste, January 29, 1979.

Ann Arbor, Energy Steering Committee. "Minutes of Meetings." Photocopied. Ann Arbor: Community Development Office, 1980–81.

———. *Ann Arbor Energy Plan: A Summary of Findings*. Ann Arbor: Community Development Office, June, 1981.

Ann Arbor, Energy Steering Committee, Building Retrofit Task Force. *Ann Arbor Energy Plan: Building Retrofit Task Force Report*. Ann Arbor: Community Development Office, June, 1981.

Ann Arbor, Energy Steering Committee, New Construction and Site Design Task Force. *Ann Arbor Energy Plan: New Construction and Site Design Task Force Report*. Ann Arbor: Community Development Office, June, 1981.

Ann Arbor, Energy Steering Committee, Promotion Task Force. "Summary of Meetings." Photocopied. Ann Arbor: Community Development Office, 1980–81.

———. "A Public Outreach Plan." Photocopied. Ann Arbor: Community Development Office, January 5, 1981.

277

————. *Ann Arbor Energy Plan: Promotion Task Force Report.* Ann Arbor: Community Development Office, June, 1981.

Ann Arbor, Energy Steering Committee, Renewable Resources Task Force. *Ann Arbor Energy Plan: Renewable Resources Task Force Report.* Ann Arbor: Community Development Office, June, 1981.

Ann Arbor, Energy Steering Committee, Transportation and Land Use Task Force. *Ann Arbor Energy Plan: Transportation and Land Use Task Force Report.* Ann Arbor: Community Development Office, June, 1981.

Ayres, Lewis, Norris, and May, Inc. *Preliminary Assessment of the Feasibility of Hydroelectric Development of Four City-Owned Dams for the City of Ann Arbor, Michigan.* Ann Arbor: Ayres, Lewis, Norris, and May, Inc., May, 1980.

————. *Assessment of the Feasibility of Hydroelectric Development of Four City-Owned Dams, City of Ann Arbor, Michigan, Phase II.* Ann Arbor: April, 1981.

Belcher, Louis D. "Charge to the Energy Steering Committee." Photocopied. Ann Arbor: Community Development Office, May 8, 1980.

Brunner, Ronald D. "Direct Testimony Before the Michigan Public Service Commission, Case No. U-6590." Photocopied. Ann Arbor: December 19, 1980.

Chapman, Reuben. "Proposals to Attract More Bikers." *Ann Arbor News,* February 16, 1981.

"City Can Help Itself on Energy." *Ann Arbor News,* January 31, 1980.

"City 'Committed to Conservation'." *Ann Arbor News,* September 26, 1979.

Cohen, Jane. *Ann Arbor and the Huron River Valley: Take A Closer Look.* Ann Arbor: Huron River Watershed Council, 1979.

"Council Clogs Shredder Plans." *Ann Arbor News,* November 14, 1979.

Detroit Edison Company. "The Hydro-Electric Plants of the Detroit Edison Company." Mimeographed. Detroit: Detroit Edison Company, 1951.

————. *Rate Book for Electric Service.* Detroit: Detroit Edison Company, 1978.

————. "Statement Concerning Professor Brunner's Recommendation." Photocopied. Ann Arbor: Detroit Edison Company, November 6, 1980.

Dunn, Nancy. "Waste-To-Energy Proposal Down the Drain." *Ann Arbor News,* June 25, 1975.

Ecology Center Staff. "Recycling: A Study of Citizen Participation in Ann Arbor." Mimeographed. Ann Arbor: Ecology Center, 1971.

"Energy Savings Classes Open." *Ann Arbor News,* September 8, 1980.

"Energy Task Forces Outline Programs." *Ann Arbor News,* November 25, 1980.

"Fuller Pool Solar Idea Sounds Good." *Ann Arbor News,* March 3, 1981.

Goyer, John. "Council Puts Off Action on Confusing Energy Plan." *Michigan Daily,* February 22, 1980.

Harris, Glen. "Recycling Plan Snagged." *Ann Arbor News,* November 16, 1976.

————. "Fuel Plan Rises From Junk Heap." *Ann Arbor News,* May 22, 1977.

————. "City Facing New Trash Crunch." *Ann Arbor News,* July 2, 1978.

————. "City Urged To Go Slow on Plan for Waste." *Ann Arbor News,* July 11, 1978.

Henningson, Durham, and Richardson. *Feasibility Study of Solid Waste Shredding Facilities for the City of Ann Arbor, Michigan.* Omaha: Henningson, Durham, and Richardson, 1978.

"Huron: 'Stream of Energy'." *Ann Arbor News,* December 9, 1978.

Jones and Henry Engineers, Ltd. *A Washtenaw County Plan for the Management of Solid Waste: Final Report.* Toledo: Jones and Henry, 1975.

LeLievre, Roger, and Klein, Pamela. "Saving Energy: A Local Perspective." *Ann Arbor News,* September 23–28, 1979.

Michigan, Department of Commerce, Energy Administration. "PACES: Public Awareness Campaign Evaluation Survey; Report on Survey of Ann Arbor Residents." Photocopied. Lansing: Michigan Department of Commerce, 1979.

"New Plant Could Extend Life of City Landfill." *Ann Arbor News,* November 7, 1978.

"News Adds Solar Data to Its Weather Report." *Ann Arbor News,* October 19, 1979.

Pyen, Chong W. "Trash Shredding Possible." *Ann Arbor News,* January 30, 1979.

————. "Mobility Outdates City Planning Data." *Ann Arbor News,* May 10, 1979.

————. "City Mounting Energy Campaign." *Ann Arbor News,* June 10, 1979.

————. "City Shredder Called Big Waste." *Ann Arbor News,* July 5, 1979.

————. "Shredder May Be Scrapped." *Ann Arbor News,* October 23, 1979.

————. "City Gets Sweeping Energy Plan." *Ann Arbor News,* January 29, 1980.

————. "City Gets Tips on Waste Disposal Problems." *Ann Arbor News,* January 29, 1980.

————. "Energy Proposal Challenged." *Ann Arbor News,* February 22, 1980.

————. "Changing Energy Lifestyle Goal of Panel." *Ann Arbor News,* March 26, 1980.

————. "Energy Panel Sniffing Out Wasted Watts." *Ann Arbor News,* June 27, 1980.

————. "Energy Panel Drafting Sweeping Plan." *Ann Arbor News,* September 30, 1980.

————. "Energy-Saving Proposal May Stir Energetic Debate." *Ann Arbor News,* November 6, 1980.

————. "How Normal Are Your Gas, Electric Bills?" *Ann Arbor News,* December 29, 1980.

————. "Solar Panel Generating Energy Ideas." *Ann Arbor News,* February 27, 1981.

————. "We're Saving Energy—But Not Money—Because of Rate Hikes." *Ann Arbor News,* February 27, 1981.

————. "Energy Plan for City Ready for Public Hearing Thursday." *Ann Arbor News,* May 11, 1981.

————. "Renters Support Forced Insulation." *Ann Arbor News,* May 15, 1981.

————. "Long-Awaited Energy Plan Ready for Action by Council." *Ann Arbor News,* June 5, 1981.

————. "Council Gives Cool Reception to Energy Conservation Plan." *Ann Arbor News,* June 9, 1981.

Resolution to Adopt 1980 Energy Work Plan. Ann Arbor City Council, filed March 17, 1980.

Resolution Promoting Improved Communications for Ann Arbor Energy Consumers. Ann Arbor City Council, filed November 17, 1980.

Resolution to Initiate Solar Applications at City Parks. Ann Arbor City Council, filed April 9, 1981.

Resolution Authorizing Continuation of City Activities Toward Reactivation of Hydroelectric Potential at the Huron River Dams. Ann Arbor City Council, filed May 4, 1981.

Senunas, Louis. "Shredder Is Not the Answer to City's Waste Problem." *Ann Arbor News,* November 28, 1979.

Treml, William B. "Is Ann Arbor Still an All-American City?" *Ann Arbor News,* May 25, 1981.

"Voters Approve Shredder Proposal." *Ann Arbor News,* April 3, 1979.

Other Energy References

Acton, Jan, and Mowill, Ragnhild Sohlbert. *Conserving Electricity by Ordinance: A Statistical Analysis.* R-1650-FEA. Santa Monica: Rand Corporation, 1975.

American Gas Association, Edison Electric Institute, Consumer Activities Committee. *1975 Directory: Customer Accounting Methods and Equipment.*

Aron, Joan B. "Intergovernmental Politics of Energy." *Policy Analysis* 5 (Fall, 1979):451–71.

Associated Press. "Earth Day Rebel's Evolution Mirrors That of Davis, Calif." *Ann Arbor News,* September 18, 1980.

Ayres, Lewis, Norris, and May, Inc. *Assessment of the Feasibility of Recommissioning the French Landing Hydroelectric Facility in Van Buren Township, Michigan.* Ann Arbor: Ayres, Lewis, Norris, and May, Inc., 1979.

Baldwin, Fred D. "Meters, Bills, and the Bathroom Scale." *Public Utilities Fortnightly,* February 3, 1977, pp. 11–17.

Baltimore City, League of Women Voters. "Conserving Energy: Baltimore City's Energy Conservation Program." Mimeographed. Baltimore: League of Women Voters, March 29, 1979.

Becker, Lawrence J. "Joint Effects of Feedback and Goal Setting on Performance: A Field Study of Residential Energy Conservation." *Journal of Applied Psychology* 63 (1978):428–33.

Becker, Lawrence J., and Seligman, Clive. "Reducing Air Conditioning Waste by Signalling It Is Cold Outside." *Personality and Social Psychology Bulletin* 4 (July, 1978):412–15.

Bee Angell and Associates, Inc. *A Qualitative Study of Consumer Attitudes Toward Energy Conservation.* Washington, D.C.: Federal Energy Administration, 1975.

Bronfman, Benson H.; Carnes, Sam A.; Schweitzer, Martin; Peelle, Elizabeth; and Enk, Gordon. *The Decentralized Solar Energy Technology Assessment Program: Review of Activities (April 1978–December 1979).* ORNL/TM-7189. Oak Ridge: Oak Ridge National Laboratory, May, 1980.

Brooks, Sarah Osgood; Wood, Elizabeth Scull; Guenther, Sue; and Graves, Thomas. *A Guide to Reducing Energy Use: Budget Costs.* Local Energy Management Program, vol. 2. Washington, D.C.: National Association of Counties Research, Inc. and U.S. Conference of Mayors, 1979.

Brown, Peter W.; Plitch, Lawrence W.; and Ringo, Martin. "Obstacles and Incentives to Small-Scale Hydroelectric Power." In *Energy Policy and Public Administration,* edited by Gregory A. Daneke and George K. Lagassa. Lexington, Mass.: Lexington Books, 1980.

Brunner, Ronald D. "Suggestions for Revision of S. 931." Photocopied. Ann Arbor: Institute of Public Policy Studies, May 9, 1979.

Brunner, Ronald D., and Vivian, Weston E. "Citizen Viewpoints on Energy Policy." *Policy Sciences* 12 (1980):147–74.

Butt, Sheldon. "Inflation and Solar Energy." *Solar Engineering,* August, 1979, p. 40.

California, Office of Appropriate Technology. *Working Together: Community Self-Reliance in California.* Sacramento: California Office of Appropriate Technology, 1981.

"A California Town Is Able to Kill a Watt in Its War on Waste." *Wall Street Journal,* May 17, 1978.

Cigler, Beverly A. "Directions in Local Energy Policy and Management." *The Urban Interest,* Fall, 1980, pp. 32–41.

————. "Organizing for Local Energy Management: Early Lessons." *Public Administration Review* 41 (July/August, 1981):470–79.

Citizen's Advisory Committee on Environmental Quality. *Energy in Solid Waste.* Washington, D.C.: Government Printing Office, 1974.

Clark, John A. "Solar Energy Economics—The *A Priori* Decision." *International Journal of Heat Transfer* 19 (1976):1095–1106.

Corrigan, Richard. "With an Off-Handed Push from Congress, Speculators Plunge into Small Hydro." *National Journal,* May 30, 1981, pp. 974–77.

Cortner, Hanna J. "Formulating and Implementing Energy Policy: The Inadequacy of the State Response." *Policy Studies Journal* 7 (August, 1978):24–29.

Darnay, Arnsen, and Franklin, William E. *Salvage Markets for Materials in Solid Waste*. Washington, D.C.: U.S. Environmental Protection Agency, 1972.

Doran, Daniel M. *Energy from a Wasted Resource: The Ames Experience*. Ames, Iowa: City of Ames, 1978.

East Lansing, Department of Planning, Housing, and Community Development, Planning Division. *Energy: Conservation Alternatives for the City of East Lansing*. East Lansing, Mich.: Department of Planning, Housing, and Community Development, May, 1979.

E G & G, Inc. *Executive Summaries, Small/Low-Head Hydropower PRDA-1706 Feasibility Assessments*. Idaho Falls, Idaho: U.S. Department of Energy, Idaho Operations Office, 1979.

Elements, The. *The Davis Experiment: One City's Plan to Save Energy*. Washington, D.C.: Public Resource Center, 1979.

Energy Conservation and Production Act, Pub. L. No. 94-385, 90 Stat. 1125 (1976).

"Energy Management Partnership Act of 1979 (S. 1280)." *Congressional Record*, 96th Cong., 1st sess., June 5, 1979, pp. S6965–70. (By Senator Jackson by request.)

Energy Policy and Conservation Act, Pub. L. No. 94-163, 89 Stat. 871 (1975).

Energy Tax Act of 1978, Pub. L. No. 95-618, 92 Stat. 3174 (1978).

"Factsheet: Solar Swimming Pool Heaters." Rockville, Md.: National Solar Heating and Cooling Information Center, 1978.

Fitchburg Action to Conserve Energy. "Handbook." Mimeographed. Fitchburg, Mass.: Fitchburg Action to Conserve Energy, n.d.

Franklin County Energy Conservation Task Force. "Franklin County Energy Profile, 1975–1978." Mimeographed. Greenfield, Mass.: Franklin County Energy Conservation Task Force, n.d.

———. "Franklin County Energy Conservation Survey, 1978." Mimeographed. Greenfield, Mass.: Franklin County Energy Conservation Task Force, n.d.

Gil, Efraim. *Energy-Efficient Planning: An Annotated Bibliography*. Planning Advisory Service Report No. 315. Chicago: American Society of Planning Officials, 1976.

Gleichman, Ted K. "Case Study: Electricity from the Great Stone Dam." *Solar Law Reporter* 2 (November/December, 1980):753–67.

Gorton, Tom. "In Ames, Iowa, They're Taking the Waste Out of Garbage." *Planning* 43 (January, 1977):14–18.

Hampshire College (Amherst, Mass.). *Energy Self-Sufficiency in Northampton, Massachusetts*. Washington, D.C.: U.S. Department of Energy, Assistant Secretary for Policy and Evaluation, 1979.

Hart, Kimball G., and the Editors of U.S. News & World Report Books. *How to Cut Your Energy Costs: A Guide to Major Savings at Home and on the Road*. Washington, D.C.: U.S. News & World Report Books, 1978.

Hayes, Steven C., and Cone, John D. "Reduction of Residential Consumption of Electricity Through Simple Monthly Feedback." *Journal of Applied Behavior Analysis* 14, no. 1 (Spring, 1981):81–88.

Hendricks, John W. "Public Participation and Democratic Decision Making on Energy Issues." *Social Science Energy Review* 1 (Spring, 1978):1–21.

Henningson, Durham, and Richardson. *State of Michigan: Interim Report on Energy Markets*. Omaha: Henningson, Durham, and Richardson, 1977.

————. *State of Michigan: Interim Report on Quantities and Composition of Solid Waste*. Omaha: Henningson, Durham, and Richardson, 1977.

————. *State of Michigan: Interim Report on Technology Evaluation*. Omaha: Henningson, Durham, and Richardson, 1977.

Hildt, Michael; Sheets, Edward; and Somerstein, Lee. "Energy 1990: An American City Tackles Its Energy Future." Photocopied. Seattle: City of Seattle, 1977.

Hill, Greg. "The Politics of Energy 1990." Photocopied. Seattle: City of Seattle, April 17, 1978.

Hitch, Charles J., ed. *Modeling Energy-Economy Interactions: Five Approaches*. Baltimore: Johns Hopkins University Press, 1977.

Hunt, Marshall, and Bainbridge, David. "The Davis Experience." *Solar Age*, May, 1978, pp. 20–23.

"Information Assistance for Local Conservation Activities (Amendment to H. R. 3000, Department of Energy Authorization Act for Fiscal Years 1980 and 1981—Civilian Applications)." *Congressional Record*, 96th Cong., 1st sess., October 12, 1979, pp. H9059–60. (By Representative Sharp.)

International City Management Association. "Managing the Impact of the Energy Crisis: The Role of Local Government." *Management Information Service Report* 12 (February, 1980):1–17.

International City Management Association, National Association of Counties, National League of Cities, and U.S. Conference of Mayors. *Community Energy Efficiency: How Local Governments Accomplish It*. Washington, D.C.: President's Clearinghouse for Community Energy Efficiency, n.d.

Kirschten, Dick. "Hydropower—Turning to Water to Turn the Wheels." *National Journal*, April 29, 1978, pp. 672–89.

Knapp, Dan; Brandt, Tom; and Carson, Don. "Mine the Trash Cans, Not the Land." *Rain*, November, 1978, pp. 4–8.

Koenig, Herman E., and Sommers, Lawrence M., eds. *Energy and the Adaptation of Human Settlements: A Prototype Process in Genesee County, Michigan*. East Lansing: Michigan State University Center for Environmental Quality, 1980.

Kohlenberg, Robert; Alberstein, Barry; Barach, Roland; and Anschell, Susie. "Washington State Electrical Rate Demonstration Project: Quarterly Progress Report." Photocopied. Seattle: University of Washington, October, 1978.

Lanouette, William J. "Rising Oil and Gas Prices Are Making Hydropower Look Better Every Day." *National Journal,* April 26, 1980, pp. 685–89.

Lescaze, Lee. "Little Dams Being Revived as Power Source; Big Utilities Balk." *Washington Post,* March 11, 1978.

"Lifeline Rates" 1980 Mich. Pub. Acts 139, to amend 1939 Mich. Pub. Acts 3.

"Local Energy Management Act of 1979 (S. 931)." *Congressional Record,* 96th Cong., 1st sess., April 9, 1979, pp. 4199–4202. (By Senator Percy for himself and Senators Domenici, Heinz, Kennedy, and Tsongas.)

"Local Energy Management Act of 1979 (S. 1537)." *Congressional Record,* 96th Cong., 1st sess., July 18, 1979, pp. S9784–89. (By Senator Percy for himself and Senators Baucus, Cohen, Domenici, Hatfield, Heinz, Kennedy, Sarbanes, and Tsongas.)

Lock, Reinier H. J. H. "Encouraging Decentralized Generation of Electricity: Implementation of the New Statutory Scheme." *Solar Law Reporter* 2 (November/December, 1980):705–52.

"Look Before You Leap Into a Solar Pool System." *Solar Engineering* 4 (November, 1979):19.

Marketing Services Company, Inc. "RECIP Program Study." Mimeographed. Hartford: Connecticut Light and Power Company, 1979.

Massachusetts Electric Company and Northeast Utilities Service. "A Feasibility Study of the Erving Paper Mills Site." Mimeographed. Franklin County Energy Conservation Task Force, 1979.

Max, Bradford J. *Resource Recovery and Waste Reduction Activities: A Nationwide Survey.* Washington, D.C.: U.S. Environmental Protection Agency, 1979.

Mayer, Lawrence S. and Benjamini, Yoav. "Modeling Residential Demand for Natural Gas as a Function of the Coldness of the Month." *Energy and Buildings* 1 (1977/78):301–12.

McCombs, Phil. "Energy-Savings Ideas Work." *Washington Post,* April 14, 1980.

McGarity, Arthur E. *Solar Heating and Cooling: An Economic Assessment.* Washington, D.C.: Government Printing Office, 1977.

McGregor, Gloria Shepard. "Davis California Implements Energy Building Code." *Practicing Planner* 6 (February, 1976):24.

Michigan, Department of Commerce, Energy Administration. *The Michigan Solar Tax Credit Program.* Lansing: Michigan Department of Commerce, 1978.

Michigan, Department of Management and Budget. *Population Projections for Michigan to the Year 2000. Summary Report: State, Regions, Counties.* Lansing: Michigan Department of Management and Budget, 1978.

Michigan, Department of Natural Resources. "Status Report on Michigan Dams." Mimeographed. Lansing: Michigan Department of Natural Resources, June, 1972.

Michigan, Public Service Commission. "Opinion and Order, Case No. U-

5502." Mimeographed. Lansing: Michigan Public Service Commission, September 28, 1978.

————. "Opinion and Order, Case No. U-5955." Mimeographed. Lansing: Michigan Public Service Commission, November 6, 1979.

————. "Opinion and Order, Case No. U-6006." Mimeographed. Lansing: Michigan Public Service Commission, March 14, 1980.

————. "Order Granting, In Part, Motion for Partial and Immediate Relief, Case No. U-6372." Mimeographed. Lansing: Michigan Public Service Commission, July 1, 1980.

————. "Order Initiating Hearings to Implement Provisions of 1980 PA 139 (Lifeline Rates), Case No. U-6590." Mimeographed. Lansing: Michigan Public Service Commission, September 16, 1980.

————. "Order Implementing Lifeline Rate Structure, Case No. U-6590." Mimeographed. Lansing: Michigan Public Service Commission, May 27, 1981.

Michigan Energy and Resource Research Association. *Toward a Unified Michigan Energy Policy.* Detroit: Michigan Energy and Resource Research Association, 1977.

Milstein, Jeffrey S. "How Consumers Feel About Energy: Attitudes and Behavior During the Winter and Spring of 1976–77." Mimeographed. Washington, D.C.: Federal Energy Administration, June, 1977.

Moore, John L.; Berger, David A.; Rubin, Claire B.; and Hutchinson, Philip A., Sr. *Organizing for Comprehensive Community Energy Management and Planning: Some Preliminary Observations.* Technical Memo ANL/CNSV-TM-27. Argonne, Ill.: Argonne National Laboratory, 1979.

Moore, John L.; Berger, David A.; Rubin, Claire B.; Hutchinson, Philip A., Sr.; and Griggs, Harry M. *Community Energy Auditing: Experience with the Comprehensive Community Energy Management Program.* Technical Memo ANL/CNSV-TM-43. Argonne, Ill.: Argonne National Laboratory, 1980.

Morris, David. *Planning for Energy Self-Reliance: A Case Study of the District of Columbia.* Preliminary Report. Washington, D.C.: Institute for Local Self-Reliance, 1979.

Mounts, Richard. "The Role of Local Government in a National Energy Strategy." Mimeographed. Washington, D.C.: National League of Cities, 1977.

————. "What Cities Are Doing about the Energy Crunch, What Remains for Them to Do." *Nation's Cities* 16 (March, 1978):4.

National Association of Counties, National League of Cities, and U.S. Conference of Mayors. *A Guide to Reducing Energy Budget Costs.* Washington, D.C.: U.S. Department of Energy, 1978.

National Energy Conservation Policy Act, Pub. L. No. 95-619, 92 Stat. 3213 (1978).

Natural Gas Policy Act of 1978, Pub. L. No. 95-621, 92 Stat. 3351 (1978).

National League of Cities and U.S. Conference of Mayors. *Cities and the Nation's Disposal Crisis.* Washington, D.C.: National League of Cities, 1973.

National Research Council, Committee on Nuclear and Alternative Energy Systems. *Sociopolitical Effects of Energy Use and Policy.* Edited by Charles T. Unseld, Denton E. Morrison, David L. Sills, and C. P. Wolf. Supporting Paper 5, Study of Nuclear and Alternative Energy Systems. Washington, D.C.: National Academy of Sciences, 1979.

———. *Energy Choices in a Democratic Society.* Supporting Paper 7, Study of Nuclear and Alternative Energy Systems. Washington, D.C.: National Academy of Sciences, 1980.

Oakes, John B. "Taking the Waters." *New York Times,* May 17, 1977.

Odland, Robert, ed. *Community Energy Self-Reliance.* Proceedings of the First Conference on Community Renewable Energy Systems, University of Colorado at Boulder, August 20–21, 1979. SERI/CP-354-421. Washington, D.C.: Government Printing Office, 1980.

Odland, Robert; Menuier, Richard; Ohi, James; Pollock, Peter; and Unseld, Charles. *Decentralized Energy Studies: Task 5323 Research Plan.* SERI/MR-53-168. Golden, Colo.: Solar Energy Research Institute, 1979.

Okagaki, Alan, with Benson, Jim. *County Energy Plan Guidebook: Creating a Renewable Energy Future.* Fairfax, Va.: Institute for Ecological Policies, 1979.

Portland, Bureau of Planning, Policy Analysis Section. *Energy Conservation Choices for the City of Portland, Oregon.* Vol. 6, *Project Overview.* Washington, D.C.: Government Printing Office, September, 1977.

Portland, Energy Office. *An Energy Policy for Changing Times.* Progress Report of the Portland Energy Conservation Project. Portland: Portland Energy Office, 1980.

Portland, Energy Policy Steering Committee. *Proposed Energy Policy for Portland.* Discussion Draft. Portland: Energy Policy Steering Committee, 1979.

"Portland, Its Energy Supply Threatened, Planning Drastic Conservation." *New York Times,* July 9, 1979.

Public Utility Regulatory Policies Act of 1978, Pub. L. No. 95-617, 92 Stat. 3117 (1978).

Rattner, Steven. "New England Again Turns to Its Streams for Energy." *New York Times,* April 8, 1978.

Reisner, Robert A. F. "The Federal Government's Role in Supporting State and Local Conservation Programs." In *Energy Conservation and Public Policy,* edited by John C. Sawhill. Englewood Cliffs, N.J.: Prentice-Hall, 1979.

Resource Conservation and Recovery Act of October 21, 1976, as Amended by the Quiet Communities Act of 1978, Pub. L. No. 94-580, 90 Stat. 2798 (1976).

Reuth, Nancy. "A Solid Waste Package Deal: Energy and Materials from Garbage." *Mechanical Engineering,* December, 1977, p. 25.

Ridgeway, James. "A City's Energy Saving." *New York Times,* January 12, 1978.

———. *Energy-Efficient Community Planning.* Emmaus, Pa.: JG Press, 1979.

Riegel, Kurt W., and Salomon, Suzanne E. "Getting Individual Customers Involved in Energy Conservation: A Printed Comparative Use Indicator on Customer Bills?" *Public Utilities Fortnightly,* November 7, 1974, pp. 29–32.

Ross, Marc. "America Needs House Doctors." Mimeographed. Princeton: Center for Energy and Environmental Studies, 1979.

Rothberg, Paul. "Energy from Solid Wastes and Bioconversion." Mimeographed. CRS Issue Briefs #IB74064. Washington, D.C.: Congressional Research Service, January 17, 1978.

Ruegg, R. T. "Life Cycle Costs of Solar Energy." *ASHRAE Journal,* November, 1976, p. 1488.

Seattle City Light, Office of Environmental Affairs. *Energy 1990: Interim Report.* Seattle: Seattle City Light, 1976.

———— *Energy 1990: Final Report.* Seattle: Seattle City Light, May, 1976.

————. *Energy 1990 Resolutions: An Update Report.* Seattle: Seattle City Light, February, 1978.

Seaver, Burleigh, and Patterson, Arthur H. "Decreasing Fuel-Oil Consumption Through Feedback and Social Commendation." *Journal of Applied Behavior Analysis* 9. (Summer, 1976):147–52.

Seldman, Neil. *New Directions in Solid Waste Planning.* Washington, D.C.: Institute for Local Self-Reliance, 1977.

Seligman, Clive, and Darley, John M. "Feedback as a Means of Decreasing Residential Energy Consumption." *Journal of Applied Psychology* 62 (1977):363–68.

Sherwin, E. T., and Nollett, A. R. "Solid Waste Resource Recovery: Technology Assessment." *Mechanical Engineering,* May, 1980, pp. 26–35.

"Simple Sizing Guides Exist in Industry." *Solar Engineering* 4 (April, 1979):27.

"Solar Predictions Show Wide Range." *Solar Engineering* 4 (November, 1979):9.

Solid Waste Management Act, 1978 Mich. Pub. Acts 641.

Southern Tier Central Regional Planning and Development Board. *Energy Situation Study.* Corning, N.Y.: Southern Tier Central Regional Planning and Development Board, 1977.

————. *Renewable Energy Resource Inventory.* Southern Tier Central Region Citizen-Based Energy Technology Assessment Program, vol. 1. Corning, N.Y.: Southern Tier Central Regional Planning and Development Board, 1978.

————. *Renewable Energy Technology Handbook.* Southern Tier Central Regional Citizen-Based Energy Technology Assessment Program, vol. 2. Corning, N.Y.: Southern Tier Central Regional Planning and Development Board, 1978.

————. *Technology Assessment Workbook.* Southern Tier Central Region Citizen-Based Energy Technology Assessment Program., vol. 3. Corning, N.Y.: Southern Tier Central Regional Planning and Development Board, 1978.

————. *Energy Conservation and Development Plan.* Corning, N.Y.: Southern Tier Central Regional Planning and Development Board, 1979.

Spangler, Don. *Establishing an Energy Office: Seven County Programs.* Washington, D.C.: National Association of Counties Research Foundation, 1979.

Stern, Paul C., and Kirkpatrick, Eileen M. "Energy Behavior." *Environment,* December, 1977, pp. 10–15.

Stern, Paul C.; Kirkpatrick, Eileen M.; and Gardner, Gerald T. "A Review and Critique of Energy Research in Psychology." *Social Science Energy Review* 3 (Spring, 1980):1–71.

————. "Psychological Research and Energy Policy." *American Psychologist* 36 (April, 1981):329–42.

U.S., Army Corps of Engineers. *Feasibility Studies for Small Scale Hydropower Additions.* Vol. 1. Davis, Calif.: Hydrologic Engineering Center, 1979.

U.S., Comptroller General. "Views on Legislation to Continue State and Local Government in Promoting National Energy Objectives." Mimeographed. Letter Report EMD-80-15. Washington, D.C.: General Accounting Office, November 27, 1979.

————. *Hydropower—An Energy Source Whose Time Has Come Again.* Report to the Congress, EMD-80-30. Washington, D.C.: General Accounting Office, January 11, 1980.

————. *The Rural Energy Initiative Program for Small Hydropower—Is It Working?* Report to the Congress, EMD-80-66. Washington, D.C.: General Accounting Office, April 1, 1980.

U.S., Congress, House, Committee on Banking, Finance, and Urban Affairs. *Hearings on Energy and the City.* 95th Cong., 1st sess., September 14–16, 1977.

————. *Hearings on Compact Cities: A Neglected Way of Conserving Energy.* 96th Cong., 1st sess., December 11–12, 1979.

————. *Hearings on Compact Cities: Energy Saving Strategies for the Eighties.* 96th Cong., 2d sess., July, 1980.

U.S., Congress, House, Committee on Interstate and Foreign Commerce. *Hearings on Local Energy Policies.* 95th Cong., 2d sess., May 22, June 5 and 9, 1978.

U.S., Congress, Office of Technology Assessment. *Materials and Energy from Municipal Waste.* Washington, D.C.: Government Printing Office, 1979.

U.S., Council on Environmental Quality. *Environmental Quality—1978: The Ninth Annual Report of the Council on Environmental Quality.* Washington, D.C.: Government Printing Office, 1979.

————. *Environmental Quality—1979: The Tenth Annual Report of the Council on Evironmental Quality.* Washington, D.C.: Government Printing Office, 1980.

U.S., Department of Energy. "Loans for Small Hydroelectric Power Project Feasibility Studies and Related Licensing." *Federal Register,* January 17, 1980, pp. 3538–49.

U.S., Department of Energy, Assistant Secretary for Conservation and Solar Applications. *Solar Energy Incentives Analysis: Psycho-Economic Factors Affecting the Decision Making of Consumers and the Technology Delivery.* Washington, D.C.: Government Printing Office, 1978.

U.S., Department of Energy, Assistant Secretary for Environment, Office of Technology Impacts. *Distributed Energy Systems in California's Future: Interim Report.* 2 vols. HCP/P7405. Washington, D.C.: Government Printing Office, 1978.

U.S., Department of Energy, Assistant Secretary for Intergovernmental and Institutional Relations, Office of Consumer Affairs. *DOE Role in Support of Small-Scale Appropriately Distributed Technology.* Official Transcript of Public Briefing and Addendum, January 26, 1978. Washington, D.C.: Government Printing Office, 1978.

————. *Energy and Urban Policies/Programs.* Official Transcript of Public Briefing and Addendum, April 27, 1978. Washington, D.C.: Government Printing Office, 1980.

————. "Communities and Energy." *The Energy Consumer,* (entire issue) February/March, 1980.

U.S., Department of Energy, Assistant Secretary for Policy and Evaluation, Division of Environmental and Institutional Impacts Evaluation. *Local Government Energy Activities.* 3 vols. DOE/PE-0015. Washington, D.C.: Government Printing Office, 1979.

U.S., Department of Energy, Assistant Secretary for Policy and Evaluation, Deputy Assistant Secretary for Conservation and Renewable Resources. *Low Energy Futures for the United States.* DOE/PE-0020. Washington, D.C.: Government Printing Office, 1980.

U.S., Department of Energy, Assistant Secretary for Policy and Evaluation, Office of Solar Policy. *Renewable Energy Development: Local Issues and Capabilities.* DOE/PE-0017. Washington, D.C.: Government Printing Office, 1980.

U.S., Department of Energy, Energy Information Administration. *Annual Report to Congress, 1978.* 3 vols. DOE/EIA-0173. Washington, D.C.: Government Printing Office, 1979.

U.S., Department of Energy, Idaho Operations Office. *A Guide for Small Hydroelectric Development.* Idaho Falls, Idaho: n.d.

U.S., Department of Energy, Resource Applications, Office of Renewable Resources, Hydroelectric Resource Development Division. *Federal Financial Assistance for Hydroelectric Power.* DOE/RA-0055. Washington, D.C.: Government Printing Office, 1980.

U.S., Department of Housing and Urban Development, Office of Policy Development and Research. *In the Bank . . . Or Up the Chimney? A Dollars and Cents Guide to Energy-Saving Home Improvements.* Washington, D.C.: Government Printing Office, 1975.

————. *Capacity-Building: Local Government Approaches to Energy Conservation.* Washington, D.C.: Government Printing Office, 1979.

U.S., Environmental Protection Agency. *Resource Recovery and Waste Reduction, First Report to Congress.* EPA Publication SW-118. Washington, D.C.: Government Printing Office, 1974.

―――. *Resource Recovery and Waste Reduction, Third Report to Congress.* EPA Publication SW-161. Washington, D.C.: Government Printing Office, 1975.

―――. *Resource Recovery Plant Implementation: Guides for Municipal Officials, Planning and Overview.* EPA Publication SW-157.1. Washington, D.C.: Government Printing Office, 1976.

―――. *Decision-Makers Guide in Solid Waste Management.* EPA Publication SW-500. Washington, D.C.: Government Printing Office, 1976.

―――. *The Resource Recovery Industry: A Survey of the Industry and Its Capacity.* EPA Publication SW-501c. Washington, D.C.: Government Printing Office, 1976.

―――. *Source Separation: The Community Awareness Program in Somerville and Marblehead, Massachusetts.* EPA Publication SW-551. Washington, D.C.: Government Printing Office, 1976.

―――. *Office Paper Recovery: An Implementation Manual.* EPA Publication SW-571c. Washington, D.C.: Government Printing Office, 1977.

―――. *Resource Recovery and Source Separation, Fourth Report to Congress.* EPA Publication SW-600. Washington, D.C.: Government Printing Office, 1977.

―――. *Resource Recovery Management Model.* Pre-Publication Copy. Washington, D.C.: Government Printing Office, 1979.

―――. *Resource Recovery and Waste Reduction Activities: A Nationwide Survey.* EPA Publication SW-432a. Washington, D.C.: Government Printing Office, 1979.

U.S., Executive Office of the President, Energy Policy and Planning. *The National Energy Plan.* Washington, D.C.: Government Printing Office, April, 1977.

U.S., Federal Energy Administration. *Tips for Energy Savers.* FEA/D-76/513. Washington, D.C.: Government Printing Office, 1977.

U.S., Internal Revenue Service. *Energy Credits for Individuals.* IRS Publication 903. Washington, D.C.: Government Printing Office, 1979.

Warren, Donald I. *A Pilot Study Relating Actual Household Natural Gas Usage to Social Organization Patterns of Neighborhoods.* Ann Arbor: Institute of Labor and Industrial Relations, 1976.

Wentworth, Marchant. *Resource Recovery: Truth and Consequences.* Washington, D.C.: Environmental Action Foundation, 1977.

Winett, Richard A., and Neale, Michael S. "Psychological Framework for Energy Conservation in Buildings." *Energy and Buildings* 2 (1979):101–16.

General Public Policy

Behn, Robert D. "How to Terminate a Public Policy: A Dozen Hints for the Would-Be Terminator." *Policy Analysis* 4 (Spring, 1978):393–413.

Berman, Paul. "The Study of Macro- and Micro-Implementation." *Public Policy* 26 (Spring, 1978):157–84.

Campbell, Donald T. "Reforms as Experiments." *American Psychologist* 24 (1969):409–29.

————. "Focal Local Indicators for Social Program Evaluation." In *Evaluation Studies Annual*, vol. 1, edited by Marcia Guttentag. Beverly Hills, Calif.: Sage Publications, 1977.

Cochran, Nancy. "Grandma Moses and the 'Corruption' of Data." *Evaluation Quarterly* 2 (August, 1978):363–73.

Cole, Richard L. *Citizen Participation and the Urban Policy Process.* Lexington, Mass.: D. C. Heath, 1974.

Etheredge, Lloyd S. "Optimal Federalism: A Model of Psychological Dependence." *Policy Sciences* 8 (1977):161–71.

Floden, Robert, and Weiner, Stephen. "Rationality to Ritual: The Multiple Roles of Evaluation in Governmental Process." *Policy Sciences* 9 (1978):9–18.

Gramlich, Edward M. *Benefit-Cost Analysis of Government Programs.* Englewood Cliffs, N.J.: Prentice-Hall, 1981.

Hoos, Ida R. *Systems Analysis in Public Policy: A Critique.* Berkeley: University of California Press, 1972.

Larkey, Patrick D. *Evaluating Public Programs.* Princeton: Princeton University Press, 1979.

Lasswell, Harold D. *A Pre-View of Policy Sciences.* New York: Elsevier, 1971.

Meltsner, Arnold. "Political Feasibility and Policy Analysis." *Public Administration Review* 32 (November/December, 1972):859–67.

Merton, Robert K. "Social Deviation and Social Conformity." *American Sociological Review* 26 (1961):177–91.

Nelkin, Dorothy, and Pollak, Michael. "Public Participation in Technological Decisions: Reality or Grand Illusion?" *Technology Review*, August/September, 1979, pp. 55–64.

Orlans, Harold. "Neutrality and Advocacy in Policy Research." *Policy Sciences* 6 (June 1975):107–19.

Rodgers, Joseph Lee, Jr. *Citizen Committees: A Guide to Their Use in Local Government.* Cambridge, Mass.: Ballinger, 1977.

Schlesinger, James R. "Systems Analysis and the Policy Process." *Journal of Law and Economics* 11 (October, 1968):281–98.

Sherif, Muzafer. *Social Interaction: Process and Products.* Chicago: Aldine, 1967.

Simon, Herbert A. "Research for Choice." In *Environment and Policy: The Next Fifty Years*, edited by William R. Ewald, Jr. Bloomington: University of Indiana Press, 1968.

————. "Rationality as Process and Product of Thought." *American Economic Review* 68 (May, 1978):1–16.

————. "Rational Decision Making in Business Organizations." *American Economic Review* 69 (September, 1979):493–513.

Spengler, Joseph J. "Social Science and the Collectivization of Hubris." In

Propaganda and Communication in World History, edited by Harold D. Lasswell, Daniel Lerner, and Hans Speier. 3 vols. Vol. 3, *A Pluralizing World in Formation.* Honolulu: University of Hawaii Press, 1980.

Stokey, Edith, and Zeckhauser, Richard. *A Primer for Policy Analysis.* New York: W. W. Norton, 1978.

Sui, R. G. H. *The Craft of Power.* New York: John Wiley & Sons, 1979.

Williams, Robin W., Jr. "The Concept of Norms." In *International Encyclopedia of the Social Sciences,* edited by David L. Sills, vol. 11. New York: Macmillan Co. and Free Press, 1968.

Yule, G. Udny, and Kendall, M. G. *An Introduction to the Theory of Statistics.* 14th ed. London: Charles Griffin & Co., 1950.